STRONG LEADERSHIP

By the same author:

The University Experience — An Australian Study (Melbourne University Press)
Politics and Personal Style (Thomas Nelson Australia)
Faces On The Campus — A Psychosocial Study (Melbourne University Press)
Political Ensembles — A Psychosocial Approach to Politics and Leadership (Oxford University Press).

STRONG LEADERSHIP

Thatcher, Reagan and An Eminent Person

GRAHAM LITTLE

OXFORD
UNIVERSITY PRESS

Melbourne
Oxford Auckland New York

To the memory of my father, Frank Little,
Belfast 1917—Wellington 1988

OXFORD UNIVERSITY PRESS
Oxford New York Toronto
Delhi Bombay Calcutta Madras Karachi
Singapore Hong Kong Tokyo
Nairobi Dar es Salaam Cape Town
Melbourne Auckland
and associates in
Berlin Ibadan

First published 1988

National Library of Australia
Cataloguing-in-Publication data:

Little, Graham.
Strong Leadership: Thatcher, Reagan and an eminent person.

Bibliography.
Includes index.
ISBN 0 19 554759 4.

1. Thatcher, Margaret, 1925- — Personality. 2. Reagan, Ronald, 1911- — Personality. 3. Fraser, Malcolm, 1930- — Personality. 4. Political leadership—Case studies. 5. Political psychology. I. Title.

303.3'4

Typeset by Syarikat Seng Teik Sdn. Bhd., Malaysia
Printed by Impact Printing, Melbourne
Designed by Ron Hampton
Published by Oxford University Press, 253 Normànby Road, South Melbourne
OXFORD is a trademark of Oxford University Press

Contents

Acknowledgements

I owe an immense amount to the late A.F. Davies and to the circle of people who approach the study of politics, culture and society with an interest in psychoanalysis: The Melbourne Psychosocial Group, The Annual Freud Conference, some of my colleagues in the Politics Department. I am grateful to Vanda Arfi and Jan Souter for their typing. Thanks, too, to Oxford University Press, and particularly to Louise Sweetland for her early interest and continuing support. My warmest thanks are for Jenny and Jessica and for those, some of them far-flung, whom I want to call my friends.

University of Melbourne,
26 January 1988.

INTRODUCTION

1
The Rage for Strong Leadership

Political leadership has taken on a special significance in our age, as if politics and its leaders have to fill a space left by God and religion. Party leaders, whether Prime Ministers or Presidents, have become symbols of who we are, personifications of our way of life and our deepest beliefs. The interest taken in our leaders' character or personality is not ultimately a distraction, though it can be manipulated into becoming one. We are interested in the leader's beliefs and conduct because that is something all of us can judge from our own experience of life. Thus political leaders are increasingly sought as moral guides through the uncertainties of the age.

For some time now, the kind of leader demanded by the public voice has been the 'strong leader'. The case for strong leadership is put most bluntly and insistently by businessmen, especially by those who are looking for wider, political influence. One well-known businessman, John Elliott, a political party president and the man behind Paul Hogan's ruggedly masculine beer commercials, complained recently of an 'excess of democracy' in Australia; there should be more doing and less talking, and talented and go-ahead people (men?) should be given their heads — especially in politics where they should be allowed to enter parliament without too much interference from local selection committees. In similar vein, the principal of a major American business consultancy has announced that the time has come for leadership, strong leadership, to replace management as the engine of business. In his view, leaders are those who 'take the company into new dimensions' and 'generate an emotional tie between the leader and the led'. Management is 'cool', a matter of tending the machinery of an organization and leaving people alone. Leadership is 'hot', aggressively active, conjuring up deep commitment and eager, yet disciplined, teams of followers.

In addition to being a strong leader himself, Mr Zenger of Zenger-Miller (USA) is a magician. His interview in a Melbourne paper carries a wry heading that happens to point to the heart of this study of strong leadership. The heading was 'Magical Cure For A Leadership Crisis'.

Much in the idea of strong leadership is good, though it is for the most part fairly obvious and often fatuous. The important thing is what it entails, such as the need to reduce the democracy. Moreover, it is a catchcry that balloons out into a faith so that 'strong leadership' has become a kind of myth which promises the earth.

My task, then, is to penetrate the foggy rhetoric that tells us strong leadership is the answer to all our political and social needs. I shall try not to overlook the benefits but I hope that even its most fervent supporters will appreciate my effort to calculate the costs hidden in their faith.

This book is primarily about three Strong Leaders: Margaret Thatcher, Ronald Reagan, and our Eminent Person, the former Australian Prime Minister, Malcolm Fraser. Any team of Strong Leaders must have Thatcher, the 'Iron Lady', as captain. Reagan's inclusion will have to be justified as we go: amiable and lazy, he must be the most notorious hands-off chief executive since Nero. Fraser is a relative unknown but his qualifications for being a Strong Leader are excellent, not least that he anticipated both Thatcher and Reagan and has involved himself with them both.

All three became their country's leader by appealing to men and women who believed they 'needed leadership', Strong Leadership. The 'strong' in Strong Leadership has a special meaning — not the moral force and visionary powers of a Sister Theresa or a Gandhi, but something else. Thatcher, Reagan and Fraser all promised to arrest their nation's decline, to bring hardness in decision-making and clear purpose where before there was irresolution and drift. Though they promised to govern for the whole, and indeed insisted on national unity, all three implicitly heralded division. This would be a highly righteous division. In future the hard-working and the productive would be rewarded, and those who 'won't work', or who worked 'unproductively', would have to bear the consequences. Strong Leaders are about will or resolve, and intend that the 'strong' shall not be pulled down by the claims of the 'weak'.

Throughout the book I am going to use this specialized meaning of 'strong', using capitals — Strong Leadership, Strong Leaders — to make this clear. *Political Ensembles*, a theoretical book, described three types of leaders (Strong Leaders, Group Leaders and Inspiring Leaders) but apart from a few words later in this chapter, *Strong Leadership* is about just the one type. I shall not be criticizing Strong Leadership from outside, as if Thatcher, Reagan or Fraser should have been, or could have been, a different kind of person and a different type of leader. I will try to show, as I would with Group Leaders or Inspiring Leaders, the internal, built-in problems of Strong Leadership.

For about a decade now Strong Leadership has been the fashion not only in politics but in society generally — in the church (including the present Pope), in schools and universities, in families, and in business. Throughout society people are favouring more structure and more authority, more rules and tougher sanctions, clearly defined goals and sharp measures of success or failure all requiring a strong, guiding hand as a tight ship needs a tough captain.

Strong Leadership's popularity followed a period beginning around 1960 that saw a very different kind of leadership. Kennedy's election as President of the United States ushered in an era in which political leadership — and, again, leadership in all parts of society — was important and potent but 'inspiring' rather than 'strong'. In Britain, Harold Wilson was elected in 1966 on the promise of a 'new frontier' of intelligence and technology. Then in 1968 there was

Trudeau, the 'Northern Magus', in Canada, and later Whitlam in Australia. Both stimulated the arts, raised national self-esteem, and rewrote the world of international affairs, installing a youthful cohort of the best and the brightest in the driving seat of social change. Dubcek in Czechoslovakia, and belatedly Lange in New Zealand, belong to the same Kennedy wave.

These and others were leaders who excited and disturbed in equal parts. They were Inspiring Leaders (as I call the type) in that their impact rested primarily on their personalities, on who-they-were. They shaped a following with their charisma. They were political Pandoras, liberating hopes and arousing fears which Strong Leaders would later try to damp down and control. They were unrealistic, inventive, imprudent, careless, enraptured with change and the future. Theirs was a leadership of hubris.

Strong Leaders, for all their talk of individualism, are in favour of traditional pieties and accepted conventions. They are deliberately unvisionary and unexciting. Throughout the 1960s Strong Leadership fought back. Reagan was elected Governor of California in 1966. Johnson could not keep up the Kennedy momentum, primarily because of the Vietnam War, and gave way to Nixon in 1968 who set out to prosecute what he called 'The Real War'. The Kennedy sheen on Wilson soon rubbed off and Wilson's own Machiavellian manipulation took over. Trudeau's long innings saw him become less Inspiring and more Strong as he became frustrated and angry. The sad end to Dubcek's 'Prague Spring' is well known, made more poignant by the Soviet's glasnost policy twenty years on. Australia's Whitlam years lasted only from 1972 to 1975, were interrupted by a forced election and ended in a constitutional scandal, while New Zealand's Lange, late to the game, is temperate about social change and has partnered himself with an economic boss of the Strong Leader type.

Fraser was elected in 1975, Thatcher in 1979, Reagan in 1980. (Kohl in West Germany and Mitterand in France soon followed, the latter originally an anomaly and out of step in his economic policies who was soon forced to conform.) Their brief was to quell the excitement and halt the drift.

As well as Inspiring Leaders, whom Strong Leadership thinks irresponsible or even mad, there are Group Leaders, whom it calls weak. Group Leaders are reluctantly aggressive and they idealize solidarity, equality and consultative processes. President Carter is an outstanding example from this period, as is Michael Foot, the former British Labour Leader. Reagan beat one, Thatcher the other, as they did their successors. Mondale was a classic Group Leader in his attachment to the solidarities of working men and women and his preachments on compassion. 'Sunny' Jim Callaghan, fruitlessly searching for peace in industrial relations, went under to the firmer bite of Mrs Thatcher. In Australia, an exemplary action by Bill Hayden brought Labor to power in 1983. Hayden, a Group Leader, resigned to make way for Hawke 'for the good of the Party', and Hawke went on to beat Fraser.

Almost a decade later, at the time of writing Mrs Thatcher commands the British political arena, the American Presidential race is still open, and Hawke's Labor has the reputation for acting less like a compassionate and visionary reform party than as a more efficient version of Fraser's government. In other words, it is not clear whether Strong Leadership will continue its dominance, whether it is faltering and will recover, or is fading out. In Britain, Kinnock has tried, like Hawke, to marry economic hardheadedness with Labour's traditional social compassion, but he is accused of media superficiality. In the 1988 Presidential campaign Bush appeared as a Reagan reduced to managerial proportions; Dukakis and Jackson — whose quip 'I'd prefer a President who rode in a wheelchair than one who sat up on a horse' encapsulates the Group Leader's appeal to triumphant weakness and sympathetic identification — would make a familiar team: a leader tending to Inspiring in his narcissistic personality and mould-breaking actions plus a leader who is warm, passionately rhetorical and a spokesman for outsiders. Instead, the Democrats, regarding the times as transitional, have allied idealism with business-like prudence. In Australia, Group Leadership is hinted at in the Prime Minister's folk-hero status but his government's actions are a compound of compassion, limited reform and the economic hard-headedness of Strong Leadership, especially those of his

Treasurer. Despite the Bicentennial celebrations, Inspiring Leadership — visionary, exciting, symbolic — is rigidly excluded, a Whitlamist deviance that the present incumbents fear would threaten their businesslike image and their hold on power. However, there is an increasingly articulate mood calling for Group Leadership, a return to Labor's traditional emotional constituency.

The fate of Strong Leadership may now be hanging in the balance, poised between the success of Mrs Thatcher and the decline of President Reagan. No one who has experienced Thatcherism, Reaganism or Fraserism — and Australians always get a dose of at least two regimes — would think leadership irrelevant to what happens in politics. Our three subjects have put their stamp on a political era, rewriting the political agenda virtually from their own personalities. This is not to say the mood was not there. At another time I hope to write about 'political climates', how they build up, how they then come to dominate before being, in turn, swept away.

However, Thatcher, Reagan and Fraser were not invented by any mood; nor are they creations of the media. They are who they are, and who they were as they grew up — in very different and what were, to them, hostile political times — even if they are enlarged and encouraged by the media and the mood. Moreover, their political programmes centre on themselves, the Strong Leaders. As they always stood no nonsense, as they eschewed irrelevant, impractical ideas and goals, as they would not back down and stayed resolutely goal-oriented, so should we. Their political message was: install a Strong Leader and expect to work or get out of the way.

This is not a book about real authoritarians, dictators and their cowed followers. Much has already been written about them and they are not, thankfully, of pressing concern in Britain, the United States, or Australia. Of course, Strong Leadership is not entirely without echoes of Fascism. The 'far right' in all three countries is a continual reminder of how simple demands for enterprise and efficiency (like getting the trains to run on time) are linked to more ominous themes. Still, neither doom-saying, even about Strong Leaders, nor name-calling would get us far and for the moment

I leave it to others to extend the analysis of Strong Leadership into non-democratic systems and apply it to extreme cases.

I was tempted to write about leaders at the other end of the scale: small-time autocrats, often disguised as sports coaches, State Premiers, or gung-ho businessmen who think politics is like running a company (not running all the companies, and much else beside). These have the comparatively simple task of motivating just one team to destroy another and are the loudest advocates of Strong Leadership. In the event, I preferred to concern myself with Strong Leaders who work within reasonably democratic constitutions and whose responsibilities are for the whole game, not just one participant in it.

So the Strong Leadership we will try to understand is 'strong' because it can master the constitutional powers at the disposal of high office and the democratic political processes. It cajoles and coerces, but any impact it has is on people whom it cannot arbitrarily punish without public questioning and possible legal redress. Strong Leadership is important (and interesting) in this ordinary, everyday form just because it reveres will and authority — the Leader's freedom of action — in a world of due process, in a complex system of office-holding and designated tasks, and in the context of an established morality and customs. The fascinating question is, how does Strong Leadership operate in our kind of society? What is Strong Leadership in Western democratic politics?

There is more to this discusssion than my preference for studying 'ordinary' politics. Strong Leaders lay as much stress on order — law-and-order — and so-called traditional values and behaviour as they do on individual enterprise. Strong Leadership is tied to a form of social life which I call 'Structure', i.e. to a view of human affairs that makes civilized life the equivalent of organized, disciplined and conventional thinking and acting. It sees nature as a jungle, and people in the natural state as brutish. Other types of leaders have a different vision of what is essential for human social life. Group Leaders stress neighbourliness, translating the experience of life in smaller groups, like the family, into the nation as a whole. Inspiring Leaders look to cosmopolitanism, innovativeness, a creative society that is diverse and changing. Strong Leaders scorn the first as ridiculous and impractical. They fear the second: societies need structuring, the way a game does, requiring an orderly system of incentives and sanctions which gets work done and prevents the fragmentation and collapse that would come from too much spontaneity and change. Controlled competition, not love and not imagination, makes the world go round.

Hence, our three Strong Leaders will be found preaching order and restraint as much as acting wilfully and impulsively. Personally, each is a great contestant and may tend to be a bully or to admire others who act like pirates or guerillas, as Reagan perhaps admired Oliver North. Equally, each is a master at controlling followers and shaming citizens into behaving 'responsibly', and they are typically highly controlled themselves. This explains why words like 'conservative' or 'radical' do not fit our Strong Leaders well. Built into Strong Leadership are two opposite tendencies, one towards individual will and freedom, the other towards moral and legal restraint, where both imagination and social activity are reined in and held to conventional standards. Our Strong Leaders, then, are not buccaneers but the creators and sustainers of Structure — of social life arranged, so that there is practical (economic) competition within strict rules, where leaders should not rely too much on sentiment (you need incentive), where it is dangerously irresponsible to question the letter of the law (constitutional reform), or to challenge the conventionally held values within which enterprise can be encouraged.

THATCHER, REAGAN, FRASER

There is a Henry James story called *The Real Thing* in which a well-born but down-at-heel couple seeks work as models for an illustrator employed on a book about the English upper classes. Unfortunately for them, a Cockney servant and an immigrant Italian ice-cream vendor, acting the part, do very much better, and the impoverished gentility have to descend to doing the menial tasks the others once had to do.

The artist-narrator concludes that 'plastic' can be more 'real' than the real thing.

The moral hardly applies to Mrs Thatcher, who is without doubt The Real Thing among Strong Leaders. Of the three, hers is the nearest to the monolithic drive and determination the myth of Strong Leadership promises. In the late 1980s, she is also the only one still in complete command. Mr Fraser, whose term of office as Prime Minister was the second longest in Australian history, was voted out of office in 1983 and, except perhaps for his role as an Eminent Person (attempting to influence the South African government to change its racial policies), has become a marginal political figure. Fraser, however, is close to The Real Thing. Years before Thatcher he spoke the language of Strong Leadership and was proposing it as the salvation of the West in Carter's day, and he had himself elected on a Strong Leadership platform as early as 1975. However, unlike Thatcher, Fraser's personality and leadership were never so monolithic or so sure. Fraser has always been divided along the Strong Leadership's central axis: feeling the urge to win, to dominate, to be Strong; feeling the equally insistent urge to limit conflict, provide stability, to shape a moral world. This stress-and-strain is in all Strong Leaders. In Fraser it is morbidly obvious, explaining much in his political fortunes and providing a window on the tensions Thatcher and Reagan cover more successfully.

Reagan is so far from 'the real thing' (or even 'the right stuff') and so much the 'plastic' imitation that he might have been created for James's story. His success seems to indicate that those who are not can do much better than those who are. Until the Irangate revelations in 1987, Reagan gave a powerful performance — though Australians and Britons, used to a different tradition of political stagecraft, found it a stagy one. He was the Strong Leader whose powers were only lightly suggested, whose self-confidence was such that he need not raise his voice and could joke away dangers and complications, a leader who barely needed to be awake and certainly did not need to know. Reagan, who moralized less than Thatcher and Fraser, was the Strong Leader languid and off-duty, the Strong Leader in jeans. Meanwhile, his programme was similar to those of Thatcher and Fraser, preaching muscle-flexing abroad (and even engaging in a small skirmish in Grenada) and a more virile capitalism at home, though casual about engendering it.

The Real Thing, The Image, The Divided — the range within the Strong Leadership type is interesting in itself. So is the extent of the overlap: three different individuals become the chief executive in three different political systems by responding to the politics of the mid- to late 1970s in highly similar ways. The profiles that follow are not exactly biographies (which would tell more complete, factual stories), nor are they just pictures in a book of political theory. I have tried to bring Thatcher, Reagan and Fraser alive on the page, to give a sense of each as an individual, as a flesh and blood person. Taken together, though, the profiles are like three panels in one overall picture. They reveal a type: the Strong Leader and his or her followers, a type of leadership and a type of politics.

These psychological studies are political studies as well. They attempt to convey my belief that politics, difficult and even impossible to comprehend as it swirls about us, nevertheless relies on a few simple themes, and these themes are accessible to us all because they are our own experiences and judgements writ large. Politics exists in people, in their passions, prejudices and plans. Though there are other types of leaders and politics, where some of us might see ourselves more clearly, in Thatcher, Reagan and Fraser all of us will see a good deal of ourselves, particularly in our time.

This may be introduction enough for readers wanting to get on to the profiles of Thatcher, Reagan and Fraser. These readers might want to skip the following section. Others will be interested in the aim I set myself of understanding not just three very significant Strong Leaders but the type — Strong Leader — they represent. The following chapter reduces the characteristics of Strong Leaders to a few essentials. I put this blueprint of the Strong Leader type before the profiles partly because too many abstractions there would destroy the individual portrait being painted, and partly to give the analytically-minded reader a framework he or she can test along the way.

2
The Strong Leader Type

The following two paragraphs give a short account of the Strong Leader taken from my book *Political Ensembles* where Strong Leadership is contrasted in detail with Group Leadership and Inspiring Leadership.

The Strong Leader sculpts in power. He is partly a raw adversary even to his colleagues and subordinates, and partly a manager who has to provide incentive and quell rivalries so that the organization or society can achieve its goal. Ideally, his strengths run the gamut of the ambivalence continuum: from confrontation as he presses for action, to constitutionalism as he calls for order and responsibility; from naked power-plays and apparently cynical manipulation, to by-the-book administration and providing a model of rectitude. In practice, even the best Strong Leader will swing between being too brutal and direct, where the struggle is made personal, and being too cautious so that he fails to win advantage for his followers. The pivot of the Strong Leader's work is his will and capacity for both contest and control.

The Strong Leader should look as if he comes from outside Structure, that he is more alive, brave and purposeful than his social learning and role performance could have made him. His assertiveness should appear comfortable and important to him, a vital underpinning of his commitment to order. He impresses by his independence, his record of overcoming opposition, his determination, all of which predate the job he will have to do. He is expected to take control, lift standards and energize enterprise by drawing on his self-confidence and determined purpose as if they were independent of other people. The Strong Leader should seem to have leverage outside society. The Strong Leader exemplifies the view that the objective, the external, the individual and competitive are the true realities, and that the only leader worth having is one for whom co-operation is an act of disinterestedness exercised by a naturally independent and reluctantly social man.

To give a close-up of Strong Leadership I shall begin on the outside and work in. First, the meaning of leadership itself. Second, the aims of Strong Leaders and their followers, and their ideas about politics, society and human nature. Finally, a list of some deep assumptions behind Strong Leadership. Following all this I give a brief account of the psychological ideas that underlie my analysis of Strong Leadership and my interpretations of the life and work of our three Leaders.

THE MEANING OF LEADERSHIP

Leadership itself is the crux of Strong Leadership's politics and its view of human affairs. These are the essential features:

1 *Crisis-orientation.* Strong Leadership announces itself with warnings. A threat looms, ultimately to the survival of nation, organization or person, and the dangers will grow unless some 'hard-headed' thinking is begun, some 'tough decisions' are made. The Strong Leader diagnoses a parlous state and blames it on drift — a confusion of aims, irresoluteness in the incumbent leaders — or on self-indulgence, leaders who 'mortgage the future' or 'buy popularity'. Strong Leadership's diagnosis may be correct or it may be a fabrication, a device, and the crisis a manufactured one. Strong Leaders' warnings contain an implicit promise: unlike

environmentalist or nuclear doomsters, Strong Leadership has a simple, political answer — its own accession to power. It disturbs people, but it quickly settles them down in the simplest possible way. It promises that decisive leadership will transform the situation and avert the crisis; it offers a programme of clear goals and a leader with gumption. Moreover, the enemy is named and therefore easier to resist.

In thus focusing our fears, Strong Leadership calms them. The hard times that Strong Leadership likes to predict are less a threat than a promise: they will simplify life and politics, invigorate us all, and are virtually certain to lead to peace and prosperity, maybe even to glory. Starting out to dispel complacency, to reduce expectations, Strong Leadership stimulates a new set of hopes. The Strong Leader offers herself or himself as an object of faith.

2 *Realism and results.* Strong Leadership spurns idealistic aims, considering itself above wishful thinking, and is suspicious of beliefs that are highly complex. It is also suspicious of people who are overly sceptical (an excuse for procrastination? a sign of cowardice?). Its own ideals merge into the one aim: to be competitively strong, whether overwhelmingly powerful, heroically enduring, or just 'plucky'. It prides itself on its realism, its practicality, and the concreteness of its goals. The Strong Leader offers not his personality, not his charm or his virtue, but his skills, above all his capacity to win or at least to resist. He wishes to be judged by the results of his efforts, nothing more, nothing less. He and his followers are beholden only to the bottom line.

Of course, the Strong Leader gives himself room to manoeuvre (the figures may be ambiguous, opponents' calculations are wrong, it is too early to tell, etc.). Ultimately, having the right attitude (talking tough, a further tightening of the screws) can take the place of measurable results until 'realism' itself becomes an attitude and the whole project of practical, hard-boiled measures becomes a kind of propitiation rather than a plan for actual achievements. Similarly, reputation can play an important part in establishing a Strong Leader's qualifications. The old bull may be held in awe though he is past any effective action, a sportsman or farmer may be allowed to carry his reputation for toughness on the field or in the bush into conference rooms and committees though he is bewildered and overawed there.

As well, Strong Leadership likes to enhance its reputation for realism and results by using the past, honouring historical fortitude in such a way that it appears inheritable. This is a selective conservatism which focuses on those among the legendary who succeeded by enterprise or 'true grit', or tells the historical story to accentuate the individual leader and the uncomplaining follower. Poets and philosophers are left out or treated as decoration. In this selective conservatism, pragmatism is given historical purpose and comes to seem like principle.

3 *Action and decisiveness.* Simple, tangible goals, minimal entanglements and reluctance to compromise allow Strong Leadership to act decisively. Indeed, decisive action can be an end in itself because the worst thing is to be inactive, passive or confused. Even incompetents can be admired for their irrepressible energy, approved for always trying something (or trying *something*). Thinking too much, and talking, waiting and watching, dreaming, hoping, these are anathema. They do not meet Strong Leadership's sense of urgency nor its sense of itself as mover and shaker. Moreover, delay breeds doubt and lowers morale when it is important to keep up momentum, or at least to keep occupied.

Action and decisiveness are possible, in the first place, because Strong Leadership has the answers already. The goals are clear and set. Strategy and logistics, practical and technical questions, are the only genuine problems. The crisis Strong Leadership is empowered to meet has been the result of a failure of nerve — not real bewilderment or the potentially creative confusion surrounding any new beginning. The 'physician's' cautious balancing of numerous factors has got nowhere; it is time for the 'surgical strike'.

This attitude also lies behind Strong Leadership's choice of problems. It looks for problems that yield a bottom-line result (economic enterprise is preferable to the slough of social welfare), that give definite reassurance of achievement, that show clearly that something is being made to happen. If the outcomes are unclear morale will sag, resolution will fail, action will falter. This encourages the substitution of selected parts of the political task (especially the economy) for the whole, so that progress in that is taken to signify progress overall. A kind of fetishism takes over (for example, the balanced budget) where the fetish (or 'indicator') wards off criticism and reassures the leader that he is doing well. Ultimately, however, Strong Leadership has an inclination to concentrate on the whole in an abstract sense — the nation, for example, may improve compared with other nations, though most of its citizens may languish. The 'parts' (youth without jobs, for instance) may have deteriorated or been lost in a forced march but if the 'whole' measurably survives (such as the regimental name and colours, the 'Great' put back in 'Great Britain') that is success.

4 *Boundaries, divisions and hierarchy*. Crisis, results, decisive action all require clarity and choice, the sheep separated from the goats, friend separated from foe and — a very important internal requirement — the strong distinguished from the weak. Boundaries have to be set up and maintained. Only clear signals should cross them: in case the opponent mistakes vagueness (or subtlety) for weakness; to get quick and decisive actions from below; to forestall criticism that the Strong Leader is being hesitant or arbitrary, criticism that could allow a coalition of opponents. Clarity — who's who; who is boss and who is not; priorities in goals, allowable means, etc. — also serves Strong Leadership's purposefulness.

Above all, the Strong Leader must steel himself against distraction, ignore alternative ideas, remove himself from the clamour of those excluded or getting hurt. This means that a critical boundary has to be established separating the strong from the weak. The weak may be well looked after, but they must not be confused with the strong who need room to move, and benefits ('incentives') appropriate to their extra 'responsibility'. Strong Leadership energetically resists empathy with opponents, competitors or strangers, but above all it resists identification with those who are defeated and doubtful. It fears being undermined, undone, unmanned.

Thus 'strength' in Strong Leadership is essentially the capacity to be separate and stay ahead. This means living in 'boundaried' social groups, whether family, party, institution or society, in groups united by the conviction that there is great danger that can only be dealt with through mobilizing the strong. Fraternizing, like too much sympathy and too much reflection, which lead to empathy, would inhibit action. Division (though not disunity) equals strength because it leads to concerted action among the like-minded and equally strong, who are protected from the sceptics and those unable to contribute. The unity of Strong Leadership is a concert of individualists who, notwithstanding their individualism, are eager to follow in a faith laid down for them (goals will not be questioned) because they have a common fear, the perpetual threat on which Strong Leadership's fortunes depend.

It follows that hierarchy is intrinsic to Strong Leadership. Just as the Strong Leader must have preferential treatment, so must the class of Strong Leaders around and just beneath, the Barons as well as the King. Moreover, a clear pecking order is essential not only for establishing the chain of command but for selecting new recruits to the strong. In its pure form, selection is natural selection, the strong being those who have proved themselves competitively, the ones who have forced their way in. Of course, reputation or status — family and class background, school, profession, money, etc. — are substitutes for real competitive proofs when 'fitness' becomes less evolutionary and more social. However, this does not alter the main intention, which is to limit participation. This exclusiveness is justified technically in terms of numbers: decisions, especially 'decisive' ones (quick and hard), cannot be made by large committees. As well, larger numbers, more participant structures, bring in those who would inevitably undermine Strong Leadership: the over-sophisticated ideas-people and the representatives of the weak, even the needy themselves, who lack the strong's hard-edge principles and long horizons.

5 *Technique and values.* There is a strength which belongs to élites and there is a mass strength. The latter is the contribution made by those who, individually or in small numbers,

would be more a burden than a help. Strong Leadership has both contempt for the mass (it is sheeplike) and fear of it should it get organized, as in trade unions, for example. Strong Leadership can believe itself stronger than most and yet feel profoundly embattled. Leaving aside the dictatorships, the recipe for the efficient management of crisis in constitutional Strong Leadership is an obedient and productive workforce led by people who 'know their own minds', 'see where they are going', 'can say no' and 'won't be deterred' — the leaders respected, the followers respectable.

It is always understood that Strong Leaders will kick against the restrictions placed on individual energies in the name of the collective task. Covert action, breaking the rules, heroic defiance, are proofs of vitality, in people and in an administration. At such time law-breakers may be called courageous and patriotic, their stretching of the rules proof of the leadership's long-term and higher aims. However, those whom Strong Leaders lead must remain in their harnesses: as individuals, or as critical coteries (or reporters protected by the law), they can only be a drag on the overall effort. A good deal of moralizing is used against the foot-soldier who dares to put initiative against sheer obedience; initiative is for higher ranks, like big crimes.

Hence the readiness of Strong Leadership to resort to manipulation. If there is a crunch, what does it matter what methods are used? If the majority are incapable of participating, yet needed for their formal support, they must be wooed somehow, and why not by whatever means will work? I mean no sanctimonious criticism of Strong Leadership for this; its candor, like Machiavelli's, is preferable to the self-deception that can accompany more obviously idealistic leaders. Nevertheless, it is a distinguishing feature of Strong Leadership that followers are means — in the mass, at any rate — before they are ends. They are excluded from goal-setting, given lesser tasks and expected to anticipate the fruits of Strong Leadership without claiming freedoms with which only the Strong can be trusted.

One of the most astonishing contradictions in Strong Leadership is that the will to manipulate co-exists with elevated rhetoric and much-vaunted spiritual values. This is not exactly a paradox. Strong Leadership is tough, competitive, and hard-headedly materialist, but it understands that we lack its capacity to be independent of mind. Intellectuals are wimps, social workers are sentimentalists, and most people are eager for reassurance, for good feelings, for ennobling objectives. Thus Strong Leadership presents itself as practical and realistic, but in the service of something glorious, a higher calling that will help us take our medicine. This is easier to understand once we recall that its predilection is for hierarchy, for leadership, and it is only extending this when it points to the flag, family life, fallen soldiers, historic destiny and even God. This satisfies its followers, who, for all their individualism, desire a framework for authoritative guidance. It confounds its idealistic opponents for whom the disjunction between manipulative actions and sincere rhetoric is a stumbling block. Perhaps it even comforts Strong Leaders themselves, whose ruthlessness might otherwise seem ignoble in the bathroom mirror.

Thus, the practical men, supporters of Strong Leadership, vote for leaders surprisingly ready to claim noble intentions and high public and personal virtues, and surprisingly vocal about policies owed not to economists and accountants but to religious fundamentalists and their secular descendants. Strong Leadership, in the end, is not noticeably more 'practical' than the types of leadership which it dismisses as Utopian and crusading. If Group Leaders and Inspiring Leaders must compromise their ideals for the material gains their electors demand, Strong Leaders compromise the other way, substituting a vague but intense patriotism and other flatulent symbols for the results that turned out harder to get than they anticipated or pretended.

6 *Innocence and experience*. Strong Leadership wants to claim both of these. It is innocent of something it calls 'politics' — above pettiness, above greed and selfishness, above politicking. The Strong Leader comes from elsewhere, he is a 'cleanskin', a law unto himself (though for the good of all), someone who has not compromised. Unlike ordinary political mortals, the Strong Leader has not curried favour or let himself be diverted from the ideas he grew up with. He is less concerned with new ideas than those he ruminates on while keeping his own counsel. Innocence means being

distant from politics, resistant to influence, faithfulness to the original teachings of youth. At the same time, Strong Leaders see themselves as offering worldly wisdom, confidence born of struggle, hope born of achievement. They believe they offer a down-to-earth seriousness and purposefulness lacking in the idealists and visionaries, who are 'all theory', and a willingness to grasp the nettle.

Strong Leadership thus claims to be both simple and knowing, both untouched and never afraid to dirty its hands, both a child of simple faith and an adult who is worldly-wise. It invokes the familiar — the innocence of hearth, toil, and faith in God and country — and warns about insidious threats, Babylonian degeneration, a world full of snares which only cunning can defeat. Good at heart, it asks for a licence to defeat an evil enemy by imitating his wickedness. It implies that it knows him of old but was never influenced by him, that is, that it gained experience while staying innocent.

POLITICAL IDEAS

Strong Leadership makes leadership a political philosophy. I have been describing what the supporters of Strong Leadership mean by a leader, what he or she should be and how they should act. I want now to present a few key ideas that lie behind this view of the leader, ideas about nature and human nature, about social priorities, about the arrangement of human affairs.

1 *Nature and human nature.* Strong Leadership has no place for the delicate ecologism of environmentalists; it is on the side of the loggers and miners, believing that benefits must be torn from an unwilling nature and that its unforgiving encroachments must be fought against. The soil from which humankind springs is hostile and unremitting, something to be subdued, or at least colluded with watchfully and without respite, as in careful farming.

At the same time, Strong Leadership is always fighting off refinements of style, intellect, sometimes even in technology. It likes to get its teeth into its work, to use its hands, and it likes its meat raw. Strong Leadership, in this aspect, seems to stand for the natural, the down-to-earth, the direct, simple and gutsy, and indeed Strong Leadership's supporters often admire it for this. Where it differs from its ecological rivals is in its fundamental motive. Strong Leadership retains some of the crudity and brutality of nature because this will help subdue it. The enemy has to be fought on his home territory. There is an unstable balance then between keeping nature at bay, subduing it and keeping alive the rebarbative elements needed for the task, especially since these become sources of satisfaction — in sport or war, or in flattening forests or diverting powerful rivers — in their own right.

Human nature is not etherealized under Strong Leadership. Self-interest and crude pleasures are given prominence while more sublimated interests and pleasures are considered insignificant and sometimes mere window-dressing. This is particularly so for altruistic or collective sentiments. They cannot be trusted because human nature, like nature, is individual and predatory.

Strong Leadership is needed precisely because social sentiments will not arise spontaneously or last through lean times; they have to be manipulated or organized with shouts and siren's songs. Strong Leadership offers rewards and sanctions to obtain order and collective action, beginning with the material ones and adding higher ones (like patriotism). It tends toward replacing autonomy with authority. Self-criticism is more important than self-congratulation or self-expression. Even enterprise, if it is to be lawful and useful to society, is ultimately a duty because, for Strong Leadership, all achievement is against the grain.

To put this another way, Strong Leadership finds personal fulfilment and social value in the harnessing of energies to overcome — to overcome nature, human opponents, or a pervasive if unnamed crisis. 'Getting somewhere' is crucial to life's meaning and to personal well-being. Human beings 'find' themselves in avoiding passivity, inertness, death. Strong Leaders all imagine less competitive and more contemplative people (and institutions) to be lacking in morale, needful of direction, languishing for lack of strong external stimulus. They are suspicious of the contented and come down hard on those who, in the name of 'autonomy', make extravagant claims about personal rights: they are seen to be probably loafers, possibly even traitors. Human nature, like nature (and including one's own) must be mastered and, through success in the approved ways, should be seen to be.

2 *Priorities: physical and material.* Military and economic concerns, followed by law and order, have priority in Strong Leadership's world of threat. The ultimate threat is to life itself, and the basics of security and physical survival must come first. Bombs, bread and only then books. A pecking order, a system of priorities, is essential in Strong Leadership's view of things. Work, then sentiments, then ideas; soldiers and businessmen, then nurturers and thinkers: these are not seen in a complex pattern of interdependence but have to be arranged on a ladder where the first are higher and command the latter. Wealth-making must come before wealth-distribution, and unfairness can even be a spur to productivity.

3 *Society as structure: contest and control.* The absence of natural solidarities underwrites Strong Leadership's offer to end discord and establish collective action and collective security. It does 'artificially' what cannot take place 'naturally', and civilization itself is a kind of prosthesis that keeps people upright and in line. (This has the added attraction of being safer, because it is more controllable than the natural processes it displaces.) Thus sentiment or imagination, unorganized, can endanger civilization, which can only survive if it is a structure of roles more or less routinely performed.

One side of Strong Leadership leans to individual initiative, to enterprise and action. This combats the individual's fear of inertia, which would mean being vulnerable to takeover because one is passive and therefore weak. The other side recognizes the need for collective security and the rewards of collective action (as in the division of labour). So there must be contest ('incentive' or individual, legally protected rewards) and there must be control (law and order, conventional morality, patriotic conformities, etc.).

Much of the instability within Strong Leadership arises from its holding these twin aims. Strong Leaders must be obeyed, yet everyone must be free to become the Strong Leader since a threatened society cannot afford to cosset its élite. Thus the Strong Leader must remain strong, perhaps grow stronger still, and continue to win. He who defeats him is the new Strong Leader, by that fact alone and with only minimal reference to the constitutionality of his victory, let alone the morality.

Among followers of Strong Leadership the problem is how to balance initiative and duty. Strong Leadership, when not sending confused signals about whether society needs more enterprise or more discipline, solves the dilemma by selecting those who will be given the freedoms of contest and those expected to be mainly dutiful, a selection that reflects its priorities (physical and material) and confirms its hierarchy (the military man and the businessman). Strong Leadership's greatest reward is that the more conventionally successful individuals become — that is, the more pious they are about social values, prospering in the 'right way', for example by becoming a tycoon — the more freedom they are allowed. As with James Bond, accepting assignments without question brings a licence to act above or beyond law and morality.

4 *Leadership: principle, policy and programme.* So, we come back to leadership. The management of contest (for example, business enterprise) and control (especially law) is the work of the Strong Leader, who must light fires under people and hose them down when they go too far. The Strong Leader is both an example and a restraint, a challenge and a servant of the constitution. He offers himself as someone who understands (has experienced, can handle) the strain of individual achievement versus social virtue. He is enthusiastic for the fray but also self-controlled, he has appetite and is not afraid to accept rewards (especially power itself) yet he is guided by the rules and the common good. He must contain these opposites to some extent in his own personality or show how they can be organized efficiently or, as they say, 'prioritized'.

Thus Strong Leadership's claim to realism and practical achievement, its promise to be competent and nothing more and therefore to demand nothing more from its supporters, is ultimately undercut by the fact that it rests its politics on the qualities of a person, the Leader. Society is a pyramid whose apex is a person of outstanding energy and fortitude and singular disinterest. He is supposed to be offering only his skills, but we are directed, in fact, first to his vitality, then to his courage, judgement, fair-mindedness and self-control. The Strong Leader is presented as down-to-earth and human but also above us, a person of such character that he can be powerful while still being controlled, ambitious while remaining devoted to the public good. A man or woman of will *and* responsibility.

Though the Strong Leader can go too far, his supporters expect him to show that he is not timid or a slave to opinion or regulations. In the end, they believe, principles, programmes and policies will not avert the crisis or overcome the enemy; some individual person must have the final say. Not 'bureaucratic', Strong Leaders must also prove that their actions are not arbitrary or selfish. There must be no lack of self-control; a Strong Leader must show his respect for due process and the impersonal institutions that constitute social structure. Still, enthusiasts for Strong Leadership will worry less about this than that the Leader might be entangled in compromise, losing momentum and even direction. Sometimes high-principled, opposing the short horizons of 'mere politicians', and sometimes opportunistic, avoiding the inertia of a fixed position, Strong Leadership is always directed at movement, action, progress. These are signs and promises of the strength Strong Leadership's supporters are looking for to repel the takeover anticipated in their permanent orientation to crisis.

As principle, programme and policy, Strong Leadership is both alarming and reassuring. The dramatic, ever active Strong Leader, and the seasoned, quiet campaigner, both dispel fear. He or she will be full of energy or will 'have seen it all before'. Enthusiastic, spoiling to do battle or calm and unwavering, either way there is a fundamental optimism which Strong Leadership uses to oppose the defeatism it sees in Group Leadership. This is not the optimism of Inspiring Leaders which is radically unsettling and can be naively Utopian. Strong Leadership's optimism is proudly realistic and closer to determination than to expectation, a signal more of the effort it will put in than of any outcome it can imaginatively project.

FOUR BASIC ASSUMPTIONS

We have looked at the meaning of leadership and at some key political ideas in Strong Leadership and arrive now at some basic assumptions it makes about human experience. In a sense, and in a highly abbreviated form, this is where Strong Leadership's ideology becomes a kind of psychology.

Strong Leadership is one response to the question, how shall love and hate be handled? Group Leaders make love tame but extensive, turning passion into a community-wide tolerance which restrains aggressiveness by making every stranger into a brother. Inspiring Leaders keep the passion in love but turn it towards exotic peoples and customs and to new ideas that it imagines will make conflict unnecessary. Strong Leaders, in contrast to both, love and hate tribally — us vs. them — holding out the promise that the two, loving and rivalling, can be kept alive while being channelled productively. One of the ways Strong Leadership channels love and hate is to distribute them between the genders, one set to nurture, the other to compete. However, the proposed segregation of love and hate that Strong Leadership promises — the promise that each of us (and whole societies) can organize and control our passions and become decisive because we are no longer ambivalent — must take place originally in the mind. So I start with thinking.

1 *Strong thinking: hard vs. soft.* Strong Leadership scorns ambiguous, tentative, highly coloured or fractured thinking, and thinking that seems too passionate or involved. It calls the latter soft. It wants ideas reduced to yes/no options suitable for decisive action. Its crisis-orientation, its ostensible realism and concern with results, its emphasis on action and decisiveness, its maintenance of sharp boundaries and hierarchy — all depend on thinking that proceeds by choosing between opposites and arrives at clear options or, at least, alternatives ranged in an order of urgency, risk or cost. The structure which Strong Leadership identifies as civilization

is a system of clearly defined rules, unambiguous roles, uncluttered chains of command *plus* the thinking that will maintain and advance such a structure. Moreover, Strong Leadership wants thinking that is forceful, that moves things forward, that facilitates action. Rumination, impractical imagination or pure aesthetics and playfulness are of little value, as is the kind of thinking that, tracing outlines (the loving observation of the natural and human worlds), neglects to search for a lever of control.

Two other linked features of Strong Leadership's thinking are its suspiciousness and its devotion to the external. Because it is about crisis, Strong Leadership's version of realistic, hard-headed thinking is attuned to 'seeing through', to doubting motives and checking proposals, especially those that offer good results without conflict. Ideas that go too directly to peace or happiness, ideas that assume co-operation, ideas that are radically imaginative, especially if there is insufficient stress on cost, are received sceptically or sent away to be hardened up. Such ideas may be mere wishes, or they will make us flabby, or they will distract us from the hard work and the resolute attack that are the real things needed.

It is true that Strong Leadership's thinking on broad human and patriotic themes seems the opposite of this — florid, sentimental, sloppy; but we should remember Strong Leadership's priorities, especially the ubiquitous physical and material threat to survival. This threat lies behind its devotion to the external world, its avoidance of introspection, emotionality and imagination. Strong Leaders are poor poets, their lifelong inclination is to run from inner realities and grasp, if they must, at ideals and symbols that are ready-made. Strong thinking prefers 'realities' that are affected, and effected, only by operational thinking kept sharply distinct from feeling, as impersonal and as instrumental as possible. The realism of Strong Leadership is philosophical here, meaning that what is outside is more real than what is in our minds, and the 'strong thinker' is one who puts his mind to grasping the 'not-I' problems and dangers with competencies determined by that external world.

Strong thinking is sometimes brashly confident, recklessly interventionist, as imperialistic as Strong Leadership can be.

At other times it is defensive, over-cautious, virtually ritualistic. In this variant — the bureaucrat, lawyer or accountant behind the business tycoon — hard-edge thinking becomes a pathology of itself, making control (rather than control balanced by contest) the main thing. A good part of the debate within parties of Strong Leadership is between supporters of the Strong Leader as single-minded entrepreneur and supporters of a more controlled, almost bureaucratic, Strong Leadership.

2 *Unity and division: dichotomies.* It is impossible to write about Strong Leadership without invoking one dichotomy after another. Looking over all the points listed so far, not one exists without an alternative to oppose it. In the previous section the dichotomies are hard/soft, internal/external, contest/control. Others spin off from these. I use this section to emphasize the fundamentally dichotomizing nature of Strong Leadership, its intrinsic attachment to division.

Psychologically, the fundamental dichotomy is 'I/not-I', or self vs. other, which is the formulation used in my book, *Political Ensembles*. Strong Leadership is defined most profoundly by its suspicion of natural harmonies, of spontaneous and lasting solidarities. Its greatest fear is of the loss of self, of the invasion of the boundaries of the self. Conversely, distinction, separateness, distance are the great values. These are defences against the tug of social life which threatens the individual with submergence and anonymity meaning death. This individualism has to coexist, in the way I have explained, with law and order, conventionalism, structure, but none the less it is real. Thus there is very little for Strong Leadership to fear in the charge that it is divisive. It is, and gladly so, embracing inequality — which allows distinction — within a conventionally ordered society, just as sheep huddle together not wishing to lose themselves in a herd of goats. (Strong Leadership is not always unsympathetic to 'black sheep', a last-ditch throw at distinction, though it might prefer a knighthood.)

Thus dichotomizing is not only to facilitate 'strong' thinking; it creates the need for it. Though it is a mode of problem solving, at a more profound level, dichotomized thinking is an expression of a particular kind of attitude and experience — a way of thinking that fits lives built on the assumption of a gulf fixed between one person and everyone else. This is the foundation on which Strong Leadership and its supporters build their crisis orientation, and everything in their political philosophy and actions flows from it. Theirs is a malignly dichotomous world, a world of win or lose, lead or be led, control or be controlled, us or them, stemming from a sharply etched and darkly coloured sense of 'I' and 'not-I'.

3 *Masculine and feminine.* We have not yet explored the psychology behind Strong Leadership far enough to understand why Strong Leaders and their supporters associate strong with masculine, weak with feminine. It is clear, however, that they do. The rise of Strong Leadership has brought the 'wets' (and 'wimps') into political discourse to be mocked and maligned. A clue lies in the link Strong Leadership makes between what it calls soft thinking (compassionate attitudes and proposals, preferences for co-operation), and being weak. These are, of old, culturally feminine virtues and limitations. It appears that distinction or differentiation is masculine, while the feminine implies loss of self from being too close to others or thinking too much like them. The rhetoric of Strong Leadership makes clear that an essential boundary in politics and society is the one that separates men from women, and it is likely that this requirement rests on the fundamental wish to keep 'I' separate from 'not-I': if women are associated with mother and mother with nature, then men and civilization (as 'dries') must be protected from women and nature.

At any rate we are alerted to look for links between the fashion for Strong Leadership and a sharpening of distinctions between the genders (as appears the case in recent advertising), not to say opposition to feminist reforms. We should also look for a view of the 'not-I' — of the social, outside the self — which is jaundiced by a baleful interpretation of its first representative, the mother.

4 *Aggressiveness and love.* Strong Leadership offers its supporters an outlet for aggressiveness both as anger and simple self-assertion. It calls for a halt to feelings of guilt and

endless hand-wringing, and aims at setting people in motion and lightening their burdens. A minimum of self-assertion is essential to obtain the distinctiveness desired by Strong Leadership's supporters, but the licence to defend and even promote oneself aggressively is not to be abused. Strong Leadership's promise is of controlled competitiveness and it recommends itself as the specialist in optimal aggressiveness, a promise that readily fails, from too much or too little. It is also subject to the hierarchical principle that the trusted can assert themselves (as in white-collar crime) more freely than the distrusted mass.

Licensed hostility is also Strong Leadership's way of getting a semblance of collective action. The well-known use for aggressiveness is to turn it outwards, unifying and energizing the group by displacing intra-group tensions. More generally, allowing and even respecting people's combativeness permits Strong Leadership to call for social unity without threatening its supporters with the feared submergence in the group. Unities are partial, revokable, a means to an end and will not be required after the collective task is completed. They are 'office' unities not 'family' ones, reassuringly finite. Thus, respect for competitiveness legitimates Strong Leadership's calls to work together, because they are only for meeting the crisis and even if the crisis attitude is to be permanent, the principle holds: privacy, reserve, rituals of conflict (as between men) reassure the Strong Leadership supporter that he or she is only partially involved in the social whole, still safely individual even though behaving as a model citizen.

It is Strong Leadership's boast that it creates a social structure that can hold this delicate balance between aggressive self-interest and collective life, but can love and hate be so simply organized and contained? In a vigorous and peaceful society, are there not unacknowledged social sentiments at work; and might not these be the real creators of social life and the effective limits on individual competitiveness? That is, the social order may owe more to trust and the enjoyment of others than to Strong Leadership's emotional traffic management.

Leaving these aside, Strong Leadership's 'cool' image of society is contradicted even in its own terms. Social feeling

— love — is only sent on a detour by the fear of submergence in social life. It turns out that the hostile and hard-headed attitudes of Strong Leadership and its supporters coexist with intense, frequently sentimental attachments — with melodramatic rhetoric, corny beliefs, bursts of patriotic passion. The nation, sports teams, veterans' clubs, along with legendary feats of heroism and self-sacrifice, bring swelling hearts and tears to the eyes. The sentiment that was barred re-enters by the back door and the social feelings denied in favour of individual safety and personal advancement become attached to larger-than-life entities, to club, corporation, company, etc. The abstract and the impersonal — toughness of mind, the structure equated with social life itself — are loved with a feeling it would be too dangerous to show to persons directly.

Hence, it is a mistake to see Strong Leadership as only aggressive, its leaders and supporters virtual sadists whose political pleasure is in kicking heads, dividing and conquering, becoming king of the castle. That takes Strong Leadership too much at face value, accepting too much of its self-image as virile, iron-willed and heroic, noble in the responsibility of command, passionless and needing no one. The true picture is more complicated. The aloofness of the Strong Leader, the reserve between his or her followers, the combativeness and self-aggrandizing, all rest on a fear of social life as homogenizing. Those qualities are stressed, or over-stressed, because the same people have an opposite tendency — to run with whooping hordes (in war or sport), to join in swelling choruses singing the praises of some banal custom or achievement, to work back-to-back in some noble, even sacrificial task. Aggressiveness and love, widely separated in Strong Leadership's rhetoric which mocks bleeding hearts, are in fact woven together like the Pentagon and prayer breakfasts, and there is as much to fear from Strong Leadership's crusading love as from its vigorous hate.

PSYCHOLOGICAL IDEAS

I have one more task before turning to our three Strong Leaders. The reader will want to know what psychological ideas I am drawing on while I, in turn, want the reader to have confidence that I am neither theoretically doctrinaire nor making *ad hoc* judgements as I go.

In general, the background ideas are from psychoanalysis, but no one can psychoanalyse someone who is not there, and psychoanalysis is a co-operative project, anyway. Psychoanalytic *ideas*, however, have the sort of depth and range we need if we are to understand something of the complexity surrounding the individual in politics. Still, these ideas have needed a certain amount of translation and reorganization and this book, though it stands on its own, draws on my work in the earlier book, *Political Ensembles.* There I employed the notion of psychoanalytic — or psychological — 'promptuaries'.

A promptuary, summarily, is a sort of theoretical toolshed, a store of ideas relevant to the bit of politics or leadership we want to understand. There are three promptuaries, each bearing on a different set of issues in an individual's life: the Oedipus complex, the separation-individuation crisis, the problem of self and meaning. In the profiles that follow I rarely refer directly to these ideas. I outline them here to reassure the reader that the twists and turns, the pursuit of idiosyncrasy and nuance, that appear in the profiles have a degree of order about them, and to show how politics — which is usually thought distant from our personal affairs — is, in fact, a shaped enlargement of the issues that concern us most intimately.

Promptuary 1: the Oedipus complex

This subset of psychoanalytic ideas is the obvious one to begin with in the study of Strong Leadership because it accentuates, in relation to personal life and development, the exact problems Strong Leadership picks out for society and politics and relies on similar key assumptions. The central problem is how *desire* will be satisfied in the face of *rivalry.* The Oedipus complex is the psychology of the crunch, or crisis, that moment when there is a collision of wills, when it is necessary to fight and win or lose. It assumes threat from outside, a real, objective obstacle or challenge to desire, a real prize that is to be lost or gained. This is how Strong

Leadership sees the world and its central problems. What Strong Leadership means by 'realism' is that human experience is essentially a triangular conflict of this sort ('scarcity' rules), the crunch always at hand in a world profoundly conflictual and objectively frustrating. Its remedy is also a species of force, whether physical or moral, requiring, above all, will.

The psychological Oedipus complex and the social-political beliefs of Strong Leadership and its supporters thus share a view of the world and the essentials of human experience. Their responses are similar too. Like Strong Leadership, the Oedipal promptuary suggests an ideal solution (the so-called resolution of the Oedipus complex) which rests on a perfect balance between individual initiative and internalized social controls (like contest-and-control). Ideally the child surmounts the crisis of desire and rivalry still zestful and determined, still desiring, but now more realistic and self-controlled. The newly installed super-ego — classically, the threatening father internalized — is the capstone in an essentially finished psychic structure which finely balances self-interest and social-mindedness just as, in Strong Leadership, an external leader/father presides over a structure of followers both enterprising and responsible.

It is the less-than-ideal outcomes that interest us most. The Oedipal promptuary gives us insights into these that can be carried over into critiques of Strong Leadership, especially of its claims to have found the solution to combining vitality with social order. The practical message of this promptuary is that ambivalence — love mixed with hate — is not easily quelled or channelled, for all the social structuring Strong Leadership sets out to do.

A too powerful super-ego, leading to loss of initiative and to over-conformity, is one obvious possibility. So is the reverse, the under-socialized, still too impulsive, follower who is disruptive and unproductive. There are many less obvious ways in which the Oedipus complex continues unresolved (which is the normal situation) but it would not be fruitful to try to list all these in the abstract. Fortunately, the less-than-perfect outcomes can be summed up in a word: ambivalence. The Oedipal promptuary teaches us to doubt Strong Leadership's claim to have set up a monolith of social order, a stable-boundaried, hierarchical structure in which clearly delineated rewards and sanctions work to ensure an efficient collective which simultaneously reaps the benefits of co-operation and safeguards individuality.

In fact, love and hate continue in a swirling confusion, despite Strong Leadership's attempts to segregate them by turning one on its designated enemies, reserving the other for its allies. Certainly Strong Leadership can have temporary successes at this (for example, in wartime), and one kind of criticism is of just those successes: they require hostile division, stereotyping, narrowed sympathies and restricted imagination, as well as heavy 'policing' costs to keep the boundaries high and strong. However, these criticisms draw on the psychological insights of the other promptuaries and on different political persuasions. The Oedipal promptuary, of itself, indicates only that Strong Leadership cannot avoid being internally unstable, that its realism about conflict, about the place or desire and rivalry in human affairs, inflates into myth when Strong Leadership claims to provide orderly enterprise, both stability *and* freedom. The real story is far less tidy.

In addition, the persistence of ambivalence — love and hate linked together behind the mask of leader-to-follower 'respect' and follower-to-leader 'deference' — calls attention to Strong Leadership's potential distortion of the world. Ambivalently loving and hating, Strong Leadership and its followers help *make* the world untrustworthy, though they claim to be only seeing it as it is. They ignore their own subjectivity and volatility, proudly claiming to be well socialized, civilized, maturely beyond such primitive, stormy states. The primitive is thus transferred outwards on to nature, on to bordering territories and attributed to dissidents within. In other words, ambivalence, the more it is disowned, is 'projected' outwards from the ambivalent person, making the outside world a reproduction of his or her own unacknowledged inner tensions.

We must bring to the study of Strong Leadership, then, the psychological wisdom of the promptuary which bids us not to accept Strong Leadership's confident assertions that it can achieve a perfect balance between self-interest and social-mindedness, that it brings order and properly channeled (efficient, purposive) achievement, that it gives the truest reading of the real world. The persistence of ambivalence means push-pull instability. It means that profoundly competitive self-interest does not yield easily. It allows for the possibility that the ostensibly objective world of bitter rivalry is a construct of divided men and women calling their inner state the state of the world.

Promptuary 2: the separation-individuation crisis

Psychoanalytic insights into a child's experience of separating from its mother provide us with another set of concepts for use in understanding the appeal and the limits of Strong Leadership. The interplay between aggression and love are as important here as in the Oedipal promptuary, though the two-person context, rather than the triangular one, dictates a difference in emphasis. However, the separation-individuation promptuary throws a more direct light on two other components in the psychology of Strong Leadership: the preference for division over unity and the devaluation of the feminine. There is also considerable overlap with the third promptuary which is concerned with the self, meaning and self-knowledge.

Whether as hypothesis or literal fact, the separation-individuation crisis presupposes a complete union between mother and child followed by a disruption which is both inevitable and portentous for the future course of an individual's life. Human experience, according to this psychoanalytic emphasis, is marked less by Oedipal strivings and eventual defeat (which individuals then perpetually battle to reverse, or deny, their socialized behaviour masking ambivalence) than by the pain of lost connection.

Ideally, individuals abandon their longing for the blissful, undifferentiated, primitive union with mother and the world, working instead for unities of a more mature and more limited kind. Thus society or civilization rests on a 'natural', though not easy, tendency to overcome isolation, on a fundamental proclivity for solidarity or community life. Distrust, division and rivalry, much prized as realistic by Strong Leadership, in this view are signs of resentment and of a continuing refusal to accept the reality of separation except as an injustice which sours all future social life. Strong Leadership, through the lenses of this promptuary, seems to adopt the attitude of the once bitten, twice shy: let down once, it will not make the mistake of trustful, hopeful interdependence again.

The British psychoanalyst, Melanie Klein, conveys this emphasis. Her 'paranoid-schizoid' position illuminates Strong Leadership's attitude to collective life very vividly. (Paranoid equals suspicious, wary; schizoid means cool, withdrawn, controlled.) It also shows that Strong Leadership's much prized objectivity — its emphasis on the external world — may be more apparent than real.

Given that the child's discovery of separateness is the foundation for its attitude to its own individuality, then it matters very much how this separation is experienced: if separateness is interpreted darkly, angrily, then the child will set about guarding itself from the influences playing on it from outside, and this installs the suspicious inner world, the powers of its own mind biased by fear, as the individual's main guide to other people and the world. Creating a hostile environment for itself, the child thus allows suspicion to guide thought, and nourishment and influence from outside are not accepted easily. Hence projection predominates, 'putting outside', not introspection or 'taking in'.

Indeed, the concept of 'projective identification' which plays so large a part in Klein's thought may describe best the way Strong Leadership and its supporters operate. Strong Leadership approaches the world to master and manipulate it. Projective identification — where an individual controls his world by reading into other people his own unacknowledged qualities, especially the bad ones — is well suited to this project. Salespersons, no less than generals and elected Strong Leaders, like to keep one step ahead of their rivals and even their supposed allies, and do so by 'reading their minds'. What they imagine in their quarry may be a projected part of themselves and halfway at least to a self-fulfilling prophecy, as the 'real world' turns out to be what the Strong Leader requires for his own mental economy.

There is a split here between good and bad, friend and foe, reflecting the pain of separation and the establishment of an angry individuality, which can see the world only in terms of hostile dichotomies, summed up in 'lead or be led'. Wisdom, in this promptuary, would be the softening of these distinctions, as the Group Leader and his or her followers try to do (though they have another set of problems to deal with). The hard-edged individualist reinterprets Eden as Gethsemane and immersion in the collective life as a kind of death. Self, individuality, can only survive in opposition.

It would seem to follow that women, nearer to mother (and nature) will be devalued in the Strong Leadership camp. Its celebration of the masculine — of activity, of hard-boiled attitudes, of 'biting the bullet', and its love of tangible, practical intervention — would then reflect its avoidance of the unjust, untrustworthy feminine, modelled in a supposedly rejecting mother. Separation is pursued with a vengeance: Strong Leadership's advice is always to 'cut the apron strings', 'throw them in at the deep end', 'apply the [political] blow-torch', etc. Women, and the qualities of attachment they appear to provide, are necessary, but in their place, subject to broad political and economic aims, to law and, ultimately, to men.

One test of Strong Leadership is its attitude to the quasi-religious attitudes the separation-individuation promptuary implicitly commends. Klein's version of maturity, the 'Depressive' position, looks for evidence that the individual no longer blames (m)others but shares blame; or moves beyond blaming altogether into unbitter acceptance of loss and the task of creating unities across the earlier divides. Our Strong Leaders will show few of these signs, seeing the world quite differently — needing to see it differently — that is, as divided and properly so except under careful control. Nevertheless, we will need to look at what evidence there is of attitudes and behaviours designed to heal wounds, of a sensitivity to bonds that go deeper than the self-interested connections and legally-enforced conformities of the structure Strong Leaders head and their followers feel comfortable in. How they handle desire and rivalry, and the resulting structure of hierarchy, boundaries, etc., will be our main focus (drawing on the first promptuary). However, how they think about and handle social sentiments, the lateral rather than vertical dimensions of social life, using the separation-individuation promptuary, needs our attention too.

Promptuary 3: identity, meaning and self-understanding

The previous two promptuaries are drawn from two developmental crises on which psychoanalysis has focused. They are linked: the more sharply pain is felt at the point of separation and the more exclusively individualism is based on self-preservation and hostility, then the more fiercely Oedipal fires will burn and go on smouldering throughout life. The ideas I am turning to now are not about crisis. They involve a shift of perspective, a look at how individuals see themselves, how they live with themselves, what they hope for in themselves. This question of self-experience directs us not to a critical moment but to a thread running through individual lives, lifting our attention as it were above the audience's view of the actor and the actor's view of the audience to the actor's view of the actor himself.

Ideas about self-experience are not absent from the other promptuaries but they are not so clearly separated. In the Oedipal promptuary the nature of the self is implied in the balancing act that must be performed. The person is to be both an agent and an object, enterprising and dutiful, and his or her self-experience will range between feeling free and effective and feeling sufficiently virtuous or obedient to avoid shame or guilt. In the separation-individuation promptuary, the state of the self has more to do with feeling adequate to the task of healing, repairing, being sensitive to the needs of others, a mixture of attitude and ability in making human connections. These are derived ideas about the self, not untrue but not allowing sufficiently for the individual's desire and capacity for viewing himself or herself, for judging the self to some degree independently of the standards of the super-ego and of the community of impressions absorbed or received in childhood. This third promptuary gives greater weight to these, to imaginative reflection on who one is.

It might seem enough to ask what Strong Leadership wants, whom it believes it must oppose in the pursuit of its desires, how successful it is. Those are its own criteria. But

I shall be pointing out another dimension in the profiles: a need for identity, which in Strong Leadership is a need to find oneself in the pursuit of desires and the defeat of enemies. To be 'strong' in order to achieve something is one thing; to try to confirm (to oneself) that one is 'strong' is another, and not obviously less important. Indeed Strong Leadership's insistence on being merely, and solely, executive — just about getting results — has to be viewed very sceptically. From this third psychological point of view that is just a mask covering the wish to 'be someone' which shapes the true physiognomy.

Having said that, we must begin with Strong Leadership's conviction that meaning lies in the critical struggle for survival, and that thinking should be practical, its first priority problem solving. For Strong Leadership, both self-examination and unfettered curiosity are at best a distraction from the task in hand, at worst potentially subversive. Both the crises we have mentioned contribute to Strong Leadership's in-curiosity. Oedipal defeat is a profound dampener on a child's questioning: its attempt to master the secret of human origins is turned back as a challenge to authority, its claims to have guessed are laughed at, and its parents retain their advantage by the secret they keep to themselves. (Secrecy is a crucial weapon in Strong Leadership politics, as 'privacy' is one of the chief values of its supporters; to know is to be master, to be known to be mastered.) The separation-individuation crisis shows how children censor themselves, not out of fear of punishment (initiative punished) as from fear that knowledge damages. In summing up what can have caused the loss of connection with mother, the child concludes: it was my insistence, my intrusion that did it, my wish to know.

Moreover, both crises shape Strong Leadership's style of thinking. The recoil from 'natural' unities breaks the lines communicating shared understanding; intimate knowledge is cut off from public knowledge, deeply felt ideas are isolated from operational ones, and so on. The maintenance of a paranoid-schizoid stance towards the world requires and facilitates ignorance about other people, leaving a void which is filled in by projections (attributions) placed on them. It also turns attention away from the inner realities of the self.

Strong Leadership favours thinking that can be expressed in a belligerent — or at least bantering — manner so that minds do not overlap too closely; it will not like lateral (playful) thinking which, being unstructured, could lead into dangerous territory where control is lost and the safeguards of continual contest are undermined. It will prefer the formal debate to the brainstorm, unless the latter is kept safely apart from executive decision-making. It will also doubt the value of the sort of therapeutic group in which feeling and thought, person and task, are difficult to distinguish and keep apart, though once again they may be used if properly segregated from serious policy-making and if properly harnessed to Strong Leadership's overriding goals.

For Strong Leadership and its followers identity lies in the position given by the outside world, or the status carved out there. Meaning lies in the demands of that world. The self feels real and valuable if something outside — above, pre-existing or even opposed (enemies grant a brave man respect) — approves. Much depends on the truth of this supposed objectivity. Strong Leadership's claim to value is that it has 'made a difference', 'made a mark on the world', that it is recognized by something or someone other than itself. This is virtually Strong Leadership's bedrock: human significance born of meeting resistance successfully, or at least in a controlled way, boldly or with endurance. The question is whether the not-I, the Other — a person, the world — is as opposed or as 'real' as Strong Leaders and their supporters believe them to be.

What if, in line with the second promptuary, the (m)other is not so hostile as it seems? If the Oedipal promptuary's accentuation of zero-sum conflict is only partly right, then Strong Leadership too can be only partly right, its formula for politics and society needs modification to allow for trust and enjoyable, satisfying co-operation. Also, what if, as in the third promptuary, nature and culture are a kind of interplay, a blend of real otherness and real subjectivity? What if, in other words, 'reality' is not really there? If this were the case the only adequate attitude would be a continuing blend of investigating oneself and investigating the world, controlling and yielding, understanding and acting. Resistance and overcoming would not lose their point in this kind of world, but they would not be the supreme values they are in Strong Leadership. What does it profit to rule over a republic of shadows?

This is certainly the drift of the third psychoanalytic promptuary. Identity and meaning are a continually adjusted composite of inner and outer, of subject and object. They require action but with self-understanding and an overview in which the actor sees himself and his world as if from outside. There is no formula here, no ultimate rebuke to Strong Leadership. Those who most support the overview — the committed universalists and ideas people who may be followers of Inspiring Leaders proposing a brilliant 'third way' — fall into traps of their own. However Strong Leadership's black-and-white thinking, its concept of identity as with-us-or-against-us, and its tribal location of meaning in fighting-the-good-fight, need to be qualified. For this task, the third promptuary collects together useful ideas about the need to be simultaneously active in the world and to be an observer of it — and of oneself in it. Even the paradox of both/and, rather than the dichotomy either/or which Strong Leadership presses on us, may not always be a sign of woolly thinking and moral wimpishness but of a truer realism and more adequate politics.

MARGARET THATCHER

3
Conviction Politics

A 'conviction' politician uses his or her philosophy like a political catechism and a set of marching orders. Its functions are to bind the troops together, to highlight differences with rivals to the point where their views are unthinkable — in all, to harness ideas to power, action, victory. A Strong Leader's philosophy must be simple and reliable, easily communicated, made to strike hard and stick. The intention is not to contribute to a debate; the intention is to overcome, and then marginalize contrary views out of existence.

There are some who say Margaret Thatcher was convinced of the futility of 'managerial' Toryism after Heath's successive defeats and went hunting for an ideology to match that of the Socialists. Keith Joseph was her tutor. About this time Malcolm Fraser had shown in Australia how to win with a 'philosophy' against an incumbent whose idea of capturing the middle ground could be shown as muddle or worse. Mrs Thatcher had little help from 'Thatcherism' in becoming the Conservative Party leader but, once she was in power, maximizing difference and providing 'a real alternative', became the successful Party strategy. There is no doubt, though, that Thatcherism is a direct expression of Mrs Thatcher herself, her personal views, her prejudices, turned into political truths. She wrote a paper at Oxford in

1946 which prefigured her leading themes, and one senior civil servant remarked that her policies, like everything she did, flowed from her character rather than from her intellect: 'The policies were the man, as it were'. Mrs Thatcher herself has been at pains to show the consistency of her views from childhood and Grantham on.

Principle, or philosophy, can have pragmatic uses. If Strong Leadership is about being on top, then it will use whatever weapons are most likely to work, and the Strong Leader — on the basis of the ultimate 'principle' that nothing succeeds like success — will not allow herself to be consistent to the point that she becomes an easy mark. A well-honed philosophy lets you trade hard punches, but you must feint too; the advantage of seeming resolute and absolutely sure of what is right must be balanced against the advantages of expediency.

Margaret Thatcher has been accused of rigid thinking, of absolute inflexibility — a civil servant again: 'she was the only Minister I never heard say "I wonder whether" . . .' — but a former cabinet minister says she can change her mind 'far more than people realize' as long as you know your facts and stand up to her. An economic adviser calls the description of her as intransigent 'absurd — she is more open to argument and logic than the majority of politicians I know'. (He went on to admit 'she followed my cases, of course! But she followed them well'.)

Complaints that a leader does not listen are notoriously hard to evaluate. Leaders can take too much advice as well as too little, and those who challenge their advisers and colleagues to put up a good case see this as necessary to protect their leadership. (Ronald Reagan's permissiveness towards his advisers shows the dangers of the opposite.) There is a balance to be found between dominating too much, so that the leader becomes increasingly isolated and increasingly confined by his or her own ideas, prejudices, 'facts', or whatever, and being dominated. Also, there are different ways of handling advice and influence. It appears that Mrs Thatcher carries division and challenge — Strong Leadership's predilection for struggle — deep into her own domain; and that she handles logic better than she handles people.

I will be saying more about the second of these points later. Enough to say here that the significance to be attached to Mrs Thatcher's workaholism, her unease in 'unstructured' conversation and her record of establishing few non-working friendships is that she thereby closes herself off from sensitive advice subtly given. Advice squeezed through the grill of debate, logical and factual though it may be, is limited to what can be communicated in that way. By contrast, Franklin Delano Roosevelt was a leader who learned as much or more from relaxed, speculative conversations as from anything resembling the sort of moot courts Mrs Thatcher prefers.

David Howell, who was in Thatcher's cabinet until 1983, says that in her world 'everything should start as an argument, go on as an argument, and end as an argument'. 'Everyone likes to win arguments', he went on, but 'nobody could deny she likes to win arguments more than others do'. Those who have resigned (the figure is now approaching a score), especially Pym and Heseltine, have blamed Mrs Thatcher's style of work in cabinet — her high-handedness, gratuitous competitiveness, and her narrowness of outlook.

A sharply etched philosophy creates division even where division is unintended and unwise. Mrs Thatcher's celebrated 'wets', her insistent question 'Is he one of us?', her linking of thought to combativeness and a narrow form of competence (the debater's skill) are characteristic of Strong Leadership's taste for invidious success. High-profile ideology linked to high-profile leadership is a powerful predictor of internal dispute, factionalism, and fragmentation, except in extreme circumstances such as war. The Leader commands the party by commanding its philosophy, so that to oppose the dominant philosophy (or the Leader's interpretation of it) is seen as opposing the Leader. The Strong Leader, even if she sees the dangers in this, finds herself powerless to avoid them, lacking the will and capacity for low-profile, easy-going solidarities. Mrs Thatcher boasted to one civil servant that she could sum up a man in a matter of seconds and that she never had to revise her decision. The civil servant commented: 'you were consigned to a very short list of saints or a very long list of sinners', and you 'couldn't work your passage' from one to the other, 'that was the difficulty'.

Francis Pym's none too subtle use of an historical example to criticize Mrs Thatcher neatly sums this up. If Neville Chamberlain is a weapon Strong Leadership can use against its 'appeasing' rivals, the latter have their own weapon in Joseph Chamberlain. Pym uses him, a thinly disguised Margaret Thatcher, as a lesson in the dangers of confrontationist, ideological politics. At a time when 'the British economy was in relative decline' and 'a staleness had crept into the nation' Chamberlain 'offered an approach that was new, radical and invigorating'. He decided 'the key to success lay in strengthening the hold of the ideology within the party' and he adopted a rhetoric that 'polarized opinion and exaggerated the differences instead of reconciling them'.

Intensifying the comparison with Mrs Thatcher, Pym describes Joseph Chamberlain as 'not a Conservative' (he was a Liberal), 'a vigorous, self-made, Midlands industrialist'. 'He had great energy, determination and charisma. He was a politician of conviction . . . preferred to implement ideas rather than to debate them . . . ideological and iconoclastic . . . ruthless in the pursuit of his ideas.' Finally — and this points to Strong Leadership's *use* of ideas as an adjunct of its overriding concern with power — 'Chamberlain came to equate loyalty to the Conservative Party and to the nation with loyalty to his particular ideology. Anyone who was disloyal to the ideology was immediately considered disloyal to the party, and was thought to lack any judgement of the national interest'. The last sentence in the quote draws attention to Pym himself, of course.

'Convictions', then, serve in the first place to strengthen Strong Leadership's hand. They are a weapon to divide and conquer, within the party and across the electorate. However, not any philosophy will do: it has to be sharply-defined, essentially oppositional, easily reduced to simple ideas and therefore widely comprehensible. There will be items of policy that can be changed or given up (though too many of these would forfeit the look of purposefulness and determination), but there will be a core which, in substance or as a kind of fetish, will be protected at all times. The balanced budget is one of those, the analogy between housekeeping and national accounts is perhaps another. So we turn now to the themes of Thatcherism.

THATCHERISM

In their itemized form the themes of Thatcherism are already well known, though I think the impact of some items has not been fully understood. Smaller government never meant less powerful government, though Thatcherism ingratiated itself with 'little people' such as small business with the plan to cut down Big Brother and see off the Nanny State. Indeed, in several of her published speeches Margaret Thatcher, as a politician, pretends to a kind of self-criticism, beating her political breast for not being helpful enough to the real wealth-creators. She meant, of course, that her Labour opponents hadn't been.

The aim is to make government leaner and stronger, better able to help the Strong for being free of the energy-sapping entanglements in social welfare, education, etc. Government will be strong against the incentive-draining pull of the unproductive poor and their idealistic, equally unproductive spokesmen in social work and local government. The market will be freed up, promising outlets for energy, initiative, imagination, bringing wealth for one and all. Strong Leadership's sense of human vitality takes this form: the production of tangible wealth. Strong Leadership offers itself and the institutions it commands as a protective framework for those enterprising people who find security and purpose in advancing themselves this way. In addition, market forces will act as a discipline on those who want to do something else, pulling more of them into this kind of productiveness, expelling those not up to it, ranking everyone, not according to need, but according to usefulness.

The chief organized representative of the opposite view, the union movement, is obviously target number one. The second target is 'direct action'. Margaret Thatcher has long been an opponent of extra-parliamentary movements which she believes, with the connivance of the media, threaten existing institutions. Having gained some dominance over the big institutions, public and private, Strong Leadership takes a dim view of those opposing groups it cannot routinely put down. 'Direct action' appears to Strong Leadership like guerrilla action, anarchic and intolerable. This strengthens the law-and-order emphasis, balancing with control the emphasis on contest, so that a Thatcherist society can seem both ruthlessly *laissez-faire* and severely conformist and even Puritan in its moralizing. In recent years Strong Leaders have turned their attack on to schools and the ('left-wing biased') communication media, convinced that their efforts are being undermined there, though not always sure how, or exactly whom, to pursue.

Thatcherism, like all Strong Leadership, means both freeing up and clamping down. As we move from the practicalities of private/public borrowing, privatization in industry and housing, anti-union legislation, etc., the same double-edged goad is used to make moral or 'spiritual' changes. The tone is now shrill. There are 'shirkers' and 'workers', 'savers' and 'spenders'; there are those who undermine our confidence and those (entrepreneurs) who have sacrificed for the good of the whole. Above all there is the family — not the warm, misty-eyed family that takes in a reformed Scrooge, but the family that has authority, teaches its children to work and save, the family that is an agent of social order and material enterprise. The right people and the right families are those that hear and respond to Mrs Thatcher's message that improvement means sacrifice, that returning to health means swallowing harsh medicine, that moral tolerance is really moral decline.

So far I've said little that is not by now very familiar — though subjecting each item to the overall character and aims of Strong Leadership gives them a twist not everyone will deem fair. However, let me say that in every one Margaret Thatcher and Strong Leadership may be perfectly correct. Also, whether they are or not depends on the rightness of two fundamental convictions that underlie the details of Thatcherism (or Reaganism or Fraserism). These are: the need to pursue greatness, nationally and individually, and the need for inequality. Both are basic beliefs and are the foundations of the itemized programme we have looked at.

The pursuit of greatness

There can be no doubt about Mrs Thatcher's wish for Britain to be *Great* Britain again. Labour's incumbency, she said in 1975, 'has led to a loss of confidence and a sense of helplessness'; in the 1979 election she described Britain as 'a great country which seems to have lost its way', and that her job was to erect a 'barrier of steel' across the path of Britain's decline. 'I am not prepared to accept second, third, fourth best for Britain. I do not believe our decline was inevitable.' 'Is it not time that we spoke up for our way of life?' 'What kind of people are we? We are the people that in the past made Great Britain the workshop of the world, the people who persuaded others to buy British — not in begging them to do so but because it was best.' These clarion calls come from Conservative Party speeches Mrs Thatcher made in 1976 and 1977. In 1986 a *Times* political correspondent summed up Mrs Thatcher's seven years in the same way: 'The essence of Thatcherism is an instinctive resistance to national decline'. The Falklands war, he said, was a test of how strong this resistance had become, a test that was almost welcomed. At the end of the war Mrs Thatcher boasted 'We British are as we always have been — competent, courageous, resolute'.

Its obvious relevance to British decline should not blind us to Strong Leadership's perpetual preoccupation with greatness. Aristotle wrote 'We can do noble acts without ruling earth and sea', and Jim Prior, an early opponent of Mrs Thatcher's (and an eventual casualty) remarks: 'Most of us are very ordinary people, and we don't aspire to greatness, and sometimes the tendency is to think that everyone ought to aspire to greatness — and when they don't succeed . . . they've somehow let the side down'. However, Strong Leadership links the good with the powerful. Like Machiavelli, who chose to advise a Prince who would abandon virtue to pursue greatness singlemindedly, and like Nietzsche, spurning the 'slave' virtues, Strong Leaders set themselves on a path towards negotiating — if they must negotiate — from strength. They set themselves against political opponents who trust to natural instincts for cooperation, and against others who, well knowing the difficulties of negotiating, nevertheless believe some mutuality is possible. Strong Leadership pursues instead the contradiction or paradox that only when we are in a position to impose our will can we negotiate as equals.

This is one of the foundations for Thatcherism's small-but-strong government theme, its celebration and encouragement of the entrepreneurial, ambitious individual. It also shapes its international politics. 'The first duty of any government is to safeguard its people against external aggression, to guarantee the survival of our way of life.' That was Mrs Thatcher in 1976. A year before she told a Conservative Party conference: 'the first duty of government is to uphold the law. If it tries to bob, weave and duck around that duty when it is inconvenient, the governed will do exactly the same thing and then nothing will be safe, not home, not liberty, not life itself'. There is no inconsistency between these two statements. Danger can come from within as well as from without, and the strength Strong Leadership wants government to have is total: physical (military), legal, and moral, where the last is in large part the government's determination to apply the law.

Margaret Thatcher became known as the 'Iron Lady' on the international scene first. She went outside the politeness which was then, as *détente*, governing East-West relations, calling world attention to an alleged Soviet superiority in conventional armaments. This was partly a tactic to keep American nuclear interests in Europe. More generally, she was frank in admitting that 'Britain's capacity to play a constructive role in world affairs is, of course, related to our economic and military strength'. The Falklands war showed this in concentrated form, not least in her determination that the military should be served without let or hinder, that the politicians should not be a drag on the military effort. She has shown great interest in the services, donning their workaday gear, posing for photographs in or beside their weapons. She draws on Britain's military past, claiming friendships on the grounds of wartime alliance (France, the United States); she visits Northern Ireland (but not, until after the last election, the economically derelict areas of the north of England) and stands her ground at the scenes of terrorism.

All this expresses Strong Leadership's conviction that effectiveness, security and even meaning rest on being able to impose oneself, or one's party or one's country. Britain's prestige in the world requires a nuclear deterrent and cruise missiles, for only that way can it influence other nations. Some years ago, and again in 1987, she drew the lesson: 'the recent willingness of the Soviet government to open a new round of arms control negotiations shows the wisdom of our firmness'.

Violence is all the more threatening when it is uncontrolled. At least this is how Strong Leadership sees it, fearing terrorism more perhaps than a well-institutionalized enemy with whom 'one can do business'. This phrase was used by Mrs Thatcher after her talks with Gorbachev in 1987, talks which apparently approached the kind of lively debate she seems to relish. However, where the enemy is out of focus, split up, and liable to disappear before reappearing unexpectedly somewhere else, Strong Leadership begins to unravel. It likes setpiece confrontations, when even covert operations have a structure there is some hope of controlling. This is as it must be, given Strong Leadership's distrust of less formal bonds and understandings that lack sanctions for when they break down.

Early in the new Cold War, Mrs Thatcher saw danger in the traditional enemy, the Soviet Union, pursuing its unrelenting aim of world domination. She has toned down her rhetoric on this in recent years, but she began strongly. Quoting Francis Bacon, 'opportunity makes a thief', Mrs Thatcher went on: 'That has been all too true in international affairs of late. I want to see that temptation reduced'. Against the Soviet Union, her answer has been a more virile, resolute Western alliance:

> There really are two political systems in the world. There is one based on personal freedom . . . and there is one based on communism . . . which denies freedom . . . Now it's always been the Russian ideology that they try to expand and to extend their system either by military force, either by proxy, or by subversion, or by propagating their creed the world over. We must do the same . . .

The immediate answer is two armed camps, ours at least as implacable and imperialistic as theirs. The West should combine around anti-Sovietism, build a combined economic and military strength, demand changes in Soviet policy (in human rights, in vacating Afghanistan), seek occasions to show its determination (Grenada?) — and only then sit down at the negotiating table. One wonders at the curtailment of imagination that makes master-strategy a lesson learned from the enemy itself.

A critical point in this Thatcher rhetoric was the wish to prod President Carter into something more like Strong Leadership. Speaking in New York she offered herself as his example: 'I have been attacked by the Soviet government for arguing that the West should put itself in a position to negotiate from strength'. She defends herself in two ways: first, 'I have done no more than echo the constant ambition of the Soviet government itself'; second, 'I am not talking about negotiations from a position of superiority. What I am seeking is a negotiation in which we and they start from a position of balance . . .'. She goes on to add, whimsically almost, that the Russians are right to call her an Iron Lady: 'I am'.

The difference between 'superiority' and 'strength' is hard to distinguish. How strong is an individual if she is only exactly as strong as everyone else? Or a nation? This uncertainty runs right through Strong Leadership: to be reduced to nothing may tempt someone to take us over; to be strong enough to raise the cost of a takeover is good sense. Real power lies in superiority, as does real safety. Mrs Thatcher's aggressive rhetoric shows, even allowing for her wish to stiffen American resolve, that this ambiguity lies unresolved at the heart of her international relations — a Strong Leader's inevitable ambivalence about letting others be equals. This suspicion grows as we look at her attitude to another kind of international threat and how it should be dealt with.

Margaret Thatcher speaks with some nostalgia of the 'periods in history when power and influence in international life [were] concentrated in the hands of a very few. Such times have often been relatively stable. A system with a limited number of players evolves its own checks and balances'. 'But', she says, 'we are now in a more uncertain arena. Gone are the days when there were only two significant groupings, the West led by the United States, and the Soviet bloc. International authority has fragmented . . .'. Focus reduces fear, and Mrs Thatcher's new East/West Cold War is a lesser evil, in which confrontation between two leviathans is paradoxically a move towards peace, where a greater number of participants threatens lethal chaos.

Strong Leadership's 'conservatism' consists above all in this: getting control of the means, military and economic, of competition and combat. Thus, for Mrs Thatcher, the mushrooming of national autonomies in the Third World is, in the first place, the fragmentation of authority, of which terrorism is just the leading edge. After her election in 1979 she forecast that the eighties would be 'A Dangerous Decade' and warned that 'the barometer is falling'. She admitted in the same speech that 'poverty wherever it exists is an enemy of stability', but Strong Leadership's Bismarckian emphasis is on power and control: The West, she says, should 'recognize . . . with respect, not hostility, what is happening in the Muslim world'; 'I do not believe we should judge Islam by events in Iran. Least of all should we judge it by the taking of hostages'. There is 'a tide of self-confidence' in the Muslim world, she says, and 'it is in our own interests that they build on their own deep traditions'. The important thing is to keep the Marxists out, and the Islamic order can do this.

President Carter's response to these warnings is not known; his pained and painful focus on the plight of the American hostages stands in sharp contrast to the Strong Leader's focus on the whole, on the broad structure of alliances, and her support for whoever is building institutions that are controlled and orderly, however alien. Where the Group Leader worries over 'people', the Strong Leader examines the political framework.

Of the two fundamental beliefs underlying Strong Leadership, one is the paramountcy of greatness, of being imposing, superior, competitively successful. The previous paragraphs have concentrated on national greatness but the paramountcy of greatness as an individual goal — often called 'excellence' — is just as easy to demonstrate from Mrs Thatcher's speeches. The individual pursuit of greatness raises the issue of equality, and it is under that heading that

I will discuss Margaret Thatcher's basic convictions about social life.

The need for inequality

Mrs Thatcher's Selected Speeches, 1975–7, have the title 'Let Our Children Grow Tall'. This is taken from a speech given in New York in 1975 in which she reassures Americans that the 'British disease' is not everywhere in Britain, that an increasing number of her compatriots share the American belief that 'private enterprise is by far the best method of harnessing the energy and ambition of the individual to increasing the wealth of the nation'.

> What lessons have we learned from the last thirty years [i.e. the welfare state years]? First, the pursuit of equality is a mirage. Far more desirable and more practicable than the pursuit of equality is the pursuit of equality of opportunity. Opportunity means nothing unless it includes the right to be unequal — and the freedom to be different.

She refers to the saying from the Middle West, 'Don't cut down the tall poppies — let them rather grow tall', and continues 'I say: let *our children* grow tall — and some grow taller than others, if they have it in them to do so'. The society she intends to build will be one 'in which each citizen can develop his full potential . . .; in which originality, skill, energy and thrift are rewarded; in which we encourage rather than restrict the variety and richness of human nature'.

Over-familiar as we are with ideas of this sort (they are standard Tory fare) it is worth pausing to notice two or three things in the light of our concept of Strong Leadership. Starting from the end: can we be sure that 'variety and richness' count heavily with the crisis-oriented, in defence and economics, with Strong Leaders and their supporters? Mrs Thatcher praises artists and scientists, it is true, but the context is inappropriately competitive, their successes made a measure of Britain's standing in the world, and the point seems crudely quantitative, the number of wins they have had. Teachers and social workers are mentioned only to be scolded; community activists are virtually reviled, as are women's action representatives, while public officials, unless in the uniform of police or soldier, are treated dismissively. Second, how does 'thrift' get into that list of vigorous, creative qualities? It signals perhaps the narrower vision behind 'originality, skill, energy' and expresses Strong Leadership's anxiety about uncontrolled originality, its emphasis on restrained energy, etc. As contest needs controlling, so vigour must be prudently watched so that it does not over-spend itself.

Finally, consider the distinction between equality and equality of opportunity. Mrs Thatcher implies that her political opponents believe idiotically that people could be equal in themselves (not just in their comforts and resources), and that they are determined to achieve a standardization of essential human qualities, not merely equality of service. Her alternative, equality of opportunity, is not of course the alternative it seems. She would not propose that the successful should return their prizes at the end of the race (in death duties) but if equality of opportunity leads, through some doing better and keeping their reward, to inequality, then she would be more candid if she said so directly. Candour, though, is rare on this issue, and typically children are a nicer focus for élite sentiments than oneself and one's own class.

Strong Leadership could not be anything but élitist. It needs the political and social means for selecting and protecting the Strong from the enervating claims of the weak, and for motivating a human nature in which it cannot see either spontaneous social sentiment or intrinsic productiveness. Incentive, especially material incentive, is critical to Strong Leadership's plans for social life, cutting against the grain of individual laziness, selfishness and shortsightedness (cf. thrift). For Margaret Thatcher, the Strong are the military and police, the ultimate boundary keepers, and the entrepreneurial who, like soldiers at the battlefront, must have priority in provisioning.

In speeches to the Institute of Directors before she became Prime Minister, Mrs Thatcher is little short of ingratiating. 'First, unlike some of my fellow politicians, I am convinced that you and your colleagues are the best suited to be the creators of wealth in society. We in government can only consume and transfer it'; 'politicians need a healthy dose of humility'; 'The most dubious pursuit of national interest is when the private sector has put aside its long-term wealth-creating role in order to conform with the wishes of transitory politicians'.

Mrs Thatcher's humility is overstated, serving before her election to dramatize her policy of small government. However, her belief in supporting business and in supporting incentive, i.e. higher rewards for the entrepreneurial, in profits and in salaries, cannot be doubted. British managers suffer most: 'Differentials have been dangerously narrowed' and fringe benefits are an understandable but regrettable result of high direct taxation — 'Our forebears would rub their eyes in disbelief . . .'; 'What a tragic nonsense this has become'. 'The living standards of entrepreneurs, managers and skilled workers have been squeezed by the impact of taxation, salary controls and inflation. There is a sense of despair and hopelessness amongst our wealth creators . . . they bear the personal cost of financing more government.' She then sums up: 'The matter can be put suite simply. There is a vendetta against success. That is the tragic truth'.

Strong Leadership is not associated with cultural élites or the mature establishment of Britain or the old élites of north-eastern USA or pastoral Australia. Its beliefs, like its tone, befit the hard core of the middle and lower-middle class, new money (as in Australia's west or Queensland or parts of the American south and west), commercial farmers, those outside the settled higher levels of privilege impatient with the old élite's mellowing. Mrs Thatcher's populism is of this kind: a middle-class populism or, better still, a revolt of those who believe themselves workers against those (above, below and to the side) who are shirkers. Skilled workers (blue-collar Tories), small businesspersons, realtors, stockbrokers etc. find common ground against salaried officials, teachers, and those socially elevated and liberal-minded politicians who seem either too preoccupied with the high peaks of the economy ('corporatists') or too attentive to 'social' issues (the rights of minority groups, etc.), or the quality of life issues of a decade or more ago.

Thus Mrs Thatcher and Strong Leadership conflict with the settled pecking order, giving Thatcherism its energy and brashness, and confusing its opponents by seeming both conservative and radical at the same time. The essential point is, as always, Strong Leadership's crisis-orientation. Wealth-creators are desperately needed, skilled workers as well as enterprising managers, and at all levels of society a bar must be put between those who are to be encouraged and the others, wealth consumers, high or low, but especially the low who use government services.

Rhetorically Mrs Thatcher is at her most candid and courageous when she exalts the word success. A 'redefined role for government', she says, would allow 'at least some encouragement for work, for skill, for effort and, above all, for success'; a Britain 'where individuals have a chance to savour the rewards of success is a Britain that will re-emerge as a self-respecting nation'. Meaning or self-respect lies in success, an idea at once very vague and, in requiring invidiousness, also hard-nosed. Success will be won, 'above all in the market place [it] will be founded upon wealth creation'. Granted that being able to 'stand on your own feet' (a favourite Thatcher phrase), is a great deal better than having to beg, borrow or steal, it is still legitimate for those whom Mrs Thatcher puts beyond the wealth-creation pale to wonder where *our* self-respect will come from. Has she not defined us, from medical professionals to labourers, from public officials to entertainers, as mere consumers of wealth? Are we all, like Tory women staying at home to smooth the life of the primary breadwinner, useful only as adjuncts, and when we obey the wealth-creators' whims? Are there not other sources of national self-respect, other national purposes?

It remains to be seen whether this is not being too hard on Mrs Thatcher. After all, politicians have to accept the limits of public rhetoric, and even small shifts of emphasis may require exaggeration and constant reiteration of half-truths.

It is worth keeping in mind, nevertheless, that though Prime Ministers are hardly spiritual leaders or symbols of life's purpose and meaning, the agenda of intangibles they set can be to some degree a substitute for religious faith and the spiritual leadership Western societies are said to lack. A *Times* correspondent in 1986 wrote 'the change in the tone of public debate has been in some ways her most important; though least tangible, achievement'. Political moods can create opportunity for leaders; leaders in turn can intensify and extend the mood — making, for example, Strong Leadership the ruling image for individuals and organizations far from politics, making its convictions the norm for all human affairs even when it fails in its specific programme. The correspondent concluded, 'There certainly is a greater sense of realism in the country now than when Mrs, Thatcher came to power . . . we see in Britain a more tough-minded approach'.

Moral inequality

Privatization in Thatcherist economics is not matched by any decentralizing drive in Thatcherist politics. Besides economic inequality, Strong Leadership requires political inequality — which, in a constitutional democracy, means strengthened central authority. One way this is sought is through more ('stronger') leadership; a more consistent and more confident firmness in applying the rule of law is another. Added to these, both of them prominent in Thatcherism, is moralizing. This is a kind of suasion that goes beyond the economic and legislative instruments of government, and beyond law, attempting to make people feel guilty and ashamed of their 'irresponsibility', etc. As such, it presumes another inequality, a moral inequality which forms, with the economic and political inequalities, Strong Leadership's three-pronged strategy for gaining consent.

Mrs Thatcher says:

> Conservatives do not regard politics as the most important thing in life. There are many other things, from religion to family life, to which ordinary Conservatives tend to accord a higher place in the scheme of things. In contrast the left-wing tends to be totally obsessed with politics.

On this familiar belief Strong Leadership builds its claim to be, unlike ideologues and 'professional sympathizers' (in churches and welfare organizations, etc.), strictly limited in its scope and practical in its methods; it allows the individual's soul to be his or her own private matter. However, the claim is a shaky one. Here is Mrs Thatcher on 'example', remarks delivered in 1985:

> Young people are impressionable. How we behave — whether as parents, teachers, sportsmen, politicians — is bound to influence how our children behave. When teachers strike and cause disruption — that's a bad example. When football idols play foul — that's a bad example. When local councils refuse to set a legal rate — that's a bad example. And when some Trade Union leaders, yes, and some politicians, scorn the law and the courts and the police — these are bad examples. So too is picket-line violence. And who can help but worry about some of the violence we see on our television screens? The standards of society are set by what we tolerate, by the discipline and conventions we set.

Elsewhere Mrs Thatcher warned: 'serious as the economic challenge is, the political and moral challenge is just as grave and perhaps even more so, because human problems never start with economics. They have much deeper roots in human nature . . .'.

Mrs Thatcher's tone is as famous as her views, 'scolding' to some ears, talking down, guilt-inducing and shaming. 'We cannot do without every family keeping some control over their young people; every teacher teaching what is right and what is wrong, and society saying "If this person has done wrong, we will not shield him. He must go before the courts and be punished."' Above all she divides society into the responsible and the greedy and envious, those who say 'my rights at all costs, regardless of who has to pay' and those with 'no consideration of the consequences', who all have the minds of children. They think 'there is no limit to resources' and their childish clamour is accompanied by ignorance of economic realities: they must be told 'more wages today means fewer jobs tomorrow'. These child-citizens must be brought under the civilizing power of our social institutions, especially of the law strictly enforced.

Throughout, Mrs Thatcher's speeches contain sentiments and phrases like the following: 'the enterprising and responsible'; 'ordinary decent people to whom both thrift and hard work are virtues'; 'people have come to believe that things will go on getting better without any extra effort on their part'; 'lack of discipline'; 'agonising about the morality of profit'; 'bourgeois guilt'; 'we must not confuse hope with attainment'; 'we shall all suffer if we refuse to face reality'; 'traditional values have been assaulted, with a growing disrespect for authority'; and: 'there used to be certain understandings in society . . . young people were trained in the family . . . trained at school that certain things were wrong, and you had certain customs and conventions which were designed to bring out the good and push down the evil'.

The sharpest condemnation is for those who will not work and those who will not save. Both lay immoral claim to other people's support and it is they, or their representatives, who have caused Big Government. This well known complaint of the Strong, that the lazy and improvident are over-taxing them, explains Strong Leadership's emphasis on work and thrift: human nature is shiftless, those who work and postpone pleasure must be rewarded, the needy must wait in line; while those who won't work and won't save and yet demand support as a right, must be opposed. In other words, a moral inequality is necessary to buttress Thatcherism's economic logic. Diplomatic the Strong Leader may be — attaching the blame to left-of-centre, Big Government, trade unions, community action programmes, teachers, etc., or just a general decline in moral standards — but finally she is claiming that she and her supporters are morally superior. Not more subtle or visionary in moral matters; merely more deserving for having always denied themselves in work and thrift, and thus more productive.

Why the scolding tone in all this? Every leader draws on ideals to lift his or her followers' aspirations and efforts and all of us can be made to feel abashed at some time or other. However, the Strong Leader insists that morality is a simple matter, a matter of will, and those who persist in not doing the right thing must miss out on the reward. Moreover, Strong Leadership, inclined to categorize, and into simple categories, is never far from a sense of danger. So to the extent that welfare expenditure, government intervention, etc. are genuinely a threat to economic viability, a sense of urgency drives them to make enemies of the needy, to see a struggle where others see a problem. This inclination to 'blame the victim' may reflect the Strong's moral complacency; deserving to succeed, the society that rewards them must be protected. However, it may also reflect a growing panic, as if the lifeboat will sink unless some undeserving occupants who are not pulling their weight are thrown overboard.

Hard justice

Justice would seem to point in the direction of equality and certainly rough justice is better than none. Margaret Thatcher has repeatedly and passionately spoken of her belief in the role of law: 'Politics is essentially about the law', and as we have seen, 'governments must not bob, weave and duck around that duty'. Mrs Thatcher was here attacking Callaghan's government for its inconsistent handling of 'direct action' in local councils. In an interview, she wondered more generally if people have forgotten the critical importance of our legal institutions to democracy and freedom — calling attention to Strong Leadership's emphasis on the restraining framework and ignoring the contribution of egalitarian sentiment and the sympathetic imagination of generations of reformers. Democracy indeed *is* law: 'Our legal system and the rule of law are far more responsible for our traditional liberties than any system of one man one vote'.

The emphasis is not on law's equalizing function, bringing order through fairness, but on its power to restrain. Law is 'creative' she told members of the American Bar Association, because it unleashes energies by guaranteeing the right to hold on to the rewards of enterprise. It follows that we must avoid the 'artificial' construction of rights, such as reformers propose, and presumably the positive justice that uncovering and institutionalizing new rights imply:

> As time passes more and more groups of people with grievances and common interests combine to press our politicians and institutions for redress and justice . . . All too often direct action outside the legitimate social and political framework is buoyed up and stimulated by an all-too-familiar debased rhetoric of 'fairness' or 'equality' . . . [Demands for a Bill of Rights are] a telling sign of the intense pressures on our constitution and the rule of law.

The impression given is of the law criss-crossing social life like tightly knotted twine, not unalterable perhaps, but not to be allowed to go slack. Impersonal though it is, Mrs Thatcher's rhetoric seems more worried about and in sympathy with the law than with the human desires and difficulties stretching and straining it. Mrs Thatcher goes on to say that 'society is a living organism resting on processes and changing relationships', a remark apparently headed towards an argument for law adjusting to change. Then she goes the other way, as if the changing, struggling life pressing up against the legal framework should be treated, on the contrary, as a threat to civilized life:

> We determine justice as much by the way in which things are done . . . justice . . . will become meaningless if each citizen can determine what is fair and just from his own viewpoint and shrug off the rights of others or the decisions of a democratic government when they displease him.

By 'the way in which things are done' Mrs Thatcher means something like consistency and firmness, correctness of form. 'You cannot have', she said in 1986, 'freedom without order', 'order without the law', and democracy demands that 'the rule of law will be strong enough to hold down the evil which is within men'.

Law in Thatcherism is thus allied to restraint not to change, especially not to egalitarian demands for redress or new rights. It is about control, and it adds obedience to work and thrift as the virtues producing and maintaining a civilized society. Mrs Thatcher once remarked that society, like science, had its laws (she has studied both) but people 'are always trying to get away from it', i.e. law. She complains that people call her legalistic when she reminds them of 'the structure of society' but for her the problem in society, as in science, is the people 'who do not like to be disciplined by the facts'. Law shows how life must be lived, how human affairs must be arranged.

I have been arguing that Strong Leadership desires greatness and that the greatness it desires is to be greater *than*; that it is invidious and means inequality. Moreover, a nation cannot be great unless resources or incentives are spread unevenly, the Strong commanding more. This introduces what might be called a third basic belief, in addition to greatness and inequality: the absolute need for leadership. Society must distinguish between those who can lead and those who must be led. This links leadership back to greatness and inequality. Strong Leadership's goals are really only open to a few — to those who can cross the divide between leaders and led, who can climb the ladder of inequality, who can become greater than those around them.

If we look again at Mrs Thatcher's speeches we see how much depends on an idea of 'ordinary people', 'decent, hard-working, thrifty people', etc. These are the obedience-givers, the followers. They are told over and over again how important they are, but it is for their hard work, self-denial and law-abidingness that they are praised, and these are the virtues they must continue to practise. Yet doesn't Thatcherism favour the individual, praise vigour and initiative? It does — but unequally.

Leading those who work, save and behave decently are 'others with special gifts who should also have their chance . . . the adventurers who strike out in new directions in science, technology, medicine, commerce and industry . . .'. Restraint is not for them. As Mrs Thatcher puts it exuberantly: 'It's not restraint that brought us the achievements of Elizabethan England but positive, vital, driving, individual initiative'. The restraints she has in mind here are socialist restraints but this does not alter the fact that the Strong Leader preaches a different doctrine according to whether she is speaking to those she believes 'strong', the leaders, or to those whose only gift is for being decent, hard-working, thrifty citizens. This is the main link between greatness and inequality. Invidiousness necessitates exclusiveness: not everyone can be a success in the way Mrs Thatcher uses the word, particularly not materially successful.

Fundamentally then, Thatcherism, like all Strong Leadership, can offer only unequal freedom. At the top you can be an 'adventurer', while lower down — or to the side doing 'non-productive' things — you must expect not only fewer rewards but also lower moral status and a more constrained citizenly role.

THE SOCIAL CONVOY

Strong Leadership is defined, politically and psychologically, by its profound doubt that fellow-feeling is as natural as self-interest and its distrust of unregulated solidarities. From this doubt and distrust comes Strong Leadership's contradictory core, its celebration of the vigorous and free individual and its equally strong commitment to structures which channel and control him. In showing the darker side of Strong Leadership — I am thinking particularly of the argument about unequal freedom — it must be understood that this contradiction cannot easily be removed; and the alternative political philosophies have problems of their own in reconciling society and the individual, collective life and personal freedom. However, this is not a reason to blind ourselves to Thatcherism's difficulty with establishing genuine social life.

Mrs Thatcher, better known for division than for unity, for distinction and difference rather than common feeling, is, not surprisingly, adamant in her dismissal of socialism:

> What is the thing that I would like in the end to have achieved? It is really to have anchored this country as a free-enterprise society under a rule of law . . . for the rest of time . . . the Labour Party . . . totally rejected — the Marxist element, in other words, because the end of socialism is Marxism.

This was her attitude in 1986. After several years in which she presided over the rout of the British Labour Party, she is upping her demands to 'the rest of time'.

Socialism encourages the indigent and the lawless, tempts people away from 'the noble ideal of personal responsibility', undermines enterprise, trucks with Britain's enemies and, perhaps above all, creates doubt and uncertainty. Ignorant of the real problems, socialism creates artificial ones, and indoctrinates us with its gloomy forebodings: 'We are witnessing a deliberate attack on our values . . . on our heritage and our great past. And there are those who gnaw away at our national self-respect, re-writing British history as centuries of unrelieved gloom, oppression and failure . . .'. The individual who would be great, the nation which could be great again, are betrayed by the Socialists, whose self-criticisms and priorities (heavily slanted to redress) sap morale. Images of strength sapped ('sucked away', 'corroded', etc.) abound, indicative of the ferocity with which Mrs Thatcher recoils from collective programmes.

Socialism stands, of course, for the primacy of the social in human nature and for fellow-feeling over individual or national greatness. Mrs Thatcher complains of the 'constant attempts to make us ashamed of the profit motive' and warns of socialism's aim to make us all dependent: 'If we go on like this [Big Government] we shall become a pocket-money society . . .'. In one Conservative Party lecture, she undertook to challenge socialism's claim to greater 'altruism and selflessness'. She said, 'we must start from the idea of self'. Self-interest and care for others are falsely polarized; on the contrary, 'Our fellow-feeling develops from self-regard. Because we want warmth, shelter, food, security, respect and other goods for ourselves, we can understand that others want them too'. This classically liberal view of the self contrasts with one that starts at the other end: that we come to know our desires and form a sense of ourselves through those around us, especially those who care for us, becoming individuals only as they help us to.

Strong Leadership, however compassionate, regards this as giving too much away to the Other. Its version of individualism requires a theory of human nature in which social feeling is a spillover from something already in the individual, originating with him or her. Indeed, when Margaret Thatcher as a schoolgirl rebuked a teacher who congratulated her on her luck in winning a competition ('I wasn't lucky. I worked for it.') she expressed Strong Leadership's greatest complaint against socialism, its insistence on gratitude. Gratitude pulls towards preferring the other person, breaks the nexus between effort and reward, and undermines the morale of those who look for meaning and purpose in struggle, competition and individual greatness.

Strong Leadership's social unities then are laboriously constructed and delicately balanced. Mrs Thatcher shows the trouble Strong Leaders can encounter in getting the balance right, even in language. She ended her Conservative Party Conference speech in 1975 with this: 'Let us resolve to heal the wounds of a divided nation, and let that act of healing be the prelude to a lasting victory'! Internationally,

Mrs Thatcher has worked hard for Western unity, although this unity depends on dividing the world in two. Her efforts have been directed, of course, mostly towards Britain's chief ally, the United States. In one speech, delivered in New York, she revealed Strong Leadership's unease about interdependence: 'Today it is painfully obvious that no man — and no nation — is an island . . .'. All her examples were of how every nation suffers from other nations' misfortunes, grain failures, oil prices, and the like. When she said, at one point, 'the bell tolls for us all', she was referring to an 'uncomfortable' and unwelcome neighbourliness.

War brings the kind of unity Strong Leadership is best at dealing with, a unity limited to the task and needing to last only until victory is achieved, and where there is enough aggressiveness around to ensure that 'softness' and extravagant pledges of solidarity will not submerge individuality. Margaret Thatcher refers often to the Second World War and in a speech in Chicago in 1975, in the published version called 'Progress through Interdependence' the war gives rise to a metaphor that more completely captures her view of social relations than any other she has used.

> During that period the convoy was a feature of our daily lives in Europe and it seems to me to provide an excellent illustration of inter-dependence in practice. Each individual ship has a purpose — to get to its destination — which it can best achieve only in concerted action. Yet each ship can only play its part if it is in good working order and keeping a certain distance from its neighbour. This is the strength of the convoy.

Although the American alliance is the main subject, the convoy metaphor sums up Mrs Thatcher's outlook as a whole. Her speech concludes with 'Self-interest is not enough. We must work together'. However, she has set careful conditions: social feeling is related to purpose, purpose is given by danger and it has a bottom line, a finishing point. The same is true for the ties that bind: these derive from the purpose and are not an end in themselves; they are not spontaneous (Mrs Thatcher calls for 'A declaration of inter-dependence'); and they continue under careful control so that one ship does not endanger the others by getting too close. Each participant must pull her weight and act responsibly, not taking more than she should of the common store of protection (Mrs Thatcher speaks of 'security and obligation'). Thus, we are given a metaphor for Strong Leadership's social order — task-focused, a response to threat, severe standards of membership (with the threat of abandonment if they are not met), limited liability and obligation, at once friendly and wary.

The convoy metaphor, however, is only half the story. This study of Strong Leadership calls attention to its double-sidedness, its contradictoriness. There is contest or competitiveness which calls up images of vigour and movement, and there is control whose images are, like that of the convoy, cool. The convoy is itself a best-foot-forward case, intended to persuade the Americans to keep Britain and Europe in mind, especially Britain, as they calculate their own self-interest. That is the point. The cool images of orderly life Strong Leadership portrays belie the striving, contentious world of the competitive life it also wants; its appeal to 'work together' beyond self-interest must be half-hearted at best, and may be deceptive. For this reason with every increase in the competitiveness it so favours, Strong Leadership has to intensify the controls (moral, legal and so on) which will keep that competitiveness from tearing society apart. Strong Leadership simultaneously encourages on one side individual success, invidious reward, emulation, private possession and, on the other side, tough laws relentlessly applied, shame and guilt for failure, moral and social conformity. Pouring on the juice, it has to pull hard on the brake as well.

4
The Leader At Work

'Every nation needs leaders of extraordinary ability if ordinary people are to prosper.' In this short sentence Margaret Thatcher encapsulates the whole project of those who want Strong Leadership and hold its view of human affairs; above all, the conviction that a crucial division (into extraordinary/ordinary or leader/led) is the way to *shared* advantage.

There is something odd about Mrs Thatcher's thoughts on leadership: she seems to have kept them to herself. Even this quotation is not about national or political leadership. They are her opening remarks at the conferring of the *Guardian*'s Young Businessman of the Year award in 1977. Her speeches and interviews, eloquent on excellence and the legitimacy of leading élites, are largely silent on leaders and leadership in a more individual sense. It is especially interesting that Mrs Thatcher spent little time openly advocating her own leadership, either before or after her election to lead the Tories in 1975 and the government in 1979. Other Strong Leaders, including Reagan and Fraser, made much of 'the need for leadership', and of their special fitness to supply it. Mrs Thatcher has done that to a lesser extent. Certainly she has frequently had to defend her leadership style but, with the exception of the leadership American Presidents should give the West, I am unable to find examples of her talking about leadership — individual, powerful, impressive — in a way that would match her actual performance of it. This is a puzzle worth returning to later.

Broadly speaking, Mrs Thatcher's image is well known and has not changed in many years: single-minded, enormously energetic and devoted to work, intelligent, combative. These are relatively neutral terms and have been used even by detractors, who can admit with an American political correspondent that 'just the word "Thatcherism" sets her apart from her predecessors'.

We shall have to juggle more emotive terms. Single-minded becomes dogmatic and rigid, devotion to work becomes a passion for having total control, intelligence becomes point-scoring or being opinionated, combative becomes contentious, quarrelsome, gratuitously competitive. As we would expect, where the leader is a Strong Leader, whose profile is likely to be sharp, opinion is polarized. The American correspondent goes on: 'The word [Thatcherism] reflects the singular determination and the accomplishments of Mrs Thatcher. It also evokes the divisive nature of her leadership'. One of her critics admits to the 'fascination' Mrs Thatcher holds, 'for friend or foe'; 'she has a power to attract and repel', she provokes people to 'the extremes of love-hate'. Already there is a hint of paradox in the response to Mrs Thatcher. The impression given by that first listing of her leadership qualities is of coolness, order, steady progress, which is her own image of the good life. Yet Mrs Thatcher creates enormous heat, so the question arises how to explain the emotional heat that surrounds a leader so determinedly practical and orderly. The list may be correct, but it fails to suggest the drama of Mrs Thatcher's leadership. What have these qualities meant in practice? In this section I rely on an excellent canvassing of the opinions of Mrs Thatcher's co-workers, originally a BBC radio documentary and now a book, *The Thatcher Phenomenon*, edited by Hugo Young and Anne Sloman.

COMBATIVENESS

'Do you remember the birth of your children, the twins?' 'Oh yes. That was the day we won back the Ashes — *do* I remember!'

Margaret Thatcher's combativeness is legendary. David Howell observed that for Mrs Thatcher 'everything should start out as an argument, continue as an argument, and end as an argument'. Lord Whitelaw, turning aside an unflattering picture of his experience with Mrs Thatcher in cabinet, says 'frightening' is not quite the right word; 'You just have to be careful about your facts, your case, and this can make you nervous in argument'. Mrs Thatcher's advisers suggest it's all in fun:

> she likes to be joshed by subordinates, and stood up to by other politicians. The story is told of a diminutive ambassador of a minor country, coming for a first meeting, whom her staff expected would be totally overawed. Instead, he stood and argued. The Prime Minister enjoyed herself immensely and so, apparently, did he.

However, it seemed more than joshing when Mrs Thatcher and Mr Gorbachev renewed in 1984 (and again in Moscow in 1987) a sparring friendship that began at their first meeting some years ago. 'He seemed to be a kindred spirit', said a British diplomat. 'It was a very frank, hard-hitting discussion — just the sort of thing she likes.' In her own words, Gorbachev is someone 'I can do business with'.

It is clearly all to the good when enemies can talk, however competitive the talk is, and Mrs Thatcher sounds eminently reasonable when she says 'You are much more likely to be able to do business with someone else, provided you have a realistic assessment of their approach, their strength, their fears, and you do not go starry-eyed . . .' Francis Pym would say that depends on how ready you are to put aside combat, and the narrowness of 'doing business', when the situation requires something else.

On the European Economic Community, Pym writes:

> I felt that my duty was to judge and to fight for the highest level of rebate . . . while avoiding bitterness and recrimination. My advice was at first criticized by the Prime Minister and the Chancellor of the Exchequor, who felt that I was not sticking up for Britain's interests with sufficient vigour.

Pym's sense of the Community as a delicate partnership advancing uncertainly towards an intangible kind of unity is his defence against the charge of weakness. His is not the only voice. Viscount Davignon, a vice-president of the EEC, spoke of 'the resentment' some of the participants bore 'at being so roughed up, which made them more negative than they would otherwise have been'. Roy Jenkins, speaking of Mrs Thatcher at the EEC, but seeming to make a more general point, says:

> I would make a strong criticism of her negotiating technique. To be a good negotiator you probably have to do two things: you have to take a strong position . . . and then you have to know when it's right to settle. I think she's good at backing a strong position and making other people slightly frightened . . . but she has no idea when to settle.

It is salutary to examine some of the transcripts of television interviews Mrs Thatcher has given in Europe. She sounds rather as British tourists can sound on Channel ferries, displaying a Britain that is touchy, pugnacious, demanding. Her efforts at diplomatic nicety are inept at best: 'Well, France is a very great nation. So I think is Britain'; 'we shall therefore be looking to our [EEC] partners to make an effort of understanding and good will' but they must not think 'I and my government will be a soft touch in the Community . . . we will judge what British interests are and we shall be resolute in defending them'. Back in London, at the Guildhall, Mrs Thatcher reported 'bullseyes — if I may use a metaphor of which you, Lord Mayor, as a military man, will approve' in her negotiations on Rhodesia and on the 'unfairness' shown to Britain in the EEC budget. The Britain of soccer hooliganism so rightly deplored by Mrs Thatcher cannot have been altogether novel for Europeans who had met or heard its Prime Minister.

For Margaret Thatcher, says one critic, 'governing is more of an adversarial than a collegial process. She has pitted herself at one time or another against every institution one can think of — even the Government itself, which she often reproaches, sounding as if it were someone else's . . .'. 'She mistakes politeness for weakness', a former minister says. Another was 'amazed' at the 'rudeness' of the letters she allowed her private secretaries to send to her ministers. Mrs Thatcher is widely thought to be distrustful of the civil service, particularly the Foreign and Commonwealth Office. 'She doesn't like the Foreign Office because it is in the business of compromise. She doesn't understand diplomacy . . . Only total victory . . .'

'Innately wary' of the whole bureaucracy, Mrs Thatcher refused to accept the facelessness of the civil service 'machine', seeing it in more political terms, a place for finding allies and spotting enemies. 'Is he one of us?' the Strong Leader routinely enquires, looking sceptically at the proposals put to her. 'She gets in behind the finely honed paper of a minister . . . In effect, she rummages through the files of ministries . . .' and, thus prepared, she runs cabinet meetings with a firm hand, less as a facilitator of discussion than as advocate and judge at the same time. These reports suggest the tone:

> 'Who wrote this?', she'll ask. 'Well, I should have known. What can you expect? That's why it's so awful'; she will let the Minister introduce the subject but then take the initiative and say 'Have you read this paper? It will end in tears if we go on this way. I read the paper most of the night. I really think you should read these things before putting them into Cabinet'.

Cabinet is where collegiality and competition find their appropriate ratios, presumably reflecting the Leader to a considerable extent. In an editorial as early as 1981 *The Times* commented: 'She clearly does not view her cabinet as a team to be guided and led but rather as a class to be instructed or a religious army to be ordered into battle'. Those who have left Mrs Thatcher's cabinet by sacking or resignation are unlikely to be wholly reliable informants, but they do sing the same song. First Pym, then Heseltine and Nott (to name three of the important ones), selected Mrs Thatcher's abrasive, bullying, 'centralizing' style as the main thing which was wrong. David Howell says that Mrs Thatcher likes to convey to the public that she is 'alone in a sea of fumblers' and she described herself once as the cabinet rebel, implying the others were all sheep.

Typically, disappointed colleagues complain that the Leader has favourites but Margaret Thatcher did give a hostage to fortune when, still in Opposition, she remarked 'As Prime Minister I wouldn't want to waste time having any internal arguments . . .'; hers would be a committed, like-minded cabinet. It is not clear, however, that her cabinet selection has reflected this attitude. Moreover, this catches only one side of the Strong Leader, the driving, success-oriented side. One minister, still in his job, indicates the other side when he says ruefully that Margaret Thatcher respects those she is sure of rather less than those who will 'stand up to her'. Both points of view are necessary for an accurate picture of her: now orderly and controlling, following the proprieties as she exercises her authority, ability and hard work; but at the same time attacking, modelling all discussion on games of victory and defeat. This is the Strong Leader's mix of contest and control.

It can be a bewildering blend. The Strong Leader is the most correct and, thanks to his or her hard work and unswerving ambition and goals, the most effective person in the meeting. At the same time he or she is full of impatience with those colleagues and subordinates who hold back the Strong Leader: Mrs Thatcher complains bitterly of 'too many meetings' and the futility of 'diplomatic minuets'. One of the reasons talking with Gorbachev is 'So refreshing. So refreshing' is that the two of them can throw away the lengthy papers prepared for their meetings, put aside the ideological baggage, and 'really talk'. The meetings are refreshing because, since they are powerful individuals meeting transiently and without prejudice, as it were, despite being enemies they are free of their usual responsibility to balance their own determination against other people's dependence. They are in a 'free' space — a kind of pugilist's gym — that is protected from real danger but above all free of debilitating entanglements with men of smaller powers and many minor worries.

WORK ETHIC

Sir William Pile, who was Permanent Secretary of Education when Margaret Thatcher was Minister, describes his first meeting with her: 'Within the first ten minutes of her arrival she uncovered two things to us: one, . . . an innate wariness of the civil service . . ., secondly a page from an exercise book with eighteen things she wanted done that day . . .'. Mrs Thatcher had skipped the getting-to-know-you stage and soon it became clear that she would work 'to all hours of the day and night. She always emptied her box, with blue pencilling and marks on. Every single bit of paper was attended to the next day'. She worked hard, and she also took control. According to Pile 'she never seriously delegated anything'; she would say '"No, I'll do it myself"'. Ten years later Mrs Thatcher is still 'master of any brief before any meeting' and thriving on 'three-and-a-half hours sleep'.

Some years ago Mrs Thatcher confided:

> I don't know what I would do without work. I would find it acutely difficult if all of a sudden I had ten days off without something specific to do. I should be at a loss, because I've always had to do things with an object in view.

She does not like 'unstructured conversations', in meetings, or off the job. 'She either talks at you or listens attentively; there is no dialogue', and she learns, or points to, political lessons wherever she goes. Her comments on the arts suggest bewilderment, and she leaves herself very little time to cultivate them. There is also little time left for friends. None of the many books and articles on Margaret Thatcher reveals anyone she is close to but her husband: her friends are those who serve with her. 'You can be absolutely brutal with her', said one. 'She is incapable of respecting anyone who hasn't worked closely and intimately with her. And she is a tigress about protecting you.' The Strong Leader who worked and worried around the clock during the Falklands war is only an accentuated version of the one who holds intense and prolonged rehearsals for parliamentary question-time and has no time for ideas and friendships not 'structured into' the vocation of Strong Leadership.

Concentrated and constant effort has many benefits of course, both in politics and in a particular life where it expresses who one is and gains one the desired rewards. It also keeps doubt and fear at bay where idling would give them opportunity. Similarly, limiting friendship to those also committed to the task can allow one to be both more productive and surer of what is right. Strong Leaders, though, tend to particularly sharp boundaries. The political reason for 'unstructured' talk and friendships is not to prove the Leader is human, or even humble, but because subtle messages are passed on and received that way. Reality is not fully or always communicated in debates or in briefs from like-minded colleagues, nor in competitive groups, nor in situations where the Leader's authority is too visible for frank exchange.

Also, a highly moralistic attitude, or a challenging one, each useful for eliciting some kinds of knowledge, cannot but inhibit both the giving of cues and the receiving of them. Mrs Thatcher, and Strong Leaders generally, are proud of their candour amongst their colleagues; Mrs Thatcher is well known for commanding 'be blunt', 'don't beat about the bush' and for liking 'straightforwardness' and people who 'stand up to her'. However, hers is the candour of an individual licensed to hold the floor — 'verbose', 'prolix', 'hectoring' are frequently used of her — and it may be difficult for others, fearful of being humiliated and exploited, to say anything that is contrary or even complex and likely to lead to an unequal wrangle. 'Free and equal' personal relations are a democratic leader's finest links with those he serves, a check at least on the crusading certainties and judgements which, of course, round-the-clock task forces, tigerishly loyal, are designed to protect and advance.

INTELLIGENCE

Margaret Thatcher went to Rhodesia, early in her premiership, with right-wing views and a great deal to learn about the black Commonwealth. After a successful settlement, which owed most to Lord Carrington, her Foreign Secretary, and to Malcolm Fraser, Prime Minister of Australia, she drew the lesson that 'even the most intractable problem will yield to the necessary combination of resolve and effort, and resolve is one of the most significant things in politics'. She then added: 'and imagination'. Imagination appears again in an odd exchange with the correspondent interviewing her for a *New Yorker* profile in 1986. She answers his question, whether being a woman had made a difference in her career, by citing her science degree and the training in logic it gave her. 'But logic is never enough', she says 'in science; you have to have the imagination for the next step. I then took law . . .'. Trying to make the point that the important distinction is not male or female but who is logical, rigorous, and who isn't, Mrs Thatcher's remarks leave us wondering whether imagination is not something she knows she lacks. This is a question of general importance: are Strong Leaders 'decisive' because they see only in black and white, are they 'resolute' because their minds are fixed?

'Margaret Thatcher lives for politics. Apart from family, the only mildly competing interest — and even this is complementary — is an instinct for finding things out. Advisers say she gobbles up information, from her papers, in conversation, almost through the pores.' When she was at school her headmistress described her as 'always ambitious and eager to learn'. Her school reports regularly described her as 'a very logical thinker', 'has a very logical mind'. She found art the hardest subject and her university tutor rated her 'good', 'sensible', 'well-read' but lacking in that 'something else' better students had, and her put-down of the young Margaret Roberts ('a perfectly good beta chemist') resembles that of an anonymous aide, years later, who said 'she would have made a good administrative grade civil servant'. In a double-handed compliment, the man who gave her her first job, in industrial chemistry, remembers her as 'though not the most imaginative chemist, she ran rings around the men' because she was 'very thorough'.

No one doubts Margaret Thatcher's intelligence. The difficulty is in describing its specific qualities. Memory stands out. Sir Keith Joseph praised her excellent 'mental filing system' while Paul Johnson, calling her a wielder of the broad brush of party philosophy, decided that she was above all an 'expert'. What teachers, aides and others underestimated was the connection Mrs Thatcher forged between rigour, which tends to pedantry and back-room jobs, and competitiveness. Airey Neave struck the right balance: 'she is self-critical, likes accuracy, enjoys a well-reasoned argument and prefers people who know their facts — she has immense powers of concentration and a quite exceptional memory'. However, he went on, Margaret Thatcher is 'essentially a fighter'.

Minds, of course, can be too broad and too flexible, as well as overly narrow and forensic. Nevertheless, as time has gone on the limits of Mrs Thatcher's kind of thinking may be becoming clearer. 'A good mind . . . rigorous . . . [not] at all reflective . . . no conceptual sense whatever' were comments elicited by the *New Yorker* interviewer from people who knew her and were not politically opposed to her. She has, in the words of a colleague, 'a searchlight mind'. Superb at taking in a brief, Mrs Thatcher's reading, off the job, seems slight and mostly the inferior detective novels, though she has memorized a lot of poetry. One senior aide seems close to summing up Mrs. Thatcher's kind of mind when he describes her as 'a problem-solver . . .; without a problem she is bored to tears and intolerable'.

A head for facts, quick comprehension and vigorous practicality are prized qualities of executive thinking, the kind of thinking that is directed at how to act strongly, safely and quickly. Whether moral convictions should be reached this way is another question. There is also the question whether executive thinking is adequate for the many intangibles a political leader must ponder, not least her 'vision'.

Sir William Pile did not think Mrs Thatcher had 'wisdom' — the capacity to deal creatively with the unforeseen — because 'she had prefabricated answers'; but 'she was clever . . . a magnificent manager of information, a user of information'. Her critics, Pym, Prior and others, complain she is not ruminative, too much 'one for her boxes' and lacks 'the broad visionary picture'. 'I must say I think she dealt with the housekeeping very well indeed', says Prior. Admittedly vision is a slippery word. Still, the mind that demands focus — that cannot see anything until the definition is ultra-sharp — will shape the world that way, will see mainly what her apparatus for seeing is most capable of. Hopes and dreams, moral dilemmas, half-articulated concerns may then be simplified into firm convictions and so-called hard proposals, and codified so that they can be insisted on or solved rigorously, whether relevant in a more sensitive way or not. Over-focused minds solve irrelevant problems or solve them out of context, neglecting the whole for the part.

In fact, Strong Leadership is driven in this direction. Sharp focus and the demand for so-called facts serve Strong Leadership's orientation to crisis and struggle. Looming defeat or the opportunity to conquer do concentrate the mind wonderfully. As well, there is an attraction to tasks that can be completed, their achievement a measure of a person's worth. If it is true that Mrs Thatcher needs to think, as she says she needs to work, with a 'clear purpose in view', then we should not be surprised if her thinking tends to outcomes that are narrow, partial and divisive; or that the syntheses she produces by way of 'convictions' and 'vision' seem forced and unintelligent compared to the analytic intelligence she shows in her executive work.

SINGLE-MINDEDNESS

It is easy to be a starter
But are you a sticker too?
It is easy enough to begin a job
It is harder to see it through.

With this rhyme from her childhood, Margaret Thatcher explained in 1986 how 'It never occurred to me not to see things through to the end — I suppose that is a question of upbringing, isn't it?'. By the first day of the election campaign in 1987 this had become 'I will go on and on and on'.

One of the *Shorter Oxford Dictionary*'s definitions of the word strong is 'steadfast', bringing thoughts of *Pilgrim's Progress*. The important phrase is 'to the end', and it is part of the job of Strong Leaders to define life and social life as Bunyan did Pilgrim's: an upward path (Mrs Thatcher favours the image of a ladder), strewn with temptations and obstacles, the prize going to those who kept on. Mrs Thatcher admits that sporting fixtures can be too much for her and she'll only watch football matches on video, when the suspense is over, and if Britain has won. It is understandable that a Leader who might have been born to lead her nation in conflict should take a game so seriously. All the more so for sport's more serious kin, war itself. During the Falklands war of

1982 one of the Americans on Haig's negotiating team paid testimony to the British leader in these terms: 'I was struck by the strength of Mrs Thatcher's convictions. She felt more strongly I think than anyone in the cabinet. She was the driving force, the leading edge. She was not at all tactical . . .'

David Barber has made inflexibility the besetting sin of American Presidents, particularly those he describes as 'Active-Negative', that is, those who are driven and inwardly divided. Mrs Thatcher fits this category better than any other in Barber's scheme, though her passion seems freer, her convictions both more compacted and more pointed, her enjoyment far greater than say Nixon's, who is the paradigm of the type. Nixon's case is a good one for approaching the question of Mrs Thatcher's single-mindedness. How real is it? Will it last? It was Nixon, proponent of 'The Real War' view of politics, who reversed his attitude on China, and it was Nixon who, having courted the conventionalities and straightness of Middle America, conducted his political life on the edge of scandal, before finally tipping right into it.

First, what is Mrs Thatcher single-minded about? And why? Clearly Mrs Thatcher has sought, as a 'conviction' politician, a mandate that is fundamentally moral. 'The Lady's Not For Turning', a line from her second general election campaign, signalled not only determination and purpose but also 'character'. To be single-minded is to be Strong; and Mrs Thatcher, to a degree, puts herself above the ordinary politician by putting herself above the ordinary wheeling and dealing, posing as a critic of politicians and even her own government. She takes advantage of a widespread distrust of politics which calls for 'statesmen' and disdains 'mere politicians' and ordinary political processes.

It is hard to understand why a 'mindedness' which juggles many possibilities and allows itself to alter its emphasis should be considered weak and merely 'tactical'. This attitude, a tenet of Strong Leadership's followers, not only devalues empathy, responsiveness and self-correction; it sets up a great pressure towards hypocrisy, where a reputation for not budging becomes a public front hiding intelligent negotiation. Mrs Thatcher associates herself and her ideas with sacred values. 'The Old Testament prophets', she snorted once, 'did not go out and ask for consensus'; nor presumably did they change their minds.

Single-minded about what? Strong Leaders will show single-mindedness about the intangibles of convictions on life, human nature, the importance of power compared to unsanctioned co-operation, etc., in moral stance and character. They will be flexible about power: the Strong Leader works first and foremost to maintain and advance her position, without which nothing can be achieved. Mrs Thatcher is not single-minded at all levels or about everything. Greatness, inequality, social control, character — yes; but much of her politics is contingent, a matter of terrain, of opportunity and dealing with unexpected setbacks.

We have canvassed some of the opinions of colleagues, aides and subordinates about Mrs Thatcher's inflexibility. The results certainly confirm her single-mindedness but they are not proof that rigidity must dominate the rest of her leadership. Mrs Thatcher, if not open to the random influences and free-play of ideas implied in the notion of dialogue, is yet a learner and an observer, and though her convictions are set hard they come down in the end to the pursuit of greatness. 'Great Britain is great again', Margaret Thatcher exulted after the Argentinians surrendered. However long the haul, I cannot see this aim changing.

It would be foolish, however, to think that the lady who won't be turned is not fundamentally a fighter; and policies are not quite the same thing as convictions. Bruce Arnold's *Margaret Thatcher: A Study in Power* is an elegant quarrel with her 'consistency': first, because the pursuit of consistency inhibits imagination and real problem-solving; more emphatically because he sees it is false, a rhetorical device for constructing a public image as Strong where all around are weak. He sees Mrs Thatcher when she is off the public stage as more pragmatic than she pretends. In other words, she cloaks her will in the legitimizing cloth of lifelong conviction, character and single-mindedness. Perhaps he underestimates the difficulty. Strong Leaders ride on two tracks, staying controlled or consistent on one, switching to the other suddenly or secretly, in defence or in attack, to snatch at the weapons of contest. This is an irreducible conflict in Strong Leadership's mode of being and critics must always take both into account.

Strong Leadership nevertheless is biased towards consistency, or at least the appearance of it. At the same time, though a word like pliable suggests weakness, the Strong Leader who can shift his or her ground without compunction, stealing an advantage from opponents, is admired too. Only saints make a welter of moral consistencies, preferring defeat to being unfaithful. The political realism of Strong Leadership consists in this: that even principles are a utility and must be judged by their effectiveness. Indeed, there are Strong Leaders who can one day castigate their opponents for being unprincipled — like Mrs Thatcher on Mr Kinnock's manoeuvres in the British Labour Party ('It's the opportunism I hate') — and, when caught out themselves, will announce the past is dead, we should get on with the task in hand; let's think of outcomes, not academic niceties.

COMMUNICATING

It is a curious feature of democratic politics that leaders are supposed to be blithely ignorant of the rules of self-presentation. (Statesmen, like heroic fathers of the past, never care how they look.) Artifice seems to diminish leaders, especially 'conviction' leaders; they should be convincing without having to learn to act the part. Mrs Thatcher has been an outstanding communicator of herself and her convictions and she is no stranger to the devices by which this is done. Her appearance and her manner have been changed substantially over the years, including a remarkable effort to lower her voice (lowness denoting strength) by half an octave. The usual strategems of modern electioneering have been employed (choosing sympathetic media interviewers, handling them in rehearsed ways, meeting media deadlines, picture opportunities with shoppers, soldiers, etc.) and Margaret Thatcher's speeches closely follow the rules for eliciting maximum response.

Strong Leadership's communications strategy is more complex than is allowed for in the conventional wisdom of the television age. Mrs Thatcher's PR advisers are said to be not entirely happy with their efforts: they 'would like to see her show some flexibility and warmth', and one commentator speaks for many when he says 'On the [TV] screen, as on radio, she seems abrasive and without warmth, let alone charm . . .'. The Strong Leader signals her strength by a studied dismissal of the media, as if it interfered with her task and wastefully questioned her goals. While using the media for all they are worth, the Strong Leader tries to look as if she is engaged on tasks more important than presenting herself; her impatience with appearances and mere talk enhances the impression of Strong, action-oriented Leadership. Better 'harsh truths' than 'smooth-talking'; better a Leader hurring to his helicopter or one, like Mrs Thatcher, who says she doesn't watch the TV news or trouble about the polls. As a spokesman for Saatchi and Saatchi told the *New Yorker*: first, 'It isn't in her character to change'; second, 'she doesn't want to be seen to change'; third, 'she likes the Iron Lady image'. It isn't easy to reconcile these, but it would be foolish to neglect any one of them. Strong Leadership communicates an image though it seems not to be concerned with image; it expresses old-fashioned strength of character but with modern legerdemain.

The strong type has always been the silent type. One final feature of Strong Leadership's communications is to limit debate — single-mindedness depends on having your mind made up — and to protect the privacy of those in government who make the decision. Margaret Thatcher's alleged leaking of documents in the Westland affair appeared to contradict Strong Leadership's taste for secrecy, but the tactical deployment of leaks has become peculiarly potent in modern government. Similarly, Strong Leadership's élitism and formalism — keeping the media 'in its place' — has to be balanced against the opportunities afforded by using it selectively. Still, the lesson Strong Leaders want learned is that leaders lead and followers follow, and the media are a constant threat to that boundary. Instead of hard-fought and properly-controlled decision-making processes, TV and radio politics encourage speculative, ill-informed chat, influencing the masses with half-baked ideas rather than finished policies and institutionally-supported interpretations. Unlike some leaders eager to present their far-reaching ideas and fancies, even to play with them in public, and others who are committed to having every view heard, however inarticulate or irresponsible, Strong Leaders fear to seem to be 'wanking' and they want to have their words treated not as 'views' to be debated but as policies needing to be heard and supported.

On TV or radio Mrs Thatcher is not often drawn into being publicly reflective, or even into unpolemical discussion. When she turns questions to her own advantage, turns discussion into hectoring debate, pursues her own agenda whatever the question, she is expressing Strong Leadership's conviction that the listening followers are easily confused and easily influenced by bad ideas, and that their morale is dependent on an image of their Leader as forthright and certain. The media, then, are a kind of loudspeaker for a few simple, clear ideas, constantly repeated. They are about confidence and for confirming the Strong Leader's reputation for a single-mindedness that has no use for ruminative discussion.

Mrs Thatcher's old-fashioned style of communicating suits her purposes rather well. Strong Leadership is not advanced by yielding too much to an 'intimate' medium with its quiet voices, partial logic, bright metaphors and homely, pastel sets.

I recall two occasions when Mrs Thatcher's television performance was superbly indicative of the Strong Leader she is. After the bombing of the Tory conference headquarters in Brighton, she spoke with powerfully controlled anger — that the British Cabinet should be at risk from terrorists!, and then she turned away, saying 'I must see to our people'. She portrayed here a virtually tribal fury and protectiveness, all the more moving because of the horror of the moment and widespread fear of random terrorist attack.

The other occasion was the day following the alleged involvement of British fans in the deaths of thirty-eight people at a Belgian soccer match. This time who was friend and who was foe was not so clear and her anger was less dignified. 'It comes down', she said in fury, 'to getting hold of the perpetrators, getting them into the courts and punishing them'. The more troubling side of a Strong Leader shows here: instead of anger made constitutional, directed, if sectionally, at accepted enemies, it runs almost to direct action — the Strong Leader tempted to take off her badge, reverse her cap, and go after the bastards; the Strong Leader ashamed as well as angry, enraged by the position she is put in by some of her own people. What we saw was the Strong Leader in two moods, protective and angry, and what we see of Mrs Thatcher seems to be what we get. The Leader herself is apparently unable or unwilling to be other than she is, making her the citizen's ally against the PR man's box of tricks. A press photographer tells the story of following Mrs Thatcher around to snap her in an unguarded moment, yawning perhaps. Finally he gave up: 'I realized she yawns with her mouth closed!'. Can he have thought Mrs Thatcher would ever be unguarded?

SUPERIORS, INFERIORS, EQUALS

Strong Leadership's world is one without equals. Human affairs can take on the appearance of mutuality only when the lines of authority (who is in charge) are established and firmly agreed. Margaret Thatcher is forever testing people, ranking them, preferring work where authority operates more, to less-structured activities where equality might be expected. To the above observations on Mrs Thatcher's political work a small rider should be added on Mrs Thatcher's dealings with those who are superior, inferior or equal to her — at the broadest level, international affairs. How does she deal with the United States, the British Commonwealth, the European Economic Community? A pattern reveals itself which is in line with what we know already: her attraction to greatness, her competitiveness, her disinclination to lead 'nurturantly'. It is a useful reference point before examining Mrs Thatcher's personality and biography.

To begin with equals. 'Mrs Thatcher isn't much of a European . . . she is too nationalistic . . . she has little patience with the way the Community works . . . through a continuing process of compromise . . . no-one . . . [is] an outright winner or loser . . .' Francis Pym portrays the EEC as a fragile partnership between equals, a web of understanding and potential misunderstanding Mrs Thatcher was quick to tear. She seems unwilling to advance beyond minimal co-operation directed at economic benefits and more importantly at opposing the Soviet threat. The latter is her constant theme in broadcast interviews in European countries. 'What is *your* Europe?' a French TV interviewer asked her. She replies with the convoy image: first, each country individually prosperous — 'we all have to concentrate on that'; then agricultural policies and the defence of 'democracy and freedom'. Another asks her for her 'vision' of Franco-British relations, especially 'in the long historical perspective'. Mrs Thatcher refers to the alliance of the Second World War and then to recent trade agreements, using a prepared list. The interviewer persists: but what 'do you consider to be the "movement" in French–British relations' (that is, the tone and feeling)? She repeats a list of agreements made.

No European leader can afford to wax enthusiastic about one country in case the others are offended. Country-to-country friendships cannot be 'exclusive' she tells the French, and Britain has friendships with West Germany and the others too. Nevertheless her reluctance to envisage the 'Community' supports the view that she is half-hearted about Britain's more intangible involvements with her neighbours. After the Milan summit in 1985 Mrs Thatcher made the tasteless observation: 'the whole thing was small-minded. I wonder if it was surprising — because we were victors in the last war. We were never beaten, we were never occupied . . .'. Tasteless and suggestive of a primitively competitive attitude, as if something like 'sibling rivalry' dominates her attitude. She can also sound patronizing: 'And so what can I say? We do go to endless trouble to consult our partners, and we go to endless trouble to be constructive. Europe will mature'.

Britain has no historic right to lead Europe; on the contrary, perhaps, given its long-held reputation for insularity. (One of Denis Thatcher's pet hates, it is said, is 'foreigners'.) Economically, Britain is barely an equal. Margaret Thatcher's prickliness in Europe may reflect a sense of being unable to command economic strength and being required to negotiate not from the security of strength but on the uncertain ground of equality. At any rate her tone with the United States is very different. Though Britain is the lesser power, the 'special relationship' is at least based on a clear understanding of who is in charge and it provides an opportunity for Mrs Thatcher to share in a great power's influence.

Then there is the Commonwealth, where Britain is expected to give a lead to her former dependents. Mrs Thatcher's attitude, querulous towards the Europeans, is both intransigent and comparatively indifferent towards the Commonwealth. Her intransigence in 1979 on the question of sanctions against Rhodesia-Zimbabwe, was overcome, though she had arrived at the Commonwealth conference with a pair of wrap-around sunglasses 'in case they start throwing acid'. She has continued to oppose general sanctions against South Africa, in the teeth of strong Commonwealth pressure.

In 1986 the *Sydney Morning Herald* editorialized: 'In a manner reminiscent of Mr Botha in Pretoria, Mrs Thatcher has enraged her opponents by a verbal defiance which disguises the subtlety and strength of her position'. In 1978 Mrs Thatcher had drifted close to Powell-like warnings about Britons not wanting to be racially swamped, and now that the main Commonwealth issue is race, Mrs Thatcher's rational-utilitarian opposition to sanctions, which puts her in conflict with virtually all the Commonwealth countries, has greatly strained its unity. It came close to collapse in 1986 when the Commonwealth Games in Edinburgh were threatened by Mrs Thatchers's attitude. A *Times* columnist may be right, that Mrs Thatcher gets her head and her heart in the wrong places: she can sound passionate about the practical difficulties with general sanctions, and sound perfunctory and unfeeling about apartheid itself.

As well as intransigence there is almost irritable disdain, a disinclination for Commonwealth matters. The summer of 1986 brought rumours that Mrs Thatcher was in conflict with the Queen over her treatment of Commonwealth opinion. The Queen takes particular interest in the Commonwealth; its largely symbolic ties suit her position and her gifts exactly. She speaks of it as a family which, in a sense, she nurtures. There is abundant testimony to how well she plays her role. Mr Lange of New Zealand, for example, called her the 'glue' holding the Commonwealth together, and leaders of many Commonwealth countries, including Mr Gandhi, have praised her for her knowledge, interest and tact. It's hard to see the Commonwealth surviving without some such leadership, without a leader who genuinely cares for it. *The Guardian* reported in July 1986 that the Queen was concerned both for the unity of the Commonwealth and at Mrs Thatcher's description of the demand for economic sanctions against South Africa as 'immoral' and 'repugnant', where she turned the moral tables as it were.

It is not possible to know the extent of the row between the Queen and the Prime Minister, nor is it a question of the rightness or not of Mrs Thatcher's stand on sanctions. What is important is the suggestion that the Commonwealth, depending on the kind of attention and protection the Queen has given it for years, does not find in Mrs Thatcher anything like the same interest nor the same care. Presumably British leadership must show these, or give up the Commonwealth.

It is a regular and puzzling feature of Strong Leadership that it courts 'great and powerful friends' with an apparent disregard for its own dignity which, the rest of the time, it insists on. Old soldiers take pride in their blind obedience to officers they admire, sportsmen pledge undying loyalty to coaches they describe as 'bastards' and 'hard-but-fair'. So it is of some interest now to look at the 'special relation' Margaret Thatcher cultivates with Britain's more powerful ally, the United States.

Mrs Thatcher takes it on herself to remind Europeans of their need for America. They should not be 'unduly idealistic' about Europe's growth in unity and strength but remember, on the contrary, 'if we are safe today, it is because America has stood with us. If we remain safe tomorrow, it will be because America remains powerful and confident'. Her remarks are directed at America too. In President Carter's day, Mrs Thatcher was worried at America's loss of confidence, beginning an address in New York in 1979 with the warning that, though 'self-criticism is essential to the health of any society . . . we perhaps have carried it too far'; too much self-criticism 'causes paralysis'. So one of her tasks is to strengthen American resolve. Another is to insinuate Britain into the role of wise counsellor, an experienced head on younger, more powerful, shoulders. Welcoming Reagan's 'remarkable triumph' in the Presidential election, she praised his 'determination', his straightforwardness, and said 'I greatly look forward to working with him. Governor Reagan's victory, like the successes of Britain's overseas policies in the last years, leaves us, I believe, in good shape to cope with the storms that lie ahead'. The 'eighties, which she once called the 'dangerous decade', now became the 'leadership decade'.

Mrs Thatcher's words of welcome and praise included the reminder that she and Britain had been there before the Americans ('like the successes of Britain's overseas policies in the last year' — i.e. since the election of the Iron Lady). In other, upmarket, speeches such as the Pilgrim's Dinner in London in 1981 she deftly and pointedly listed what America owes to Britain. First, 'How often for instance the same Nobel Prize has been shared by our two countries . . . Our poets and playwrights, our actors and film makers are as at home in one country as the other. They dominate the scene in their professions . . .'. (These are terms other people would want to see her use about Europe.) She goes on, 'More important even than [these] has been our role in political thought and practice . . .'.

Leaving aside the pros and cons of the American alliance, weighed against a stronger commitment to political unity within Europe, the images and tone of Mrs Thatcher's message reveal the importance of the American alliance to her. She is admiring and almost coquettish in drawing the attention of the American administration to Britain. She evokes the memory of their wartime co-operation, of Churchill and his rhetoric; she exploits the common tongue, scattering her speeches with literary and historical references like a travel agent courting American tourists.

Margaret Thatcher was Ronald Reagan's first visitor after his election to President. (Helmut Kohl was his second.) Each claims to admire the other's 'straightforwardness', a reference to Strong Leaderhip's resoluteness and purposefulness. Broadly, and especially rhetorically, their policies have been very similar though there is detailed divergence. Personally, Reagan is amiable, likes amusing and being amused, is abysmally prepared for negotiations, while Mrs Thatcher is reserved if not forbidding, lacks humour, is thoroughly prepared and knowledgeable. Reagan, of course, supported Mrs Thatcher against General Galtieri, and she in turn supported him in the attack on Tripoli; Grenada may have been an embarrassment for Mrs Thatcher but the fall-out has not been great. In recent years, after Reykjavik and in the 1987 nuclear arms reduction proposals, Mrs Thatcher and Reagan may not have readily agreed. In the beginning she appeared to achieve her aim to stiffen American resolve, to put the American President in the forefront of a new Cold War against the 'Evil Empire', and after the Geneva summit in 1985 she spoke for Nato: '[we are] very supportive . . . very supportive indeed, grateful to him for his efforts, grateful in particular for the amount of work that he personally did and for the amount of direct negotiation that he did with Mr Gorbachev'. Elsewhere she concludes 'we in the West could not have a better or braver champion than President Reagan'.

How does the Strong Leader handle the ally who is stronger still? It is reported that Mrs Thatcher 'has no illusions about Mr Reagan', that she recognized his intellectual and negotiating weaknesses and did not have the pleasure dealing with him that she has dealing with Gorbachev or Mitterand. (The first panegyric quoted in the previous paragraph is targeted a bit too obviously on criticisms that Reagan is personally incompetent and lazy.) This need not trouble her, though. It may have allowed her to be a more influential power-behind-the-throne than would have been the case with a shrewder President, and Reagan as it happens was well used to leaning on advice, specifically, on a woman's advice, according to reports of Nancy Reagan's influence. He was a man used to allowing others to harden his resolve.

However I suspect that Mrs Thatcher would operate the same way with any American President. The main thing is the Strong Leader's sharp eye for power, how it is deployed and where advantage can be found. The *New Yorker* columnist, interviewing her in 1986, commented: 'listening to Mrs Thatcher talk about America left me wondering if she didn't sometimes think about what it would be like to be President of the richest and most powerful country in the world'. This thought is owed perhaps to Mrs Thatcher's admiring remarks about America being the home of business, of free enterprise, vigour and success. Her answer to the interviewer's question was oblique: 'Which [country] could save the world if called upon to do so?'. In other words, the security Strong Leadership seeks in riches and might are ideally its own, but the next best thing is influence over a rich and powerful friend.

This suggests that one explanation for Mrs Thatcher's sliding scale of interest in Britain's three major sets of alliances is to be found in Strong Leadership's orientation to crisis and its belief, in the face of danger, that accepting and even accentuating the inequalities of power is the only solution. Inequality is where the action is, where power is. Strong Leaders are, or get with, the strength, treating moves to equalize power, thus minimizing its influence, as a frightening denial of reality. The world is to be handled through stable rank-orders. Hence Mrs Thatcher's impatience with the efforts of equals to establish closer ties (the EEC), and her indifference to inferiors who, though unequal, have no power to hurt and indeed are a drain on one's own powers (the Commonwealth). As well, there must be gratifications in playing in the big league. The Strong get their sense of value and purpose from being as close as possible to effective action. Britain, under Mrs Thatcher, spurns the EEC and the Commonwealth for a place in the biggest game in the world, the game between West and East, a place it would be hard-pressed to join on its own account. Mrs Thatcher wants to emphasize to the United States its essentially British lineage and continuing 'cousinhood', to stave off British decline.

A personal element is involved too. By the end of this profile it will be possible to see the role Mrs Thatcher plays with the American President as one she was brought up to. Though she is a powerful leader in her own right, Mrs Thatcher's personality is built on the role of consort, in this case, a political consort. As consort to a Republic, Britain's alliance with the United States under Thatcher royally reproduces the Prime Minister's deepest political lesson.

5
Life Into Politics

We must 'confront reality' — 'yes, confront is the word I use'. Why go on from a leader's politics to studying her life? One answer lies in Margaret Thatcher's personal *High Noon* world of evil and ultimate crisis, where duty is clear and the only choices are heroism, death, or the living shame of the film's frightened townspeople. There are many realities and many ways of apprehending them, and Strong Leadership's version is embedded in a familiar political tradition. The questions are what are the ideas rooted in, how are they embodied? Supporters want to be sure the programme is more than skin-deep, that it will be adhered to, that the leader will resist its opponents, that he or she will thoroughly and comprehensively apply it. Critics want to know the leader's limits. Is she open to influence? Will she debate, or tolerate, contrary views? How objective or realistic is she in fact — or is her 'realism' so much part of her own personality and development that it amounts to a fixed subjectivity? Is she responding to the world or marching to the tune of her own desires, defences and particular experience? All this is quite separate from the adequacy of the leader's ideas and programme. She may be 'subjective' and yet quite correct, the right Leader for the place and time; good politics need not come of good stock.

A second reason for studying the Leader's personality and biography is to understand her meaning exactly. The teller of the tale does influence the tale's impact. For instance, if Margaret Thatcher is personally and deeply contentious and competitive, what exactly is the meaning of the calls she makes from time to time for co-operation and unity? And what does peace mean to her? How are we to understand her commitment to the individual and to freedom when they come from a self-confessed 'bossy-boots' and a moralizer who preaches social obligation and national spirit? It is true that all these can be understood by tracing the system of ideas involved, the philosophy or ideology. However, it would be odd to trace the ideas and then stop short of the pattern they form in the Leader's own personality; it is here that they come alive, taking their energy from the person who entertains them and propagates them. It would be particularly odd, given Mrs Thatcher's success in personifying Strong Leadership's ideas in Britain and elsewhere. The question, then, is what is she made of and how has this shaped her politics?

A CONTROLLED UPBRINGING

At the declaration of the polls in 1979, the new Prime Minister was exultant: 'the passionately interesting thing to me is that the things I learned in a small town, in a very modest home, are just the things that I believe have won the election'. Though bent on changing the face of Britain, Mrs Thatcher has never been slow to align herself with the past, when Britain was both great and decent. At a personal level her message to youth is to listen more to their elders, watch less television, join 'the workers, not the shirkers'. It is a message at least implicitly critical of the sophisticated, the spectacular, the whole range of contemporary cosmopolitan values. This message is delivered, above all, in her own life, pointing to the success an old-fashioned upbringing brings. 'I was taught self-discipline and to help others. I couldn't have got where I am without it', she told a group of secondary school children.

Nevertheless, we ought to be wary of her own account of her upbringing; Mrs Thatcher's tendentiousness and moralizing are unrelenting. The first part of this section follows her life fairly closely, though drawing on other observers; but this will yield only a half-truth. It then proceeds to try to fill in what Margaret Thatcher leaves out in the 'official' story, the contest obscured behind the picture she draws of a smoothly operating escalator from childhood obedience to adult achievement.

Alf Roberts owned the leading grocery shop in Grantham, a provincial town in Essex, where his family — Beatrice, his wife, Muriel, their first child, and, four years younger, Margaret — lived above the shop. Until Margaret (who was born in 1925) was ten, Beatrice Roberts's mother, Phoebe, also lived there. Theirs was a family of some distinction in the town. Apart from the shop, Alf Roberts was an independent alderman (or local councillor), a leading figure in the Methodist church, and sat occasionally on the magistrate's bench. They were distinctively ambitious, too, and earnest. 'They weren't wealthy, by any means, but Mr Roberts had a very successful business';

> I think this poor background has been overdone . . . Most of Margaret's life was spent with a father who was an eminent citizen of Grantham . . . He worked very, very hard and indeed so did his wife. The story goes they had no real family life . . . never had the sort of meals where they all sat around the table together, because father was so busy in the shop and in politics.

'The Roberts family were very strict Methodists and used to go to Church twice or three times on Sunday . . . Mr Roberts . . . wouldn't take a Sunday paper.' 'They were all very, very serious-minded. They worked too hard. Life was a serious matter, to be lived conscientiously . . .'

As Margaret Thatcher put it later: 'The toughest thing of my childhood was that father taught me very firmly indeed you do not follow the crowd because you're afraid of being different. You decide what to do yourself and if necessary you lead the crowd, but you never just follow'. The 'afraid of being different' and 'if necessary' could perhaps be left out as polite gestures, leaving a family not so much part of its community but different, and determined to be better.

Mrs Thatcher tells us that at her 'parents' insistence' there was a very regulated pattern of behaviour. It was important to learn how to be responsible. She and Muriel helped in the shop: 'there was always something to do and it made us feel very grown up'. This was apparently effective because at school Margaret, sitting up straight at her desk, hard-working in class, insistent about putting questions to visiting speakers, was described as 'very mature for her age'. There was work and there was morality, the two closely associated. 'We were taught what is right and wrong in very considerable detail . . . Duty was very very strongly ingrained into us.' 'I got the books I wanted, but no pleasures. I never went to a dance until I got to university . . .' Her friends of the time emphasize Alf Roberts's insistence on this Methodist regimen, but there was also his mother-in-law, Margaret's grandmother, who was 'very, very Victorian, and strict'.

Margaret Thatcher legitimizes her success with her account of duty and books and 'no pleasures', and backs up her moral programme for Britain. 'The family' in her rhetoric must exert control. She shows a provincial's anxiety about the pleasures of *Vanity Fair*. There was the 'magic' of London shop windows at Christmas, occasional cinema treats, a summer fortnight at the seaside. She caught glimpses of a 'glamorous life' — though she quickly adds 'which doesn't really exist . . . No one I know lives a glamorous life. I don't think it exists'. Indeed, following her first pre-selection defeat she complained of the unfairness in being beaten by a man who had nothing more than charm, and 'a glamorous wife'.

'Snobby' Roberts, as school friends knew her, would always have the best-quality knickers. She worked to the same high standard, though she seems never to have been thought gifted. Her satchel was 'always bulging' with homework. Ambitious and well behaved, she was never afraid to speak up. According to one friend, she was not isolated from her peers but was full of proud conviction: 'She would say "It's a fine day" with conviction, emphasizing the words'. 'You wouldn't make a joke to her that might reflect on her.' In adult life her lack of humour has often been remarked on; more precisely, its combativeness. President Reagan was rebuffed when he tried to joke at Williamsburg that, if an English King had behaved better . . . 'I know', Mrs

Thatcher cut in, 'I'd be hosting this banquet'. Pierre Trudeau thought he could joke about their differences in an after-dinner speech. Mrs Thatcher was not disarmed: 'I only disagree with you when you're wrong!'.

Margaret's father had not been to university but made himself knowledgable through library books, especially on the First World War, politics, biography. 'Somehow it was always assumed that I would go [to university]', Mrs Thatcher recalls. This took some doing, particularly when she chose Oxford against her headmistress's suggestion of a humbler choice. Alf Roberts's willingness to pay the examination fees and Margaret's determined catch-up in Latin took her to Somerville College to read chemistry.

Her interests there were work and Conservative politics, first in the student society, then in the Party itself. Her tutors found her, as she had been at school, able but not noticeably imaginative, studious but not creative. Socially she was competent but hardly interesting.

> She wasn't an interesting person except as a Conservative. I used to entertain the young a great deal [as Head of Somerville], and if I had amusing, interesting people staying with me I would never have thought really of asking Margaret Roberts. Because she wasn't very interesting to talk to, except as a Conservative.

Her predecessor as a female president of the University Conservative Association remembers her

> rather as a brown girl. She had an attractive brown head of hair, was quiet, neatly dressed and very pleasant to be with . . . It wasn't that she hid her light under a bushel; I don't think she had false modesties. I think she just did a good job without any show . . .

She had 'a deep, sincere and zealous wish to do well for her country. The roots of this wish, I would say, were . . . her Methodist background . . . fed by her discovery at school that she had abilities'.

Margaret Roberts went on to complete her degree (with upper second class honours) and then find a job in industrial chemistry. However one of her closest friends was convinced that Margaret's real aim was to enter politics:

She was single-minded from the beginning . . . Politics was her thing, and she just loved it . . . soon after she'd taken her degree . . . we were walking together . . . and she said 'You know, I've simply got to read law . . . chemistry is no good for politics, so I shall set about reading law'. And she did.

The picture is clear enough: a tightly structured family, much work and little play, pleasures taken rarely and even then remembered as innocent in an Enid Blyton way; a sense of constraint but also of advancement, especially through schoolwork; drive towards mastery, adulthood and responsibility; involvement in the public world through provincial office-holding and good works (even Beatrice Roberts made an appearance there, taking her daughters with her to distribute cakes to the needy of Grantham) and through Alf Roberts's political activities and self-education.

The story Mrs Thatcher tells accents order as if that were all. Her Grantham contemporaries, broadly confirming this picture of the Roberts family, sound still a little bemused at the 'brown' girl's extraordinary success. Like the tutor who saw no spark in her chemistry work, like the aide who saw her as having the mind of a clerk, they underestimated her passion. Can this ordered life be the whole story? Was there no sound and fury? Were there no battles lost and won? Was there no feeling? The adult Margaret Thatcher is self-disciplined, hard-working, scrupulously conventional, but she is also a zealous crusader, combative and charming, ruthless with her enemies and tribally attached to her own supporters, passionate about greatness and entirely at ease with her success and dominance. How did this come about, this *contest* side?

Contest and control coexist in the same party, the same programme and the same person. Mrs Thatcher will not complain if we take a leaf out of her own book, the book of Hobbes and Burke. This book says there is no order in the world that has not been fought for. Societies do not begin with constitutions and laws; these are achieved, to the extent they can be, through struggle, just as they must be maintained through vigilance and readiness to return to force. Family life and childhood cannot be exempted from this understanding of human affairs. Indeed, the Oedipal drama conveys the same message about individual lives and the interior of families.

First there is the clash of desire and rivalry. Only then comes the more or less firm structure that controls family life. There is a passionate, unruly phase, then crisis, then a phase of settled hierarchies and agreed tasks. The latter, which Mrs Thatcher emphasizes, is more visible to the outside world and stays more visible to the person concerned than the struggle and threatened chaos of the phase before it. This makes it difficult to trace family 'contest' accurately, but it must be attempted if we are to understand the contradictory, conflictual character of a Strong Leader. The next section turns back to the Roberts family in search of the sound and fury that has been passed over. The family is now interpreted in political terms, its tightly-structured life viewed as a 'political' achievement in which conflict is subdued, fear is focused and guidelines are established that release action and shape goals. It is a search for a Margaret Thatcher who was not manufactured but a Margaret Thatcher constructing herself and her future in an intimate political world, constructing at the same time a public world to inhabit by confronting and controlling it.

FAMILY POLITICS

All Mrs Thatcher's contemporaries agree on the importance of her father to her life. She herself claims to have been closer to him than to her mother, but before we investigate that relationship it is important to take a second glance at the picture Margaret Thatcher draws of a family notable for its orderliness and, indeed, efficiency in the job of bringing up children.

This time we notice dichotomy and division. First, father and mother: they take separate holidays (so the shop can stay open); work in the shop is divided from above-the-shop family life — Beatrice would take her turn in the shop but it was Alf who 'opened early and stayed open late' and did the books on Sunday while his wife baked; above all Alf was bookish, active in local politics, a man oriented to the world outside, and Beatrice was not. 'My mother', says Mrs

Thatcher, 'was a good woman who was intensely practical, and I learned a lot of practical stuff from her'. A schoolfriend remembers Alf Roberts very well but not Beatrice:

> Few people did know much about her mother. She was very much a homely person. I believe she sewed well, she was a good homemaker and, perhaps, let's face it, she wasn't an academic in any way. Margaret admired academic ability as much as anything else, so I used to feel, just occasionally, that she rather despised her mother and adored her father.

This same woman says of Alf and Beatrice 'They were devoted to each other'. It is not my intention to enquire impertinently into that relationship. What is relevant is the opportunity given a child — a temptation, even — to cultivate one parent and repudiate the other, and thus to build into her experience at the deepest level, a drive to discriminate, to achieve by accepting and repudiating.

We are familiar with Mrs Thatcher's unrelentingly partisan, either/or view of life and politics; 'Is he one of us?' is a phrase, according to one Tory MP, that sums her up completely. More significant is Mrs Thatcher's profound belief in choice. 'To govern is to choose', she says, and she makes choice the foundation stone of her whole philosophy. 'Choice', she said in 1977, 'is the essence of ethics: if there were no choice there would be no ethics, no good, no evil . . .'. Like all Strong Leaders and their supporters, Mrs Thatcher can see no meaning and no security without sharp discriminations, returning ultimately to the conflict between good and evil. Deeper still, embedded in a child's experience rather than in an adult's ethical system, may be the division between pleasure, security, hope, or whatever with father, and pain, insecurity, disappointment, or whatever with mother. Is this the fundamental choice Margaret Roberts made? If she did choose, is there a problem of conscience about accepting one and repudiating the other? Might Mrs Thatcher be forced towards further and further division — a more exclusive passion for the good as she sees it and a more extreme repudiation of those who oppose her — just to keep faith with an initial, fateful commitment to 'choice'?

Other dichotomies and divisions are built on this one and begin to reveal what Margaret was choosing between in preferring father to mother. The most obvious is between those in the family who do 'women's work' and stay at home and those allowed to do 'men's work' and join the public world. One of Margaret's jobs was to collect books from the library on her way home from school. For her father and herself there would be current affairs and political biography; for her mother and sister, 'general fiction'. Alf Roberts, 'a tall, dignified, white-haired man', 'at one time the most respected Grantham citizen', made Margaret his confidante and companion, 'explaining his political work as he went on'. One point made here is that of a daughter taking the place of her mother; another is that of a younger sister displacing the older. Muriel, born four years earlier than Margaret, never had the attention Margaret had from Alf. She was probably closer to their mother and the domestic world of 'women's work'. She went on to train (not at university) for work with handicapped children.

How were these divisions forged? How were they maintained? In Strong Leadership's view a structure of rewards and sanctions ensures that people do the right thing. Mrs Thatcher puts great store by law ('Our legal system and the rule of law are far more responsible for our traditional liberties than any system of one man one vote'). She has tried to persuade us that a good family is one that insists on right and wrong, exercises control, holds Burke's view of representative democracy — i.e. parents should be strict, hard-to-influence representatives of the child's interests and her future, not indulgent or permissive although ultimately responsible. However, we would be closer to Mrs Thatcher's view of the world (as a political world) if we included as well the rewards sought and the satisfactions gained for the various parties to these divisions; the desires and rivalries, defeats and victories; the interests served and trade-offs arranged. This yields a more realistic picture of the Roberts family structure: tense, unequal, costly and requiring continual vigilance to restrain moves that would upset the balance, as in international affairs.

This approach casts the young Margaret in a far more active role than she writes for herself retrospectively. She had to come from bottom of the family to next-to-top. The upward mobility of the family, its ambition and sense of being better than much of Grantham, has a matching pattern in the inner politics of the Roberts family, with Margaret the most determined and the most successful. This is not to say there was obvious sound and fury; it is entirely possible that, as in any stratified society that is well run, desires and rivalries are expressed secretly and indirectly.

As well as the struggle and the sanctions, there are the incentives and satisfactions to be enjoyed. The divisions in the Roberts family were made and maintained not by sanctions and force of personality alone. There were also gratifications, promises, hopes. This is why I cannot fully accept the division Mrs Thatcher boasts of — the division between pleasure and work, between self and duty to others.

Margaret Thatcher says she had 'books' but not 'pleasures'. Can these books have been so unpleasurable when they were the coin that passed between herself and her distinguished, confiding, encouraging father? Were they not stepping stones first to father, then to the world? Strong Leaders insist on contrasting duty and selfishness, work and pleasure, to deflect any criticism that they enjoyed their push to succeed, and enjoy their pre-eminence, or that they can be held responsible for the casualties of the struggle. Even critics of Strong Leadership sometimes exaggerate its stoicism, as if ambition was not for something desired and could thrive without reward. Mrs Thatcher freely admits to her father's influence on her values and the cultivation of her abilities; what must be added is the pleasure she had in his company, the hope engendered by the special attention he paid her. These make the love between them at least as powerful as the example and training he gave her, and begin to make sense of the passion and drive in her politics.

Remember, though, that Margaret faced the hurdle of her sex, a very great hurdle fifty years ago when the pull of the 'women's world' was stronger than now. Alf Roberts had to do more than guide her education in public awareness and Margaret had to find inspiration in him as well as instruction. It is said loosely that she was the son Alf never had. It may be enough to say that he did not hold it against her that she was a girl; perhaps the contrary was true, because Alf Roberts appears to have established a relationship with his daughter that did not detract from her femininity while it opened up the public world to her. An equivalent relationship with a son might have been stormier and less successful.

PROTÉGÉE AND CONSORT

The question of protégée and consort is especially intriguing because this Strong Leader is a woman. What was Alf Roberts to his daughter? What is he still? Is Mrs Thatcher's Strong Leadership built on something in her relationship with her father? Is it a continuation of it?

She is his protégée — this is one answer, the most obvious and simple to demonstrate. Mrs Thatcher's pride in 1979, on the day she became Prime Minister, was for Alf Roberts as well as for herself: 'Well, of course, I just owe almost everything to my father. He brought me up to believe all the things that I do believe, and they're just the values on which I've fought the election'. Mrs Thatcher speaks of values and beliefs. Others remember a more precise and practical education: political talk ('she always listened to him') and political work: canvassing, running messages between polling booths, taking notes for him at meetings he couldn't attend, and so on, including Alf's own elections to the local council. There was also the law, Margaret accompanying her father to the magistrates' court to watch him deliberate and hear his judgements. Then there was always his example: in addition to the local council he was active in the church, in Rotary, the Grantham Chamber of Trade, her school's Board of Governors and many other organizations and activities. It was an involvement in public life that, with hard work and study, provided Margaret Thatcher with her values — including her admiration for small-traders — and an inside knowledge of how a useful life might be lived. Above all, Alf Roberts was not just interesting; he was interested in her. Margaret's headmistress recalls: 'he encouraged her in everything she wanted to do'; a friend remembers: 'He was devoted to her'. Special financial arrangements were made so that, in the event that he died before Margaret had her degree, she would have the money to complete it.

The protégée is rather more than an apprentice. She is not only taught but personally invested in. Nevertheless there is a lot of the master–apprentice relation in Margaret's eager, obedient attention to the lessons her father taught her. Psychologically, we would speak of identification — the apprentice learning how to be like the master, readying herself to take his place in the future. However, identification, though it is subtler than mere copying, tends to conformism and simple continuity, and this interpretation fails to capture much of Mrs Thatcher's personality. There is more than this, more than apprenticeship, in the relationship between Alf and his daughter, taking us to a type of relationship both more inspiring and more dangerous. What this extra dimension is I have tried to sum up in the idea of consort.

Strong Leaders are wary of 'hypotheticals', fearful of confusing the troops with irrelevant speculation, of committing themselves before they are ready, of revealing uncertainties, errors and sins that show them weak or unworthy. Disarmed perhaps by an admiring biographer, Mrs Thatcher did once respond to a personal hypothetical: if not herself, who else would she have liked to be? Mrs Thatcher's reply was: 'Anna. Anna from *Anna and the King of Siam*'.

Margaret Landon's *Anna and the King of Siam* was published in 1944 when Margaret Thatcher was nineteen and at Oxford. The author described it as 'seventy-five per cent fact, twenty-five per cent fiction', a romanticized version of Anna Leonowens' 'recollections' of six years in the court of King Mangkut, published in 1870. Landon's version shapes the film of the same name released in 1946, with Irene Dunne and Rex Harrison. Both convey something of the dark, repressed sexuality of a mid-Victorian woman fascinated by the sexual life of an Asian court. There is also an impression of Anna's shady, lower middle class background struggling with her pretension to something far grander, though this is muted. Harrison, as the film King, is in a continual state of exasperation, while the real King described Anna as 'that tiresome naughty and meddlesome Mem Leonowens'. By the time the story had become the musical comedy *The King and I*, and a film starring Deborah Kerr and Yul Brynner, the dark hints of sexuality — undoubtedly closer to the actual sexuality involved — had been replaced by a sunny and simple love story. Gone were

Anna's 'hidden emotional depths, such as might have led to romantic ideas about her royal employer', and gone was her malice towards the King, her voyeuristic prejudice against his private life (it was his duty to father many children), the heated imaginings of backstairs events she could not have known about, and her grandiose claim to have been the main civilizing influence on Siam's first modern ruler despite the evidence that she 'did not loom large in the royal concerns'.

Politics and personal life come together in this fantasy of being consort to a King who is at the same time a kind of Queen Victoria bringing British civilization to a backward people. Anna, in the story, and also, it seems, in life, gives herself a role which is not quite wife and not quite mother but as intimate as both. She consistently overstates her position and influence but insists at the same time on her dutifulness and her good character. She is a consort who need not claim to be married, a mother whose son (Anna was engaged to teach the King's son) is already made. The real Anna, in fact, seems to have been trained for such a role: as a fifteen-year-old girl she travelled for three years as companion to a certain Reverend Badger, who lacked a wife. The important thing, however, is the fantasy. It has all the characteristics of a girl's wish to replace her mother in the affections of her father, of being herself mother, without being naughty or over-ambitious, a fantasy of achieving eminence and power innocently. Mrs Thatcher's choice of Anna as a model is a useful condensation of her adult politics, which combines power, femininity and a mission to civilize what she regards as an unruly world. It points, as well, to the *roots* of her politics, to the relationship the young Margaret might have believed she had with her father.

Protégée, yes; but also partner in a mutual-admiration society in which Margaret had the role of consort to a childhood King. The sheer pleasure of it, the meaning and purpose it gave, these must be counted when we consider the energy and passion of Mrs Thatcher's political career. Besides hard work, thrift, self-control, and all the other virtues her father taught her, there was love; and, as always, there was frustration as well, disappointment at the limits of love, displacement and redirection. A child cannot really be a wife. Consorting with her father, she is also a protégée, unfinished, and her attention had to turn to this aspect of her life. Mrs Thatcher's wish to be special — or great — is all the more competitive for having been cultivated in a childhood success with her father that, while it stimulated, had to be governed too. The consort, in other words, is blessed by a position beside the King, which is both highly energizing and profoundly frustrating at the same time. The trick is to become an apprentice too, and turn the excitement into work.

Strong Leadership's pursuit of greatness, personal greatness then national greatness, has this as its core: to be a child, like being a follower, is to be in a humiliating state of weakness. In the Roberts household and in its lower middle class ambience, this was shown in the family's aspiration to rise, an attitude reinforced by religious counsels towards self-improvement. Yet Margaret's aspirations had more than social and religious encouragement. She had her father's explicit encouragement and, as well, the powerful stimulus of a partnership with him — a partnership which a wife might have valued. He invited her to ignore the facts that she was 'only a girl' and the youngest in the family, and she responded eagerly.

The Oedipal promptuary schematizes some key elements in the experience of childhood. The promiscuous loves, the passions of an early phase give way to a tamed, organized pattern of attachments, loyalties and learning. The parent who denies himself the most, civilizing himself the most thoroughly, might yet realize his least-tamed dreams in the daughter who is protégée and *de facto* consort. She in turn retains some of the passion which a highly ordered family life is supposed to suppress. This is both energizing and, since it raises questions of legitimacy, very troubling. It is also made invisible behind a story of homilies, lessons learned, obedience and hard work. The 'politics' of growing up disappears; a life becomes a moral tale of good 'administration' leading to adult success.

Why can't the politics of her upbringing be admitted, and why are Mrs Thatcher's politics not the politics of gratitude and love? We have already seen that she sees families as agencies of control, of repression even: they have to 'keep down all that evil'. Was the young consort then close to doing wrong?

A curious paragraph in one of her speeches begins predictably enough for a Conservative, then its direction changes:

> it is arrogant to claim that our generation is any wiser than previous generations. We are here, they are gone. We can stand on their shoulders, as I hope succeeding generations will be able to stand on ours. But we should not be too hasty in judging them . . . because to judge requires so much knowledge, such an effort of imagination to put ourselves into their shoes, that could well be spent — barring the professional historian — on understanding our own pressing problems.

It may not be going too far to see this as a personal comment that shows how Mrs Thatcher has dealt with that fraught period in her childhood before she entered the groove she now recalls and recommends to schoolchildren. She states that the secret of life is to 'make 99 per cent of it habit', ruling out the contribution passion makes, and the contribution it made in the past. That might be because she fears to locate her success in something — a relationship — both more potent and less comfortable than mere habit.

Out of sight is not out of mind. Strong Leaders project inner conflict on to the outer world, or freight real, objective, difficulties with unrecognized personal ones. They colour their past in black and white and rewrite it in us/them terms, idealizing one side and depreciating the other. They find causes and arm themselves against criticism by fiercely committing themselves to the 'right' side in a deadly dichotomy substantially of their own making. Instead of attempting to integrate the various sides of themselves, they divide internally — and then 'discover' these divisions in social, political and global forms. Instead of examining themselves, they search for ways to act. Because they have created in themselves an evil alternative, they dare not relax or play (as in the arts), loosening the structures. This is not to say that there really is evil in them; it is the Strong Leaders who believe that human beings are inclined to evil, and it is they who carry forward into adult careers the threat of retribution that childhood's pleasures and successes seemed then to entail, and the child's exaggerated fears.

In this reading, Mrs Thatcher's politics rest on a coupling between the success she made of her family's politics — gaining a privileged position, bypassing better-placed rivals, escaping a stultifying structure by mastering its lessons so well that she could seem obedient and yet be vaultingly ambitious — and her fearfulness that she had no right to have succeeded so well. Father and daughter (Mrs Thatcher's first 'special relationship') together opened a Pandora's box. They liberated hope but unleashed worry too; they set up the conflict between ambition and self-control which continues to the present in the push-and-pull that sees Mrs Thatcher demand and dominate yet also try to cool things down with the moralizing of a governess attempting to be master and mistress at the same time. Mrs Thatcher shows little of this strain herself, appearing completely convinced that her cause is just and even noble. Others feel it, however, as she calls on them to enjoy their freedom and scolds them for exercising it.

THE CONVOY AND THE CONSORT

The convoy suggests wariness, individuals keeping their distance, and rough equality, though there is an awareness of American superiority and Mrs Thatcher's moral is greater interdependence between the two countries. This is the caution Strong Leadership and its supporters have towards social unities. The consort, on the other hand, is clearly about unequals, about finding a role that is valuable and influential though ultimately safe, which allows passion, eagerness and drive. Together they show the tension in Strong Leadership between needing society and the fear that other people are determined to take one over.

Margaret Thatcher turned from industrial chemistry to the law soon after her marriage in 1951. As she tells it, she was pregnant with the twins, had nothing to do and the Bar exams were not far off. So she entered, studied and passed. Her mother's kind of work was not for her, though she had substantial help in the house. Indefatigable in public service, she confesses 'when children are very tiny, it's very exacting because they need a lot of feeding and a lot of washing'. She sounds astonished at what they 'exacted' from her, and she says as much when she speaks of the children's upset reaction when she went away for a fortnight. Her 'help' had to explain to her the importance of talking to them more. Within a year, Mrs Thatcher was back doing tax law. This worked well, she believes, because she was only twenty minutes away 'if I was needed'. It was not, apparently, her job to anticipate their needs. Later the children were sent to boarding school.

Mrs Thatcher told a group of schoolchildren that she tried to give her children more of the treats she had not had. There is no sign that she reproduced the strict, close parenting she received. One example she gives is the twins' fear of the dark. She found it simplest to leave the light on; there is no hint of an interest in what frightened them nor of the patience a more complex solution would need. Mark, who more than once has been the object of public interest for seeming to exploit his mother's name for business purposes, says 'we haven't always been able to discuss matters'. The order of the day seemed to be live-and-let-live, or *laissez-faire*. His sister, Carol, wrote: 'If I did what was expected of me as far as work was concerned, and behaved in a reasonably civilized fashion, it was fairly easy-going'. Carol went to Australia after a troublesome relationship with an older member of the Tory party, coming back to write a book about her mother's second election win.

Sir William Pile tells of how, in a briefing session with Mrs Thatcher when she was in charge of Education in the Heath government, 'she suddenly stopped and said, "what's the time?" . . . "Oh, I must go and . . . get Denis some bacon"'. Pile offered to have the staff do this but: '"No", she said, "they won't know what kind of bacon he likes"'. When she came back 'we resumed discussing the Chancellor's proposal that thirty million pounds should be cut off the public expenditure bid'.

Denis Thatcher was a company director, divorced and ten years older than Margaret Roberts when they married in 1951. The contrast between them is captured in the words used of him and his friends: 'clubbable' and 'cronies'. He is gregarious, stuffily amusing, relaxed. *Private Eye*, in a series of invented letters between Denis Thatcher and a friend, has made much of his secondary role (in real life he calls his wife 'the Boss'), but the testimony of others is that this underestimates his influence. One conservative MP, a woman, says Margaret has been 'very lucky with Denis'; 'he is immensely kind and thoughtful'; 'he adores her'; above all 'he has believed in her'. Another says 'She is more relaxed when he is around', and he can get her to stop and go to bed when it's late and she is too wound up to realize she needs rest. He also has business expertise. An adviser to Mrs Thatcher suggests Denis will sometimes interpret balance sheets for her. It may also be important that Denis Thatcher is, or was, a successful businessman, representing at home, as it were, what she admires and works for outside.

Denis says, though, 'with Margaret work comes first. It's always the work'. Mrs Thatcher made one unsuccessful attempt at pre-selection before being pre-selected for Finchley, where she won the seat in the 1959 General Election which saw a Tory landslide. Between 1965 and 1970 she rose to a number of Shadow Ministry jobs and became Secretary of State for Education in 1970, when the Conservatives were returned. In 1975 she became Leader of the Party, and therefore of the Opposition. She did so unexpectedly, if not accidentally. There was widespread feeling that Heath, who had lost two successive elections, had to go but there was no obvious candidate. The likeliest challenger was Sir Keith Joseph who had been Mrs Thatcher's political mentor through the seventies. He withdrew, and this was the trigger for Airey Neave, a distinguished member of the party and another friend of Mrs Thatcher's, to begin a campaign on her behalf. Eventually, on the second ballot, Mrs Thatcher beat four rival candidates, including William (later Lord) Whitelaw who had entered the race late, and represented, as most of her rivals did, the more liberal side of the Conservative Party.

Mrs Thatcher certainly worked shrewdly and hard for the leadership once Joseph had withdrawn and Neave had appointed himself her campaign manager. However, Joseph's withdrawal surprised her and I think Mrs Thatcher was always less interested in jockeying for position than with making herself invaluable, in letting the rewards come if they would. That is to say, at the distant focal point of her ambition there was a slight blurring which it took Neave and others to remove.

Margaret Thatcher was an outsider to the Conservative Party on a number of counts. She was from the lower-middle class, had gone to a grammar school, had done science, was closer to 'trade' than to the 'learned professions'. Secondly, she was of the Right, and abrasively so. At Conservative Party conferences in the sixties she was even then working up her own ideas, and as time went on, helped by Joseph, she increasingly sought to remake the Party that she believed relied too much on appeals to the middle ground and on governing in a non-ideological, 'managerial' way. Particularly attentive to Party matters, Mrs Thatcher attacked the conventional wisdom of two decades of Conservative Party success and failure, fighting her own party's mainstream as a first step to fighting socialism.

Femininity

There was also her sex. No woman had led the Conservative Party before and Margaret Thatcher had few illusions that being a woman was anything but a handicap. In 1974 she told a reporter 'It will be years before a woman either leads the Party or becomes Prime Minister. I don't see it happening in my lifetime'. This in itself would have been enough to blur her vision of ultimate success. When she was at Education, Sir William Pile, the top civil servant there, asked her about her goal: 'Chancellor of the Exchequer', she replied, 'but the Tory party will never allow a woman Chancellor of the Exchequer'. Pile continues:

> Later on, when she was Leader of the Opposition I wished her well for the next election, her first election of course, and she said 'Well, if I lose I will be out tomorrow'. And I said . . . 'the Tory party lets you lose two elections before they fire you'. And she said 'Not if you're a woman'.

Images of Strong Leadership tend to be masculine, though Margaret Thatcher has provoked some florid attempts to accommodate her powerfulness with her sex: 'Attila the Hen', the 'Leaderene', etc., and some men have recalled the terrifying female figures of the Englishman's nursery and early school days. Undeniably 'strong', Mrs Thatcher remains clearly a woman. This is important because, if she were less a woman, it would be difficult to sustain the argument that the idea of 'consort' lies at the heart of her political ambition and work. The androgynous do not need to consort.

It is a trifle ridiculous that journalists poll people on how 'feminine' Mrs Thatcher is, and it is hardly surprising that the replies are vague. Nevertheless, there is a trend to seeing her as feminine. Sir Keith Joseph said 'she is very womanly, and always looks very nice'. Al Haig described her as 'every bit a woman, from head to toe'. Barbara Castle, who had been a Minister in the Wilson Labour governments, recalls seeing, in the Lady Members' room at the House of Commons, a row of pegs 'filled with Margaret Thatcher's clothes'. They were for quick changes between parliamentary scenes, 'half-a-dozen garments' and 'at least eight pairs of shoes'. Mrs Thatcher is frequently described by those who speak about her in articles and books as 'attractive'.

The comment by Dr Brzezinski, President Carter's security adviser, that 'She doesn't strike me as being a very female type of woman', points to a different aspect of the question: how to respond to her aggressiveness. Many of the men questioned spoke of being wrong-footed. An EEC negotiator said: 'it was more difficult to be rough with a woman . . . being challenged by a woman disconcerted them. If it had been a man they could have said "shut-up" . . .' Labour's leader, Neil Kinnock, said: 'I think Mrs Thatcher is more difficult for me to oppose . . . I've got, however much I try to shrug it off, an innate courtesy towards women that I simply don't have towards men'. A Conservative MP commented: 'the English middle-class male of a certain age . . . [has] always been brought up to believe that it's extremely rude to shout back at women. So she has been . . . able to hold the centre of the ring . . .'. It is also believed, in Lord Whitelaw's words, that Mrs Thatcher is not 'in the least afraid to use the feminine touch to get her way if she wants to'. Dennis Healey, former Foreign Secretary in the Callaghan Labour government, adds 'She's happier arguing with men than with women. In fact I'm not aware of her ever arguing with women — or having very much to do with them. She's very much the sort of woman who does well in a man's world . . .'.

The protégée needs only to have learned her lessons well; the consort has to have been inspired. The special relation with Alf Roberts (with whom she could fancy herself playing a sort of Anna), is the source of the vital side in Mrs Thatcher's political career. The pattern is continued. Even as an adult Mrs Thatcher is a kind of consort. To the chagrin of many women, she needs a 'man's world' to make her achievements feel big enough.

If there is anything Mrs Thatcher is in flight from it is 'woman's work', the world of her mother's 'sewing and practical stuff' and her sister's 'caring' profession. Having babies was not, in her eyes, 'work', and plainly she was impatient to get on with her work at the Bar. She did not take on family or welfare cases; her work was largely in tax law, when she was already a helper of business and could sharpen the financial and advocacy skills that would be a shield against being undervalued for being a woman. Years later, President Reagan said 'she's a great Prime Minister, not because she's a woman, but because of what she knows, what she does . . .'. While Mrs Thatcher was still on the Shadow front bench Lady Neave, wife of Airey Neave, was sent by her husband to hear Margaret Thatcher make a speech in the House opposing the then Labour government's Capital Transfer Tax:

> I was immensely impressed. I went with an open mind entirely, and by the time I'd heard her final speech I felt no longer that I was listening to a man or a woman, but to somebody who had an enormous grasp of the facts . . . [later] we both agreed . . . her grasp of this very difficult subject . . . was so immense that it didn't matter if she were a woman . . .

This is the protégée attending to her lessons, the 'eternal scholarship girl', as somebody called her, distant and a little cool because her eyes are fixed on a distant goal, one little ship in a large convoy.

In the consort role it does matter that she is a woman. Barbara Castle:

> She's . . . shown almost a contempt for her own sex in the way she has used her power as Prime Minister. Of course she has sex consciousness

. . . she wouldn't bother so much about her appearance, her grooming . . . if she weren't sexually conscious. But that's different from what I mean. Her treatment of the services that matter so much to women, that liberate them from the domestic servitudes, all the social services . . . these don't arouse her interest at all.

It is strange to see one of the most powerful women in the world so conventionally feminine, hair carefully set, handbag in hand, and so bored by other women — though I do recall a short, patronizing speech she made twenty years ago at a Conservative Party Conference on women and law which suggested that women who want to follow her into the 'man's world' should do as she did. Margaret Thatcher said 'Mrs Seel, who proposed the motion' had put forward the best claim for the better treatment of women; 'she was completely relevant, direct and to the point'. Needless to say, Mrs Thatcher doesn't speak of Anna, or that to be vital and successful she might need to stay feminine in a 'man's world', impressing men still more powerful than herself, measuring herself against lesser men. Skilled far above what she needs for it 'not to matter' that she is a woman, Mrs Thatcher nevertheless prefers to retain and exploit distinctions between the sexes. Her achievements save her from being confined to a 'woman's world' of sewing, feeding, nursing and 'general fiction' reading, but her passion to consort requires that she remain a woman with a challenge — the challenge of a man — continually there to confront.

6
Conclusion — Enchantment and Ambivalence

Strong Leaders most frequently describe themselves as people who 'like challenges'. Challenge equals purpose, directions given by a real world outside yourself and not just figments of imagination or psychological quirks. Furthermore, such 'real' challenges, if they can be met, seem to promise a reward of meaning as if nature or society had personally signed each challenge and when your collection is complete you will have 'done well'. The criticism that sees Strong Leaders and their supporters concerned only with practical and material matters misses the search for meaning behind their claim to realism. They want the hard and challenging world to give them directions and tell them their own worth. They may look like 'mere calculators and economists' (Dennis Healey said Mrs Thatcher has taken the Conservative Party from the landowners and given it to the real-estate agents); but not far below the surface of business rationality is a wish that the world be an enchanted one, that it be about something real and big and that one has a significant part to play in it.

Margaret Thatcher has offered her supporters an enchanted world, a world full of meaning. Max Weber, early in the century, doubted how civilization would survive the disenchantment that followed increasing rationality. However, precisely the same thing occurs in the individual life: childhood magic is given up for 'thinking as an adult', as St Paul wrote. In people's lives, as at this end of the century in society, we see how Weber and others exaggerated the change. Superstition and fancy, ritual and hoping for miracles continue in and around 'rational' procedures, never letting them be pure. The leading edge of Mrs Thatcher's Strong Leadership is the tense combination of high, narrow abilities and sweeping faith. This is what she has carried forward from childhood. In her shopkeeper's home, dour and 'disenchanted' in its strict Methodism, there was an opportunity for inspiration. Margaret's special relation with Alf never explicitly challenged the climate of the household but it released in her great energies and high hopes.

Thatcherism is thus built around a child's faith in what was vitalizing and liberating, a child's understanding of what was worth doing and how to be a person of worth yourself. It brings to adulthood and politics an enchanted world, a world saturated with meaning. Glory is again possible (we need think only of the effects of the Falklands victory on British self-esteem) and there is greatness waiting for those who will shrug off the Socialist conscience and abandon their dampening scepticism. Mrs Thatcher set out to lift the morale of the West, turning international politics into a Tolkien-like struggle between the greatest of all powers, good and evil. Like all crusaders, she has a holy contempt for those who won't catch the mood, while she herself has the look of someone who expects to go on to greater and greater heights.

Two things about this faith. First, it is inescapably unequal and divisive. The world and the nation are first divided — sheep and goats; good and evil — before there is any possibility of their being united again. Strong Leadership, though it favours productive individuals, has its visionary eye on the whole. The nation should prosper, though not all members of it will do so. The alliance should hold, though some of the allies will suffer heavy casualties. Just as Mrs Thatcher's Britain was 'great again' after defeating the Argentinians, though some Britons were dead, so it can be 'Great Britain' again though unemployment rises and the north decays. In Thatcherism, the hiking team does best that refuses to go at the pace of the slowest; on the contrary, each is licensed to emulate the fastest.

Thatcherism, no less than other faiths (or myths), requires sacrifice and duty. Meaning which is said to lie in individual success or contest also lies in serving something or someone outside yourself, something alien and worthy of respect. Strong Leadership wants us pushy but pious as well. It pictures society as an endless, rising series of self-assertion and bended knee, where the wish to believe is as keen as the wish to be free. This crystallizes the significance of Mrs Thatcher's consort role. Alf Roberts, whose attention energized her, is also her guide and mentor, her conscience and ideal. If, for Margaret Thatcher, meaning resides in high achievement in a 'man's world', this requires that she keep the faith. Sheer self-assertion, mere aggrandizement, a candid appetite for power and riches cannot be countenanced. They are not enough, and they do not fit the pattern that moulded her vitality and hopes. That pattern — which, in other variants, is common to Strong Leaders — requires the maximum of both initiative and restraint, both profound radicalism and deep piety. As consort, Mrs Thatcher pulls these poles together, liberated by the father she also serves.

Shall we hold Alf Roberts responsible for Thatcherism? Are we all to be consorts of the great, thanks to him? The answer is clearly no. What counted was the relationship, and the relationship as seen through the child's eyes. 'She really does think he was a great man', a friend says, implying that in other eyes Alf could seem something less. Thatcherism carries forward into a dull world the glamour of a child's devotion and the starkness of a child's choices, childhood's illuminated hopes and dark fears. Indeed, this immoderateness may be the real secret of its power.

It happens that the real Alf Roberts might not have been a Thatcherite at all. He was known as a kindly man with an interest in welfare matters in the town; his strictness was on religious matters, not social economics, and he was no Tory stereotype on the magistrate's bench. That he gave himself so fully and warmly — companionably — to Margaret is testimony itself to a quality Thatcherism lacks. Moreover, he was an Independent, never became a Conservative (even after Margaret did), and it is even claimed he was 'moderate Labour' in his views. Margaret Thatcher, it seems, is less the protégée than it first appeared. The heroic Alf Roberts, patron of manly enterprise and model for British greatness, exists in his daughter's mind. His role is written for him, the being who must be great so that she could be his great consort. This may be why gratitude has no place in Thatcherism while inequality and self-interest are praised to the skies — what counts with the Strong Leader is not quite what her father gave her, protégée-like, but the fire she took (stole?) from him.

From another woman of power, Barbara Castle, we get a striking pen portrait of Mrs Thatcher. She had just been elected Conservative Party leader. Mrs Castle wrote in her diary: 'The papers are full of Margaret Thatcher . . . What interests me now is how blooming she looks. She has never been prettier . . . I understand why — she's in love, in love with power, success and herself'. I have pointed out that Mrs Thatcher did not advertise herself as the Strong Leader the Tory Party and the nation needed, at least not as explicitly as have other Strong Leaders. I've also suggested that when the leadership came, though she was ready to take it, ambition for the top spot was not fully focused.

Feeling herself an outsider would have something to do with this, also taking into account her gender, and her dependence on Joseph, Neave and other mentors seems to confirm this self-limitation. However, the important thing is her consort role. The consort is a power behind the throne and must not plan to take it for herself; she must not openly covet the top position. Mrs Castle's sketch (and she is frank about having the same wishes and hopes as Mrs Thatcher, and is not sitting in judgement on her) reminds us not to be naive about Mrs Thatcher's motives for making Britain great again. The Oedipal promptuary which agrees so well with Mrs Thatcher's own political philosophy and her philosophy of human nature, agrees in particular with the belief that social feeling always comes second, that the ambitions held for oneself always come first. Certainly Strong Leadership cannot escape this conclusion, even when it wishes to be pious too. Thus, behind her Thatcherite faith and behind any 'special relationship' — be it with her father, the United States, Gorbachev, the 'Great' past of Britain and its greatest leaders — stands the single person, Margaret Thatcher. This Oedipal realism suggests that serving others is against the grain, that there is always reason to be sceptical of claims that what one does is done for others.

In other words, there is no relationship, however sacred, that escapes ambivalence. No one could doubt Mrs Thatcher's commitment to Britain. What needs a second look, though, is her conception of Britain. We have to watch for when Mrs Thatcher's 'Britain's' is reduced to an identikit of herself.

RONALD REAGAN

7
A Strong Leader?

'Reagan goes mourning again.' Thus reported the *Guardian* in mid-1987 following the death of thirty-seven American sailors in the Persian Gulf.

> The US was to have stood tall in the Reagan era. But the President's actions have produced a rapid-fire series of memorial services, backdrops of draped Stars and Stripes over caskets coming home, and cascades of tears. . . . The poignant scene in the simple hangar — as Mr. Reagan trailed by his wife, Nancy, applied the balm to the country's wounds — has become a tragically familiar television image of the Reagan presidency.

Mr Reagan's 'soft tones', 'his voice breaking toward the end of his eulogy', may have soothed the American people, but he gave them no comforting explanation of the tragedy. As with the marines in Beirut and the *Challenger* disaster, hard facts would come later; indeed the President seemed at a loss for an explanation when he said the deaths of men in the Second World War were 'easier to bear then because it was easier to understand why we were there, why we were fighting'. Mr Reagan, the Great Communicator, communicates sympathy, but bewilderment as well.

Six or seven years before, everything had seemed very much simpler. Reagan's speech accepting the Republican nomination in July 1980 emphasized 'the American tradition of leadership': 'The United States of America is unique in world history because it has a genius for leaders — many leaders — on many levels'. President Carter's 'mediocre leadership' was 'eroding our national will and purpose': 'he gives us weakness when we need strength, vacillation when the times demand firmness'; 'the ship has no rudder'. There could be only one answer to the question of whether the United States was stronger and more respected than when Carter took office. Carter failed to show proper leadership even in foreign affairs (his special interest); what was needed now was 'a firm and principled foreign policy', one that was realistic and sought 'to change [the world] by leadership and example; not by lecture and harangue'. America had to do more than talk. The would-be President promised that his 'Number one priority' would be 'to insure that the safety of our people cannot successfully be threatened by a hostile foreign power'. America's moral and political decline would be arrested, above all by becoming militarily strong again: 'we know only too well that war comes not when the forces of freedom are strong, but when they are weak. It is then that tyrants are tempted'. Like Mrs Thatcher, Mr Reagan frequently invoked this psychology of the bully.

US. NEEDED STRONG LEADSAR

The Reagan Presidency presents the following conundrum: how a man of black-and-white thinking, a man with a 'mad-bomber' past and a programme of action and unrestrained entrepreneurial individualism could be, at the same time, so vague and sentimental, so passive and even detached. How was the economic and military 'realism' he symbolized combined with impenetrable optimism, carelessness and cheerful ignorance and a probably unique attachment (in so high or public on office) to make-believe and popular myth? Was Ronald Reagan at once a Strong Leader (according to the model outlined in Chapters 1 and 2), in the same camp as Margaret Thatcher, and a jelly-bean man, naive, indecisive?

Our answers lead, as they must in the analysis of Strong Leaders (and their followers) to ambivalence. Love and hate, supposedly 'structured' into personal and political harmonies, in fact challenge, intertwine, awkwardly accommodate each other. It is these dynamics which shape personality and politics, not the smooth appearance of clear goals and firm disciplines.

This is not to say that, after the Thatcher profile, the Reagan profile will be more of the same. The puzzle of Reagan's personality will lead us in novel directions where we can explore how a leader might be a Strong Leader (or at the very least, a would-be Strong Leader), though he seems sincere in offering reconciliation, harmony and love. The destination is ambivalence, but the starting point can be either love and togetherness or aggression and dominance. In the case of Mrs Thatcher we had to penetrate an emphasis on difference, dominance, self-assertion and 'realism', before we could catch a glimpse of the passionate attachment to her childhood father and the magic of their relationship, though it is not acknowledged in her politics of ingratitude. In Reagan's case, unities, sentiment, dreams, myths and make-believe were in the forefront; it was love that acted as the screen, with self-assertion, ambition and anger hidden behind it. Moreover, Reagan's ambivalence, unlike Thatcher's, which is suppressed under sharp, stern manners and absolute convictions, was masked by ambiguity, which is at once a better clue to the underlying tension and a better disguise. A great many opponents of Reagan have not bothered to become informed critics, thinking him shallow, confused and simple. Our job is to see what is under the Teflon surface.

'How could anybody send these young kids off to be killed?' Thus spoke Reagan, at Arlington, with tears in his eyes, though he was their Commander in Chief. This, too, from the President setting out to have America stand tall again, respected for its military and economic strength, and the budget-slasher who tells his Office of Management and Budget director: 'On defence we don't determine the budget. The other side does. You have no choice but to spend what you need'. Both sides of Reagan are important.

The conflict between them — between power, action, decisiveness, and a penchant for mourning, for sadness and retreat into jokes, long vacations and sleep — resulted in an ambiguity that may have been no less significant for world affairs than the bellicose Reagan of the 1960s. Reagan often boasted of the progress his administration made over

Carter's, because 'they [the enemy] know where we stand'. The supporting evidence, especially in his first term, was not strong. Moreover, as some have said, Reagan seemed not to believe death and destruction would actually occur; there needed only to be movie-like costume battles — like offering the 'protection of the American flag' to Kuwait's tankers — because the enemy would fade away. Far from assisting his armed forces, the President must surely have unnerved them with his confusing signals. The commander of the USS *Stark*, later relieved of duty, implied that it was all very well to say 'we will protect our own', firing on anything that appears threatening, but to be asked as well to avoid any incident that could lead to a Middle East conflagration put him in an impossible position.

In Reagan, then, we will discover both the sincere 'Go for it, America' and, also deeply ingrained, an inhibition of action and thought. I shall try to trace how fundamental ambivalence turns into observable ambiguity, how an administration trumpeting Strong Leadership's forthrightness and determination could follow its Leader into spectacular confusion, slackness and a preoccupation with gesture. Garry Wills says of Reagan's foreign policy in the early years of his incumbency: 'the astonishing thing was that he was perceived as following a consistent course through all the zigs and zags'. He quotes Jeanne Kirkpatrick, former Ambassador to the UN and an early Reaganite foreign affairs specialist, exclaiming that Ronald Reagan resembled Jimmy Carter 'more than anyone conceived possible'. Reaganism had been, first and foremost, an attack on 'weak' leadership, its confused signals to the enemy, its indecisiveness and disorder.

REAGAN AS STRONG LEADER

Before we explore the ambiguity and ambivalence in Reagan, in his life and his politics, we have to touch base with the Strong Leader type. In Chapter 2 I set out Strong Leadership's broad characteristics: its crisis mentality, its pride in being realistic and getting results, its belief in action and decisiveness, its reliance on boundaries, division and hierarchies, its belief in technology and at the same time in faith, the value it places on both innocence and experience. I also set out the key features of its political philosophy: its ideas about nature and human nature, the priority given to physical, material concerns, its use of structure to both stimulate competitiveness and limit it (contest-and-control) and, finally, its making leadership a basic principle of life and politics, a programme in itself. I will touch on all of these.

Leadership

The emphasis on leadership is familiar and unmistakable: firmness, resolution, decisiveness. As early as the Goldwater campaign and Reagan's celebrated speech at the Republican convention at that time (1964), this was the central theme. It was again central in Reagan's campaign for the governorship of California in 1966, and Norman Podhoretz called the 1980 campaign a campaign about leadership. He added:

> The demand for 'leadership' is a demand for a strong president, and a strong president is one who will see to it that the country is no longer 'pushed around' and who will not hesitate to take action, including military action, in defense of the national interest

The American people, he said, have 'a hunger to be great again'. Reagan's campaign plane was called *Leadership 80* and by the time of his inaugural address in January 1981, Reagan was quoting Churchill, Lincoln and FDR to make the subliminal point that his administration would be about 'fine leadership', not about partisan politics; perhaps not even about policies.

Threat

There was, too, the orientation to crisis. The Goldwater convention speech hammered the theme that America had reached 'A Time of Choosing'. Its language was strong. 'We can preserve for our children this, the last best hope of man on earth, or we can sentence them to take the first step into a thousand years of darkness. The question is "Appeasement or courage".' 'The guns are silent in this war but frontiers fall while those who should be warriors prefer neutrality.' Strong Leadership mobilizes, not with problems to be solved, but with battles to be joined. Reagan went on to preach the nobility of patriotic martyrdom, of being 'dead rather than Red'.

Reagan learned from Goldwater's mistake and distanced himself from the far right in the subsequent years. However, crisis and the need to arrest decline — apparently not a British and Thatcherite theme alone — remained central to his leadership claim: 'America was not made to be second'. In his acceptance speech he listed 'three grave threats to our very existence, any one of which could destroy us'. They were: a disintegrating economy, a weakened defence, and an energy policy based on the sharing of scarcity'. America was like Gulliver: 'Adversaries large and small test our will and seek to confound our resolve'. The Soviet ('The Evil Empire', the 'focus of evil'), and Iran were both implicated here, but Reagan had domestic enemies in mind too. Along Thatcher lines, Reagan saw economic dangers as well as military ones. Tax cuts, smaller government, linking help for 'minorities' to general improvement, these underlay a crusade to re-establish 'doing well' in the value system of Americans. Reagan quoted Plutarch and warned that 'government is never more dangerous than when our desire to have it help us blinds us to its great power to harm us'. Against the liberal agenda of environmental protection and direct assistance, 'we are going to reaffirm that the economic prosperity of our people is a fundamental part of our environment'; 'we cannot support our families unless there are jobs; and we cannot have jobs unless people have both money to invest and the faith to invest it'. In these extracts, though more softly spoken, is the same shift towards the Strong — the entrepreneurial and the wealthy — as was engineered by Mrs Thatcher, and with it came the 'trickle-down' theory of later notoriety.

Realism, results and action

Strong Leadership's emphasis on realism and results appeared in Reagan's snipe at Carter's *détente* and 'human rights' policies — 'we will take the World as it is' (i.e. avoid being starry-eyed) — and in his use of the energy crisis to symbolize Carter's defeatism. Instead of 'sharing scarcity', 'America must get to work producing more energy'. This was 'realistic' and practical but also uplifting, an appeal to self-esteem, especially when set against Carter's 'regulations, taxes and controls'. The Republican programme, targeting military strength, economic revival and energy, was to bring America back to what it did best, the basics. Remembering the Laffer curve and other supply-side novelties associated with early Reaganism, it was odd to hear the candidate promise no 'new form of monetary tinkering or fiscal sleight-of-hand'. Instead, 'we will simply apply to government the common sense we all use in our daily lives'.

A strategy and a clutch of up-beat labels shored up the idea that the Reagan administration embodied Strong Leadership's commitment to decisive action. 'A strong break with the past', 'the Reagan Revolution', etc. and a strategy of 'boldness, urgency and momentum', of a 'planned string of successes' and avoiding any association with failures — these show the importance the administration placed on early and continuous momentum, as well as on 'steadiness'. It did not accept Stockman's recommendation that the Reagan administration declare a state of emergency in the economy, but Strong Leadership looks good when it looks eager to clear the decks. Stockman's book, in which he sulks with a forced smile, aims to show the President as a 'politician', a compromiser and wheeler-dealer, who undermined the OMB director's genuine revolutionary zeal (a lesson he pretends to be grateful for). However, in the course of *The Triumph of Politics* Reagan appears rather more as a man of stubborn purpose, especially in regard to military spending, tax cuts and the balanced budget. Indeed, much of Stockman's work was in 'fixing' the budget to convince the President he could have the impossibles he wanted.

There was more than image, then, in Reagan's attempted break with the past. Simplistic though his thinking on economics and public policy was, and perhaps because his ideas could be wrapped in a fortune cookie, he put up a Strong Leader's fight to stay on his revolutionary course, albeit ignorantly and passively.

East/West

Internationally, Reagan's ideas, like Thatcher's, tended towards polarization, with the Soviet Union not only politically unscrupulous but behind all that was evil in the world. Decisive international action was not easy to arrange. Grenada had the appearance of a sideshow designed to display the Strong Leader's muscles without any serious danger. Reagan is said not to have wavered in his support for Mrs Thatcher in the Falklands–Malvinas war, though in the early days there was clearly a wish to elbow free of the entanglements with allies that hampered American freedom of action. Despite the emphasis on steadiness, clarity and will, shifts of ground, confusion and drift marked Reagan's conduct of foreign policy as much as clear, swift action. It was also marked by gesture: apart from the Grenada invasion and the troubles in the Gulf there was something much less than clear policy and firm resolve in the use of the marines in Lebanon, and there was Reagan's astonishing rush to agree with Gorbachev in Reykjavik.

The Iran/Contra affair also had the marks of uncertainty or vagueness. The President (at best) left matters sufficiently vague so that men like Oliver North, who claimed 'I knew the President loved my ass', could infer what tacit support they desired. All this is ironic in the light of the attacks on Carter for indecisiveness, confused signals and humiliating backdowns. Embarrassing though it was to the supporters of Strong Leadership, it was still a puzzle for its critics. Should they oppose the Reagan simplistics and bellicosity? Or be grateful that his resolve was weaker than they thought and thankful that, as Henry Kissinger put it, 'Recklessness will be the last problem with Reagan'?

'I am in control here' — this is not Ronald Reagan speaking but Al Haig at the time of the attempted assassination of the President. He was responding in the classic Strong Leadership way: panicking and rushing to take charge before the panic spreads. In contrast, Reagan's amiable informality hardly squared with Strong Leadership's dependence on hierarchy, division, boundaries, and domestically the Reagan appeal was vague and inconclusive. His patriotic appeal, though, implied a sharp boundary between

Americans and the world, as America set its own terms again. Differences with European allies, and in world trade (especially with Japan), were added to the West–East divide. New Zealand was reminded that sentiment was not enough to buy American protection, while Australia was invidiously praised, except when it acted unilaterally in the South Pacific.

Hierarchy

It is perhaps not in the American culture, nor in Reagan, to be explicit about social distinctions as Mrs Thatcher is in Britain. The myth of the ever-expanding frontier cloaks the invidiousness in the American message of enterprise and success. Nevertheless, it is possible to detect implicit divisions and priorities hidden in the haze of 'traditional values' and patriotic solidarity: between the successful and the rest, for example. The lavish first inauguration, a follow-up to that in California in 1966, was privately paid for (a millionaire's snub to government as well as a celebration) and heralded a period in which the 'New Luxury' was blatant and insensitive. Mr Reagan had always said 'America must always be a place where a man can get rich'. There is also a distinction between the worthy and the unworthy: businessmen, the military, policemen and conservative clergy on the one hand, government workers, intellectuals, secularists, and of course 'liberals' in politics and lifestyle, on the other. Men were back in charge again, especially older men; women were divided between the traditional and the irresponsibly modern, while entertainers outnumbered scientists in the White House limelight.

Moreover the Reagan administration, for all the claims to the contrary in Reagan's campaigns and inaugural addresses, did not place minority groups and related social questions high on its agenda. None of this was surprising. It was the same Strong Leadership programme as Mrs Thatcher's, only softened in presentation by the studio smoke-screen of sentimental patriotism and the intimate promises of a brilliant, low-key television orator.

We shall see that Ronald Reagan was a great admirer of successful businessmen. He always had an eye for Top

People and how to please them. At the same time, he was sentimental about ordinary folk, about small, nameless heroes, somehow managing to link the fortunes of the two. The story about one Veteran's Day speech may point towards an explanation. The occasion was for servicemen killed in the Vietnam war and Reagan chose to extol their sacrifice at the Tomb of the Unknown Soldier. In doing so, he spurned the memorial erected by veterans and their families that lists thousands of actual names. This preference for the vague, for the blank screen on to which heroic fantasy can be projected, is characteristic of the man. It blurred his outline as a Strong Leader and softened the outline of Strong Leadership's programme in a way that suited not only the man but also his culture.

Strong Leadership's sense of impending crisis adds weight to its belief that the only true measure of worth is results, winning, success. It also underlies its comparative indifference to the means used. It is hospitable to technological solutions in general and, in politics, at ease with the techniques of persuasion. It is true that Strong Leaders — like the 'strong silent type' — are supposed to be born, not contrived; nevertheless, the charge of hypocrisy or manipulation need not be fatal if the victory is won. Strong Leaders know this. Moreover, Strong Leadership puts little store by egalitarian participation. As Mr Reagan said of nuclear freeze proponents:

> I would hope that some of these people . . . would . . . consider that no matter how sincere and well-intentioned, only in this position do you have all the facts . . . therefore I would ask for their trust and confidence . . . that they would allow us to take the actions that we think are necessary . . .

Strong Leadership is intrinsically patronizing, even when it is apparently benign, and this frees its hands for using whatever tools of political influence will work.

Contrivance

When running for Governor of California, Reagan, writes Wills, 'The spokesman for rugged individualism, was prepackaged more than any major candidate up to that time . . .'. As one of his handlers described it 'we were with him every waking moment . . . You'd follow him into the rest room . . .'; they were always 'goofproofing' him 'with last minute advice'. His mind had to be stocked with one-line answers, backed up with an array of easy-to-consult cue cards. His mood was carefully monitored and he was watched to see that he had enough rest. 'Reagan had to be spared all unnecessary stress — long days, painful staff conflict, the critical decisions', Wills writes. 'While entertaining an ambition that might dizzy the most brazen man' — the Presidency was already in his backers' mind — 'Reagan submitted to a tutoring that would have been insulting to most people of even ordinary pride'. Wills contrasts Reagan with Goldwater, whose mantle Reagan had assumed. Reagan had been afraid to fly since his first short plane flight in 1946; Goldwater piloted his own plane; Reagan was managed; Goldwater ran his own show.

There was a submissiveness in Reagan, but the point to be made here is Reagan's ease with contrivance. Strong Leadership is at home with manipulation, and of course it fits Reagan's own life, which was built around a career of contriving to convey human passions through complex and distant machinery, first on radio then in the movies, and recalls his career as front-man for General Electric's 'all-electric' view of life. Indeed Reagan once defended television's move from live to prerecorded shows, asserting that the latter were just as convincing and just as real.

Michael Rogin makes an intriguing interpretation of this untroubled reliance on technology and technique. He recalls an Edgar Alan Poe story about a certain General Smith, introduced as 'a presence singularly commanding'. Six feet tall, he had a 'splendid head of black hair', 'superbly modelled' arms, lower limbs that were 'superb' and carried 'an air *distingué*' about him. It turns out, though, that in the privacy of his own room the General is reduced to 'a large bundle on the floor'. All the parts are artificial, giving retrospective meaning to the General's frequent approving comments 'upon the rapid march of mechanical invention'. Entering the room the narrator is at a loss for a time, then, 'making squeaky protest, the bundle proceeded to attach to itself a very capital cork leg, artificial arms, shoulders, chest, wig, and teeth . . . Finally, General Smith installed an artificial palate, and his voice resumed all that rich melody and strength which I had noticed upon our original introduction.'

There is an irresistible evocation of Disneyland in these grotesque mechanics. Like Reagan's employer (General Electric), Walt Disney, who was an early Reagan backer, saw in the spread of the mechanical, the wholly controlled, impersonal illusion of life, a vision of progress. It is the sort of 'progress' Strong Leadership tends towards, ambivalently. Heroic and individualist in part, its anxiety about controlling contest — in itself as well as in others — makes it suspicious of the haphazardly organic, the 'jungle' of natural human life. Civilization has to be built on automatic and regular responses and needs to be programmed; it is a kind of prosthesis without which human beings are vulnerable and impotent. Needless to say, there is an élite of those who can be both Strong and self-controlled, heroic and yet conventional; the ideal being the patriotic entrepreneur like Disney himself. These are heroic just because the rest of us cannot achieve such balance. Rogin takes General Smith as a model of Reagan, signifying 'the manufactured, violent, deadened quality of the actor's promises to make the body politic whole'. To an actor aspiring to Strong Leadership the Hollywood 'factory' is not, as it is to others, an enemy of life and wholeness, but an awesomely effective manufacturer of lives and communities as 'real' in his eyes as any other.

Rhetoric and values

Strong Leadership likes technology and technique because they link it to the 'objective' tasks it prefers to undertake, and underwrite its promise to minimize unruly 'personal factors' while maximizing social control. This is Strong Leadership's claim to practicality and realism. Strong Leaders also express another desire: the desire to be a hero, to contest valiantly, to emerge with the laurels of a mythic victory. Strong Leadership's rhetoric, far from being always the language of accounting and finance, becomes at times the most overblown of any leadership type, both more mythical and more sentimental.

Paul Erikson in *Reagan Speaks* examines Reagan's rhetoric.

There was humour, often self-deprecating, pride, nostalgia and, above all, stories. The same stories were told again and again, filling the place of reasoned argument. In these stories Reagan assumed the major roles, where he was always heroic, in a folksy, down-home way. They were often about children, especially sons and especially soldier sons; all the characters were drawn vaguely, becoming flexible tools for the story-teller's political purposes. The imagery was warlike — in the last speech before his 1984 re-election, Reagan gave three examples, all of them military — and sporting, for example around the time of the Los Angeles Olympics America was 'a nation of winners'. The vocabulary was limited, the delivery was 'simple, clearly drawn, unconfused', language equivalents of the white middle-class men and women who monopolize a Norman Rockwell drawing.

One broad theme in the Reagan rhetoric was the superiority of heart over mind, of faith over reason and of ordinary folk over college professors and other intellectuals. (Reagan once described social science courses as a symptom of a sick society.) 'Hyper-intellectualism' was portrayed as a threat to humanity and intellectuals were described as automatons, like the Soviets. The significance of this theme is that Reagan's rhetoric was justifying itself as it went along: its moral absolutes, its sentimentality, its vagueness were all simple, heartening and unifying, and in contrast to the ideas and style of his smart-aleck, discouraging opponents. Sharp questioning, doubt, dry eyes — resistance to Reagan's appeal — were, even before they appeared, already linked with deficient patriotism.

Erickson uncovers the framework of faith in Reagan's ideas. He describes his speeches as 'sermons' and shows that the religion in them is specifically Christian, with only gestures to Judaism. America's divine mission is legitimized by the Bible, which also shows the Soviet to be the anti-Christ. Moreover, in this 'fusion of politics and belief' there is always the spectre of Armageddon, the great 'shoot out'. Ahead there always lies great peril, or great glory, and Reagan, following the uniquely American tradition of optimistic Jeremiahs, put the emphasis on the latter. Reagan's rhetoric, says Erickson, 'apotheosizes the people and the future of this land'; he 'applies the tropes and strategies of his ultimate optimism to nearly every issue which he raises'. Erickson writes of the 1984 campaign as 'an orgy of re-illusionment'. The 'New Patriotism' reflects Strong Leadership's belief that, while the leaders might need to study the facts, what the followers need is 'motivating', they need faith. President Reagan wept easily in the presence of obvious symbols of America, poeticized its history, glorified its future in the struggle between good and evil.

The crisis we are facing today . . . [requires] our willingness to believe in ourselves and to believe in our capacity to perform great deeds; to believe that together with God's help we can and will resolve the problems which now confront us. And, after all, why shouldn't we believe that? We are Americans.

The fact that Reagan seemed sincere only added to his impact as a Strong Leader, concerned with morale amongst the troops. Carter, in Reagan's view, had undermined American self-confidence. The crudeness of the patriotic appeal derived initially from Strong Leadership's patronizing attitude to its followers; but also from its limitations when once it put its mind to creating solidarity. Because it could not trust to natural human sentiments or spontaneous identifications, it could only bang the patriotic drum and sharpen an 'us' in opposition to 'them'. The mawkishness, the legerdemain of anecdote, the untruthfulness, all reflected Strong Leadership's disdain for the fine, day-in-day-out work of maintaining living social bonds, the work of extending imaginative sympathy to strangers; and they showed its vulgar inexperience in these. Love and hope — and even 'poetry' — only matter when they are associated with mighty rivalries, on sports fields and in foreign affairs.

INNOCENT EXPERIENCE

Strong Leaders present themselves as if they were from outside, uncontaminated. They have been drawn from innocent, worthy pursuits outside politics only by the urgency of the crisis and the incapacity of the compromised professionals. Mr Deeds will be eager to get back to his real work in the honest world far from Washington. Coming from outside not only guarantees the Strong Leader's honesty but implies he or she can act more freely and decisively. Thus Reagan was in the Strong Leadership tradition when he announced periodically 'I am not a politician' and when, like Thatcher, he talked of 'government' as if he were not part of it.

In fact, of course, Reagan has been a politician most of his life, and his autobiography is an odyssey of an ordinary man finding in politics the reality and substance he could not find in his only other job, entertaining.

By the time Reagan was elected President in 1980 he had been involved in politics for almost fifty years. There were links through his father and brother to Roosevelt's New Deal machinery; he says he was leader of the student strike at his college and certainly took a leading part in the student organizations. He talked politics throughout his Hollywood days, attended meetings and was twice president of the Screen Actors' Guild. In 1946 leading Democrats invited him to run for Congress and he spent the greater part of his years after Hollywood and before he became Governor of California in 1966 writing political journalism and giving lectures on behalf of political candidates, most notably Goldwater. He tried for the Republican nomination in 1968 and in 1976, before getting it in 1980; even with General Electric he was giving a political spiel (which was probably the reason for his being sacked). After he left the governorship he returned to the team of backers who supported him on nation-wide lecture tours, thus keeping himself always among the presidential hopefuls in the Republican camp.

There is artifice in presenting Reagan as too nice to be a politician. Throughout *Where's the Rest Of Me?* (published in the mid-sixties), Reagan is at pains to show how innocent he is, how naive and reluctant to absorb the lessons of political sophistication. He castigates Hollywood communists for knowing the rules of meetings, for using procedure to win votes! Like America confronted by the wily Soviet, he becomes worldly-wise only in self-defence and, it is implied, only on the surface, enough to get the job done. He remains a small-town All-American at heart. This had substantial political use, of course: amongst other things it showed Reagan as not really a product of Hollywood glamour, not really a spokesman for Californian Big Business, and above all, not a 'mad bomber' of the Goldwater far right.

Nevertheless, the appeal to innocence tunnels deep into the Reagan psyche. Some leaders play up their early struggles (and even Jimmy Carter confessed his 'lust') but Reagan presents his life as sunny and smooth. 'I had an idyllic, Huck Finn type of boyhood', he claims. Garry Wills has shown the double falseness in this. First, it does not fit the details of Reagan's life; second, it relies on a false impression of Twain's classic book. Huck Finn's life was anything but idyllic, closer indeed to nightmare and full of despair. Reagan insists on his good fortune and his unworldliness. Asked once if he looked on Mike Deaver, a young and close aide, as a son, Reagan replied: 'Gee, I always thought of him more as a father figure'. This ambiguity lies close to the heart of Reagan's character. He is part-boy/part-man, the former giving his Leadership its distinctive quality. Not only does it resonate with the tradition of innocence in Americans' sense of themselves and their still-New World; it also gave Reagan a freedom of action more experienced leaders — leaders who were more professional, more committed to a complex programme — could not plausibly claim. It allowed the President and his administration to trade on popularity, using Reagan's personality to confound 'professional' opposition and defuse 'sophisticated' criticism.

Thus Reagan chiefly communicated vague personal feelings, ducking responsibility for the meaning of his commitments and the real outcomes of his policies. 'Don't worry about our mistakes — we'll make more' he said with disarming candour. Other mistakes he called by the show-business euphemism of 'bloopers'. In all this Reagan found a way to make Strong Leadership the work of a hero-worshipping boy, and the Presidency a work of innocence rather than experience.

It is established in this section that Reagan was a Strong Leader in the sense outlined in Chapters 1 and 2. All the components are present, though given a distinctive twist by the pervasive ambiguity that surrounded his attitudes and intentions, smoothing the sort of hard edges Mrs Thatcher candidly displays. There was crisis, Armageddon even; there were military and economic realism and putting prosperity first; there was praise for action and decisiveness; there was faith to enoble and enable renewed emphasis on self-interest and hard-bargaining; there was innocence as a way of dealing with experience. Elements of what I call Strong Leadership's political philosophy have been touched on too. The 'jungle' of nature and human nature was called a 'swamp' by Reagan but he meant the same thing. Priority went to building up military and economic strength and to civilization as a bulwark made up of patriotism and conventional morality, derived from the Christian God and an idealized past.

I have said nothing directly about Reagan's fit with the psychology of Strong Leadership; that will be discussed in the next chapter. There is one overriding theme — Reagan's pursuit of innocence. This leads to other themes: his optimism, his living through other people and in make-believe, his so-called management style, the evidence of aggression denied and held in check. When we have pinned these down, we will try to answer the question why? or how come? by re-examining his childhood. We will then consider the consequences. What kind of Strong Leader was Reagan? Where did his Leadership head?

8
A Case of Dorian Gray

I ran across a forgotten, enormous collection of birds' eggs and butterflies. The colors and textures — and most especially the fragility — of these objects fascinated my imagination. They became gateways to the mysterious, symbols of the out-of-doors they represented. Here, in the musty attic dust, I got my first scent of wind on peaks, pine needles in the rain, and visions of sunrise on the desert. I could sit for hours in that wonderful attic, looking at those glass-encased collections . . .
(Reagan: on his childhood)

THE MEANING OF YOUTH

I link innocence with youth, denial of experience with denial of ageing, and hence Wilde's novel. *The Portrait of Dorian Gray* turns on Dorian's outburst when he first sees Basil Hallward's portrait of him: 'How sad it is . . . if only it were the other way! If it were I who was to be always young, and the picture that was to grow old!' Dorian had 'a wild longing for the unstained purity of his boyhood', and the moral of the story is that infatuation with youth and innocence leads paradoxically to wickedness and destruction. Avoiding experience — avoiding ageing — turns out to be a sure hastening of psychological death. Wills has described Reagan as at once youthful and old, appealing both to the future and the past. He also describes him as a man who could 'will his own innocence'. Reagan came to the Presidency under the cloud of his advanced age and yet he portrayed a youthfulness many marvelled at, albeit a youthfulness somewhat painted and artificial. Only late in his second term was his hair allowed to go grey.

Of course 'youth' is not the same thing to everyone. John F. Kennedy for example, born six years after Reagan, also appeared youthful and appealed to youth, but the word meant something different. Kennedy's youthfulness stimulated idealism and his appeal was to the post-adolescent, to those whose political ideals were already established (ready, for example, for something like the Peace Corps) and to a point in the life-cycle where knowledge and skill are seeking for full-grown social and moral tasks. Moreover, youth in the Kennedy lexicon was sexually mature, and the appeal was to both sexes. To look at Reagan, even as we note his youthfulness, is to know the word means something very different — not political sophistication but home-town virtuousness, not political debate but train-sets in the Governor's mansion, and football. As Dorian Gray longed for his 'rose-white boyhood', so Reagan's nostalgia is for a *Saturday Evening Post* version of youth where a freckle-faced boy, tousle haired, leans on a white picket fence, baseball mitt in hand. There is no image of young women. The male version — conveyed in the President's jeans and horses, his sports talk, his innocently quizzical tilt of the head that makes dissension seem unfriendly — is pre-adolescent: before sex, before religious and moral doubts, before the formation of universalist ideals and mature politics.

There is a way to understand this, using the psychosexual and psychosocial stages of childhood outlined by Freud. A. F. Davies has observed how Rousseau came to his idea that 'naturalness' was the supreme virtue and to his political programme for rolling back the encroachments of civilization, sophistication and even knowledge. Rousseau's conversion on the road to Vincennes was 'a singular conversion — to himself'; 'the turmoil came from his rediscovery, as by one dropping through a trap-door, of a whole subterranean system of personal values still alive — *the naive and candid ideals of his pre-aspirant youth*'.

Rousseau's assumption that in boyhood there is innocence is not one Freud could support; indeed the main offence of Freudian ideas is still that they undermine that belief. However there is, in what Freud called the stage of 'latency', a kind of innocence, which from Rousseau to Norman Rockwell, from Dorian Gray to Little Leagues, has been a peg on which to hang the wish for an innocent past. At that time of 'middle childhood' the tensions of desire and rivalry, which are at their height in the Oedipal phase, are relaxed and puberty has not yet arrived to revive them. This is what Erik Erikson calls the stage of 'industry', where so much is learned and done because of the comparative absence of conflict. This is also a time of simplistics, of black and white thinking, of simple loyalties to 'us' and sharp (if often harmless) opposition to 'them', of enthusiasm for sports, hobbies, collecting, puzzle-solving — but not for widening sympathies, self-examining, framing moral outlooks and political goals, which will come with adolescence. Its shallowness is latency's charm.

An English psychoanalytic theorist has related the qualities of latency to leadership or, rather, the absence of leadership: 'creative leadership is lacking, except for the most rare instance, among children of latency'; 'in the latency period social leadership is lacking in creative impulse'. All it can manage is 'the lower level of imaginative power' in which 'baddies' fight against 'goodies'. It takes puberty or adolescence, with the 'conflictual ferment' of desire and rivalry to liberate heroic, creative leadership. The latency child acts grown-up, parades his or her 'readiness for adult life', has an outward 'docility, readiness to be taught, marshalled, tested'. Meanwhile with a gang rebellion is planned, though this is less a plan to act than an exercise in the pleasures of being 'highly secretive', a naughtiness not of deed, but of ideas and talk, of the locker-room rather than the battlefield. Melzer could be contrasting 'Reagan youth' with the 1960s followers of JFK when he contrasts the fantasies of latency with those of adolescence: 'How different the pubertal excitement! The sexually attractive grown-ups must be seduced and subjugated. The old and impotent — and thereby envious — must be defied. Merlin must yield his secrets before being imprisoned in the tree'.

It is not obvious how Rousseau's party of innocence can be aligned with the 'realism' of Strong Leadership, nor with Reagan's avowed belief in virtually tangible evil. All Strong Leaders mix the two. Scornful of idealists they expect to be believed and trusted and are the last to grant the right to know or to take part in decision-making. In the end the 'right' people claim heroic public virtues and are offended if they are doubted by 'cynical' journalists and intellectuals. Presumably all evil belongs to the enemy. Reagan appears to have taken this further than most, and this is what we have to understand. Did he stay young, in a latency sense, to avoid the stresses and strains intrinsic to the adolescent experience, itself a revival of the desires and rivalries of the Oedipal period? Did he flee experience, did he retreat from ageing? And how would this have affected his view of the world and of himself, how he acted and how he felt, the goals he set himself and the desires of others he would recognize or try to frustrate? How could it be done, this withdrawal from desire and rivalry, from love and power? Of course, this overstates things a bit. Still, we will see how well Wilde's story fits. Also, Melzer's contrast between docile conformity and secret, stillborn wish on the one hand, and passionate conflict, curiosity and creative leadership on the other, makes eminent sense of the Reagan personality and leadership style.

You deal

We turn now to Reagan's strategy of using other people as a shield against experience, or as a filter. The first topic is his 'management style'. It was to this that Reagan turned (for an alibi) when the Iran/Contra inquiries reached the point where he had to assume some semblance of responsibility.

An excellent sociological study comparing the executive leadership styles of Governor Reagan and his successor in California, Jerry Brown, shows clearly how 'hands-off' Reagan's leadership was. From the beginning he set up a decision-making structure which allowed him 'to be part of the deliberations, without having to have them depend on him'. 'Reagan', the authors say, 'refused to decide issues alone or to adjudicate disputes'. His cabinet and his aides each met separately, then met together, going to Reagan only when they were doubly prepared and could present a fully united front. The authors concluded that the Governor was thus transferring considerable power to his assistants, and did not mind doing so. 'I'll go for that' is said to be one of Reagan's favourite phrases, indicating his wish, as one commentator put it, to be the cheerleader rather than a player or even the coach. His wish was to limit his involvement to approving compromises others had sweated blood for.

In the White House, 'round-tabling' was Reagan's chosen method, adversarial debate was discouraged and oral briefings were preferred to being presented and left alone with written submissions. (These must not be more than four paragraphs long, if they must be used.) He claimed to lead by 'gathering talented men around me and leaving them free to do their work as they see fit' and he described himself as 'Chairman of the Board'. Well before Reagan's style of work began to gather opprobrium with the Iran/Contra affair and Oliver North, with Ed Meese's alleged corruption and other 'scandals' beginning in 1986 — and leaving aside reports of the President sleeping late and even nodding off in meetings — Reagan showed that he could be a little sensitive to criticism of his management style. One journalist reported that in the White House Reagan 'often hesitated to make decisions, including important ones, when his senior aides could not agree on a proposal'. The same journalist received a phone call from Reagan, upset by their discussion of his 'passivity'. He boasted that things 'get pretty spirited' and, though he admitted his belief that 'constant confrontation . . . is a sign of weakness', he added 'behind the scenes I have really stomped around a bit'.

Some have described Reagan as like Eisenhower. Revisionist political scientists now portray Eisenhower as only outwardly passive, as in fact active behind the scenes. There is no similar evidence for Reagan. It is more useful anyway to compare Reagan with Truman, or at least with Truman's 'The buck stops here'. Reagan may boast of his cabinet-style, collegial administration, but as one commentator sees it he delegated 'far more to cabinet officers than most of his predecessors had, granting them broad authority and a long leash'.

What really distinguishes Reagan is that, in his forgetfulness, carelessness, ignorance, or sheer deception and self-deception, he did not hold himself responsible. His management style should be seen in the context of a strategy for managing a life, a strategy of avoiding experience by having others experience it for him.

'The secret of remaining young', Dorian is told by Lord Henry Wooton, 'is never to have an emotion that is unbecoming'. Wills says of Reagan, 'like much of America, he constrained contradictions but never experienced them'. Reagan's aversion to personal conflict is noted by every commentator. Cannon, a sympathetic biographer, reports him complaining about conflict among his staff: 'I go out and have these good days and then I get these knots in my stomach when I come back here'. Reagan did not nurse grudges and welcomed differences of opinion but what he could not abide was 'acrimony and discord'. Deaver's job as Deputy Chief-of-Staff at the White House, was, with Nancy, to give Reagan 'tranquillity' at work. In return, he did his bit by being always placid. 'He has more jokes than any human being I've ever known' said a Californian aide. As Governor he was described as friendly but not intimate and above all he disliked 'firing and disciplining personnel'. In the White House, even in private, passion rarely appeared, especially anger. He was protected by his manner of hail-fellow-well-met, his humour, his lack of curiosity and knowledge and the structures he built around him which provided a routine 'as comfortable and as undisturbed as possible'.

Truman's desk-top motto ('The buck stops here') referred to the buck-knife used in frontier poker games to show who was to deal. Reagan seems never to have wanted to deal. Fellow actors remember him in Hollywood with some irritation, resenting the earnestness with which in real life he maintained his screen image of the boy-next-door while, at the same time, he would complain of not being given the sword-and-saddle roles and first leads that more worldly-wise actors were given. Jane Wyman may have summed up their feelings in her own exasperation, after their divorce. She said Ronnie made her seem unworthy and unserious because he had cornered the market on virtue and political commitment. Reagan's legendary optimism put people of more sober judgement in the camp of the Jeremiahs carrying the worries. Nancy Reagan spoke of 'the eternal optimist in him': he believes 'that if you let something go it will eventually work itself out', adding 'It almost never does'.

Mrs Reagan was the keystone in the wall of protectors Reagan surrounded himself with. When he moved to California, Reagan took family and friends, a slice of Dixon, Illinois, with him. When he met Nancy Davis, he was freed from the cocoon of inactivity his divorce had kept him in. Nancy went on to become a key figure in his political progress, as an indefatigable encourager and, particularly with the staff, playing a crucial role in protecting him from the consequences of his wish to idealize people.

Nancy Davis seems to have been well-prepared for the dirt-carrying role. Though Wills softens the impression given in Cannon's book of a hard life — abandoned by her father, virtually abandoned by her mother, rescued at thirteen by the rich, powerful and ultra-right Loyal Davis, still pursued by memories of the 'small rooms and locked doors of her childhood' — everyone agrees that she sees the world in harsher terms than her husband does. 'Nothing she does is by accident', writes one Reagan biographer; she 'always had more push than Ronnie'. She is his 'most passionate admirer', notorious for the 'Gaze' (loving, controlling, owning?) she fixes on him in public. A 'strong and complicated woman', she is rarely apart from her husband. She is not hesitant to complain to the press and as 'a detail hound', unlike her husband, 'occasionally makes life difficult for the staff'.

She, rather than her husband, disciplined the children, though the relation with Reagan took precedence; 'we were basically raised by nannies and maids', said one son. Barrett speculates that Nancy's reward is complete: Reagan calls her 'mommy' and 'it is as if she [had] totally exclusive rights to his emotional reservoir. Not even his children [can] drink there'. Mrs Reagan came from a theatrical family and had important contacts in theatre, radio and film, and a good start in Hollywood herself, without the pain of poverty and anonymity. Even then she said that her career was only a stop-gap, a pause while she found the man to marry and devote herself to. Reagan could hardly have hoped for more: an infinitely devoted supporter who, on the side turned towards the world, is a champion who is not afraid to appear tough or act rough. (It is even said that Nancy is a fair hand at salty stories.) Thus as President, Reagan could stay young and innocent, optimistic, amiable, an inspiration for those supporters of Strong Leadership whose hopes lie in the simplistics of latency youth and a vision of America that reflects a love of themselves before they grew up.

STAYING STUPID

'There are more people in the Reagan administration thinking about fundamental questions than our highly pragmatic political tradition usually allows.' The words are those of Dr Jeanne Kirkpatrick, formerly US Ambassador to the UN. In *Where's the Rest Of Me*? Reagan lists his passions as 'football, drama and politics'. He tells not a single story of the classroom, the books he read, the ideas that were current. His intellectual shortcomings and his ignorance are legendary, if admitted only in circumlocutions: 'a turn of mind that resists ambiguity'; 'as in other sensitive and important situations, the President had not tracked the details closely'; 'by temperament, he is not a details man'; he has a 'knowledge gap'; 'Carter was a slave to logic. No one has ever made that accusation of Reagan'; 'he thinks anecdotally, not analytically'; 'he fails the essay questions but gets the multiple choices'.

Reagan's ignorance of policy matters he was supposed to be expounding, at press conferences for example, was often patent and embarrassing. Reasons given were that he over-delegated, did not work hard enough ('hadn't done his homework') but above all that he was an intuitive politician, consummately right when and where it matters. These were not defences of his intellectual shortcomings but excuses for them, implying that his patchy grasp and fuzzy reasoning did not matter. On a similar tack are those who emphasized his beliefs, his 'absolute convictions', which, they said, it would have been wrong to tamper with and which rightly concerned him more than detailed policy; these gave him judgement and protected his principles. In this view, his intellectual limitations, for from weakening him, made him a decisive leader.

What does Ronald Reagan believe in? The answer is not hard to give, and yet any listing of Reagan's political convictions is likely to be misleading. Individualism, small government, lower taxes, a balanced budget, communist expansionism, security through strength, etc. — these can all be listed. However, in Reagan's case the conservatism is, as Wills expresses it, 'sub-ideological', and hardly a philosophy. Moreover, vaguer but still powerful themes count more with him, above all America's divine mission, its uniqueness, the supremacy of 'heroism' both in American history and in human achievement, and the power of dreams, 'practical dreams', as Reagan calls them. Electorates used to judging policies that are highly explicit and closely argued (or electorates which fancy themselves judicious and wise) were likely to underestimate the reach of Reagan's ideas just because they were so intangible and overblown.

Critics, even within the United States, did not find it easy to criticize Reagan for precisely this reason. The best of them ended up demanding rather lamely that the President be a professor. Stanley Hoffmann's early critique of Reagan's foreign policy ideas lists the presuppositions, sums them up as being 'too simple' and concludes 'above all, we need a president keen on educating the public'; with Moscow there should be not just confrontations but 'a mixed relation'. Reaganism was a choice for a simple world, and continual reminders to Strong Leaders that the world is complex are undoubtedly necessary, especially since Reagan expressed Strong Leadership's fear that complexity undermines will and paralyses action. In his confident version of American history simplicity was the key: 'We found the right values, the right answers, to all the big ones long ago. They paid off for us in the past. Now we must simply tighten our grip on them'. Reagan believed in belief and worked by faith and its symbols, and it was not enough to educate him. We must take as our topic the broad, even illusory, themes that were his true mental home.

The obvious way to do this is Wills's approach in *Reagan's*

America, which puts the man and the President into historical and cultural context. The approach here is different. We are looking for some understanding of Reagan's thinking, what it was like, where it was headed. In particular I want to put up an alternative to the view that his thinking was hard-edged, authoritarian, black-and-white. These are certainly present in his thinking, but only as a part; the whole is a far more complicated affair, involving make-believe and fantasy as well as simple, stubborn oppositions. In Reagan's mind there was a studio haze that kept us all guessing. That haze contained the innocent hopefulness of nostalgia for boyhood suddenly turning dark, and an eschatology that promised salvation to some and eternal damnation to others. Ideas were faint and blurred, then suddenly cast in metal. Imagination was sentimental, parochial and banal, then, shockingly, out of the haze loomed the Evil Empire. Reagan's mental world was a world of appearances that would suddenly become solid, of proud verities that dissolved as quickly into mush.

Mrs Thatcher is said to have 'a searchlight mind'. Reagan's was more like a fluorescent sponge, his attention caught by flickering images and travellers' tales. His sources were his own feelings, anecdotes culled from 'half-remembered magazine articles', regular reading of the *Readers' Digest* and *Human Events*. He could handle short memos but liked talk ('oral communication') better. He learnt 'by trial-and-error, acting in ways that worked before and trying to find out what is expected of him'. Professor Glad made a good case for Reagan's black-and-white thinking in international affairs, but against this paranoid element (which tends to sharpen choices) we have to put the sheer fuzziness, the penchant for make-believe, the sentimentality. To these we must add his lack of curiosity, and even the lack of embarrassment at his ignorance. Cannon remarked that 'Reagan does not know enough about the policies and processes of his administration, and doesn't know how much he doesn't know'. The candour of 'Don't judge us by our mistakes — I'm probably going to make more of them' is really a detachment from self-judgement, a lack of self-criticism that governed Reagan's thinking as crucially as it shaped his slack management style.

These are what I want to examine in Reagan's thinking: make-believe, sentimentality, lack of curiosity. All, but especially the last, contribute to the argument that, like Dorian Gray, Reagan was in retreat from vital elements of experience, fleeing life and death by fleeing the knowledge of them.

Make-believe

Reagan and Hollywood are virtually the same age. It has not been emphasized enough how unique is the American experience in being the first country to have itself comprehensively mirrored as it grew to prominence in world affairs. Everyone went to the movies. For the first time in history a whole nation had a twin of itself always at hand. The mirror was not, of course, passively reflecting, nor always correct in its portrayals, but that is not the point. No other art form was ever so available for a people to see themselves writ large and lit for effect. It was, of course, a highly standardized view, establishing a widely shared view of a history, a set of values, a self-image. The movies gave American politicians a uniquely common, if often vulgar, culture to base their appeals on — for the most part implicitly — and without recognizing they were using it. Make-believe, in other words, which we might associate with individual acts of reading and viewing or with special public occasions, became with the stream of movies we call 'Hollywood' a permanent moving frieze. Like gazing into the fire, or at a slowly moving river, a century of movie-going prepared a people for finding their nation's future — and their own — in a cavalcade of images.

This is almost literally true in Reagan's case. It is an understandable error to think that a man or woman who enters the world of illusory effects from the production side would lose some of his capacity to receive or consume its products. Magicians presumably don't ooh! and aah! over a new trick but try to work out how it is done. We have to see Ronald Reagan as not so much a maker of movies as the quintessential movie-goer. Ironically, Reagan kept himself aloof from the intricate confusions of image and reality that brought ruin to many who worked in Hollywood. Thus he saved his soul. But this only kept him vulnerable to the spell the 'movie alternative' — the real American history — offered to believing customers like himself.

There are many examples of the power the movies had over Reagan, though there is one theme that dominates. This is the heroic: the rescuing hero — the legendary cowboy, cavalryman, lawman; or the hero who suffers-only-to-rise-again — Knut Rockne with his legs cut off, the young footballer, the Gipper, and the young First World War soldier, both powerful from the grave. The characters are always male, sometimes older (as if fathers), sometimes younger (as if sons); there is danger overcome, aggression avoided, reconciliation achieved.

One particularly potent example is Reagan's story of the young rear gunner trapped in a stricken plane coming back across the North Sea in the Second World War. Everyone has left the plane except the captain, who is about to jump. Then he comes back to join the frightened boy, sits down beside him and says: 'We'll ride this one down together, son'. I will leave aside the question, who lived to tell the tale? The important thing is that Reagan told this story over and over as if it were true. Certainly he used it to point to a black-and-white political moral. (Reagan discovered that the Soviets had belatedly decorated the Spaniard who killed Trotsky and he would say: that's the difference, they honour assassins, we honour self-sacrifice.) Certainly, too, the story has an important personal significance in its central theme: aggression is turned inwards, fathers and sons are reconciled in serving America, sons are patricidal in the Soviet. Far more important, though, is the fact that the story actually comes from a film, with Dana Andrews as the bomber captain. It is a Hollywood fabrication, told as if true and set alongside a true Soviet event.

The point about Reagan and make-believe is not that he took a story-teller's licence. Films, novels, old stories were presented not just as morals but as real events, with himself frequently the one who experienced them. 'What would you know?', Reagan shouted to demonstrators, 'You've never been there; I have'. (He was speaking of Nicaragua.) He hadn't. Or there was the time when he told two different Middle-Eastern leaders of the horror he felt when he was with a camera crew filming the opening of the death camps. Again, he was never there. Journalists have written of their dizzying experiences hearing slabs of well-known texts come from the President's mouth, as if he was minting new words. One, indeed, affected by Reagan's sincere, confidential remarks in a face-to-face talk, was later disappointed to find them word-for-word in Reagan's ghost-written autobiography. Perhaps the most complete example was Reagan's submergence in the Hollywood propaganda about his own war service. In *Where's the Rest Of Me?* he is eloquent about the dislocation it caused, and the difficulties he and Jane Wyman had in settling back. The fan magazines had shown him leaving for war and intermittently published accounts of Jane Wyman playing the part of the good soldier's wife at home. Reagan was actually at work making training films only a few kilometres away, and he came home each night, as in civilian days. In the autobiography Reagan writes as if he believes the studio publicity about him, pinning his post-war decline from stardom on the difficult readjustment he had to make after being away, and even mentioning the problem of sexual readjustment!

'True magic' was Reagan's description of the films he helped to make simulating in miniature the bombing runs US pilots would have to make over real-life Japan. The phrase neatly encapsulates the puzzle of Reagan: how he combined living-in-the-movies — in a starstruck, make-believe America, glittering with noble thoughts and heroic deeds — with his achievements in a real political world. Other political actors, like John Wayne, employed the magic of fame and storytelling, but more directly and knowingly. The legendary star of True Grit was never so unsure — or so blithely unconcerned — about the boundary between truth and magic. Why could Reagan not be more direct, a more powerful, more mature actor, like Cooper or Wayne; a more knowing, assertive politician? Why did Reagan's ambition, his desire, detour through make-believe?

'What I'd really like to do', he said, 'is go down in history as the President who made Americans believe in themselves again'. This was a good and reasonable ambition, but why the exaggeration, the roll of drums and the swish of parting curtains, as he continued 'there is the greatness of our people, our capacity for dreaming up fantastic deeds and bringing them off to the surprise of an unbelieving world'? Hollywood made hundreds of movies in which great inventors, industrialists, aviators, medical scientists and so on were made to seem like a combination of circus magician and frontier salesman; Reagan seemed to want America to startle the world, bring it off (whatever 'it' was) to loud gasps of astonishment and admiration. There is, surely, a child's doubt here, hidden in the excitement and boastfulness, as if he, and America, could not feel wholly secure unless they had an endless supply of amazing tricks up their sleeves. Reagan's America was built on his idealization of American history, and this was the basis for his optimism. That optimism depended, in turn, on Reagan's capacity to make truth (the realities of the world) magical, and to turn his magical world into the real one. 'True magic' gave Reagan an America to love and serve which was not real enough ever to worry over, but yet not too fanciful — his films have Hollywood's blend of the ordinary and the unreal — to make it only a story-line, emphemeral and unsustaining.

Sentimentality

The corny and the homespun have a special appeal to Strong Leaders, whose 'common-man' rhetoric sets them apart from effete and even unpatriotic intellectuals; it also disguises the Strong Leader's wish for power and eminence and suggests that he identifies with ordinary folk. The sentimental streak in Reagan appears to have been very deep, even after we allow for the peculiarly American vulnerability to 'sincerity'. He and Nancy readily wept on great occasions, and the President was never better as a communicator than when he was communicating sadness and regret.

There are two particular features of Reagan's sentimentality: its association with war and death (the Arlington communication) and its focus on reconciliation between males, where one party seems to be father, the other son (for example, the bomber captain and his young gunner). Sentimentality is the outlet for those whose emotions are dammed up, or whose emotions are inexpressible because they are thought unacceptable. Reagan is presented in the journalists' accounts as a 'convivial loner', his brother says that was how they were raised, to bottle up their feelings. There are no accounts of close friendships, though there has always been a fraternity-like atmosphere around Reagan. Everyone attests to Reagan's even temper. It seems reasonable to conclude, therefore, that Reagan found some expression, in his thinking and communicating, for feelings — often pity, regret, sadness — kept out of his relations with people. When linked to patriotism and the right occasion, these are acceptable feelings. Less worthy feelings, like rage, may have to be held back.

The ultimate corny act of Reagan's Presidency was his letter-in-longhand to Brezhnev. As Reagan tells it, we are reminded of the dozens of filmic 'Rosebuds' that have traded on Welles's device, a small 'human' touch which supposedly turns the tide. Brezhnev was supposed to reply in longhand too, and supposedly these informalities and intimacies would affect the state of the world more than all the apparatus of official negotiating. Where real intimacy is difficult, sentimental gestures are looked to as sudden cure-alls, as if the subtleties of human intercourse need not be learned. Love is resistance overcome, magically, a sudden clinch, then fade-out. Tears are for the dead and the dumb and the derelict, while there is coolness towards the self-confident, articulate and angry who are demanding their rights. Reagan's sentimentality is Strong Leadership's prized soft heart. 'We are both soft touches', his brother, Neil Reagan, says, 'but we don't like to show it'.

Make-believe and the corny personal gesture are present in a late speech of the President's. At the Brandenburg Gate in June 1987 Reagan spoke of freedom in a series of clichés, designed it seemed for the arranged applause of his invited (largely military) guests. The overall impression was of an occasion that was stage-managed. This penetrated to (or, more probably, reflected) the centrepiece of his speech: a call for Mr Gorbachev to 'come down here and open the gate', to tear down the wall. I don't know if Mr Reagan had Jericho in mind, or some film, but he combined stereotyped ideas with a projected climax Cecil B. De Mille would have liked. Reagan was close to tears at the end. One felt that an overflowing heart was calling for an ending no one would believe and no director could supply.

Lack of curiosity

It is as important to understand the thinking of a President who is not a thinker as it is to understand the thinking of one who is. I've tried to characterize Reagan's thinking as the complement of his flight from ageing — ignorance, make-believe, corny beliefs, suggest latency-youth's fear of the knowledge that is to come. The absolutism that accompanied them suggests the pre-adolescent's parochialism and narrow mastery, where what works in the gang, the home town, or the football team is all a man will need to know. A final feature of Reagan's thinking suggests how growing up can be avoided in thought.

Thought is the capacity to establish links, and the capacity to continue tracking them as they become complex and loaded with emotional significance. Linkages, between cause and effect, for example, make the world more manageable if individuals and cultures can grasp and operate them. This takes courage, because a world understood 'objectively' is a world that is independent of oneself and resists: causes are or are not linked to certain effects, and even True Magic may have to yield. The question arises, then, whether Reagan's lack of curiosity, along with his make-believe, was a way of detaching himself from the world, breaking or attenuating his links with realities that were more or less given and immutable. More specifically, I'm going to speculate that the Dorian Gray complex was a product of resisted truth, the truth of experience and, though we will need the biographical section of this profile before the argument is persuasive, that the truth avoided was the conflict of desire and rivalry called the Oedipus complex.

In *Where's the Rest Of Me?* Reagan tells the story of an adolescent love triangle. He falls in love with his best friend's girl. She falls in love with Reagan. What will happen between the two men? Reagan goes and speaks to the friend, whom he describes as 'a rare person'. As a result of their talk the friend gives the girl up gracefully and tells Reagan the girl must go with him, Reagan, to the college dance.

Reagan's ending to the story is a prize example of True Magic: 'disappear triangle but add one very wonderful friendship'.

On the psychology of thinking, Wilfred Bion says, first, that the Oedipus myth casts light not only on the fortunes of love and hate but on the fortunes of curiosity too. Secondly, that the Oedipus complex is part of the mind's structure, not just one of the things (ideas) in it. Thirdly, that unconscious attacks on the self's link with objects (or persons) can be so violent that the personality making them can virtually disintegrate — short of that, curiosity is curtailed and mental capacities are dulled, while the passions shrink back to what a diminished self can handle. In other words, stupidity and incuriosity may be willed and can become vital, load-carrying components of a man's character. To a degree, this is a universal experience: a hint of hubris surrounds all unconventional thinking and curiosity that is too pressing. Staying stupid and not asking questions (however useful in the army) are nevertheless a frightened, angry response to the reality of the familial triangle which, when the child first apprehends it, seems to place him in an impossible position. Indeed, reality itself appears impossible. The child is excluded from the creative relationship its parents seem to have, but in its ambivalence (its 'wickedness' or self-interest) the child itself is hopelessly compromised in any attempt to be peaceably included.

Extreme detachment is one recourse, a radical destruction of the links between self and other, self and reality, that leads to madness. This leaves the individual 'without an apparatus which would enable him to comprehend the parental relationship and so adjust to it'. There are less drastic modes of drawing back from unwelcome knowledge, and Reagan's little story of the triangle that is 'magicked' away — not comprehended, not adjusted to — suggests the direction he took. Interest is attenuated: for one thing, Reagan at his election must have been the most untravelled President of the century, and on his short visit to England in 1946 for *The Hasty Heart* he seems to have been the classic post-war American boor, complaining about the cold and the absence of large steaks. Ignorance is accepted: Reagan would seem to be unembarrassed by being out of touch (for example, sleeping through important events), getting things wrong in the conduct of his job, or exposing his inanities and misapprehensions. Strategies of denial are adopted: optimism, the 'movie alternative', sentimentality and corn, all heavily scented with idealization, which makes things nice rather than known, sanitizing what he fears to see and understand. Finally, thoughts for the most part litter the mind like bric-à-brac, unlinked, with loose ends and containing contradictions the thinker takes no trouble to unravel. Reagan appears to have picked up items, stories, examples, and put them out again, with little internal processing. He may have been vulnerable to passing influence but for the most part fragmentary thinking, like a disorganized group, is hard to influence deeply and comprehensibly. A few fixed ideas, especially ideas attached to major figures of influence, are not incompatible with this, so that stubbornness appears as depth of commitment.

The world held its breath over Reykjavik, and Americans in particular, still wait for the full story of Reagan's involvement in the Iran/Contra deal. At the very least there is the question whether Reagan's left hand knew what his right was doing, and vice-versa. Ignorance and forgetfulness have always played a prominent part in Reagan's career: Gary Wills has outlined the suspect dealings Reagan was involved in with the agency Music Corporation of America (MCA) after the Second World War, where 'ever-widening circles of forgetfulness' formed his chief defence. At one time he said he was on his honeymoon and understandably distracted. When that wouldn't fit the dates, he said he was making a film, but that didn't fit either. Where to draw the line between conscious manipulation of the facts and a mind structured for ignorance is not easy to decide, even with the resources of the US Congress. Nevertheless, there is abundant published testimony to Reagan's intellectual style which at least does not undermine the suggestion that he has had a lifelong reluctance to see the world clearly and completely, i.e. to trace the linkages that constitute a 'reality' which cannot be rescripted or reshot.

David Stockman, not perhaps a reliable authority and to be treated with caution in his recollections on Reagan and his other ambivalently valued mentors, writes persuasively of the President's resistance to being educated. This was not because he had strong ideas of his own; on the contrary the President 'gave no orders, no commands, asked for no information, expressed no urgency'. Stockman believed 'the tax-cut was one of the few things Ronald Reagan deeply wanted from his Presidency' but he goes on to say that Reagan did not understand the *link* between the federal tax structure and the budget and could not see the *connection* between economic growth and continually increasing deficits, which only a tax rise would break. Stockman drew cartoons to try to link the two for Reagan — but 'What do you do when your President ignores all the palpable, relevant facts and wanders in circles?'.

Similarly Barrett, in his long account of Reagan and Reaganism, writes of the 'two facets of Reagan's mind-set': stubbornness in the face of facts and his 'difficulty seeing the *connection* between related goals and understanding the tensions between competing needs'. Reagan had 'immense difficulty choosing among his own priorities when they came into conflict'. He found in his 'stay-the-course syndrome', and the idea of showing strong leadership, places where he could hide from real thought. Barrett makes Reagan responsible for the 1982 recession, as he pursued his tax cut, because again he could not see the relevant linkages. He wishes Reagan had announced, with 'brutal candour', that the recession would have to be unequally paid for: 'Reagan wouldn't do that because he didn't believe it. He will not accept the *strong links* between his . . . policy . . . and the recession'.

It is not always a damaging criticism of a leader that he is stubborn and resistant to what others, including his advisors, call facts, though one would expect him eventually to announce his own ideas and plans, and begin to press them. Reagan seems to have had only a few isolated ideas — increased military spending, decreased taxes (the Right agenda in a fortune cookie) — and little energy for developing them or bringing them together. It is not wholly irrelevant perhaps that he suffers from both shortsightedness and deafness; and though he has the manner of a good listener one Republican leader complained 'but he doesn't seem to really hear'.

DORIAN GRAY AND OEDIPUS

Ronald Reagan, in the view of all the commentators, has had a remarkably 'sunny existence'. Until very recently he seemed enviably youthful and his optimism rarely failed him. Moreover, his youthfulness and down-home innocence were critical for his political appeal; a simple mind arouses longings for a pure heart. Dorian Gray 'had the look of one who kept himself unspotted from the world' and when he entered a room 'gross men fell silent' — 'his mere presence seemed to recall to them the memory of the innocence that they had tarnished'. Reagan was a kind of Back-to-the-Future President, recalling his constituency to a past (real or not) he was deeply attached to in order to make a new beginning. I have tried to show the psychological nature of this past: a post-Oedipal but pre-adolescent, or latency, 'youth', a Dorian Gray nostalgia for innocence and an innocent world. Then there were the unconscious strategies, beginning with a management style that protected Reagan from the hard edges of political work. Next there was an arrangement by which Reagan was shielded from direct experience of the tensions inherent in love and power in ordinary human interchange. Finally, there was a deep strategy of staying stupid, of not asking questions or trying to master the world intellectually, and of substituting make-believe. These continue the Dorian Gray idea. They made it possible for Reagan to embody youth and innocence, Dorian's 'rose-white boyhood'. Others carried the can for him, any complications were beyond his field of vision, he was superbly in touch with an alternative, magical world, a world that was attractive to many who supported him.

The 'Dorian Gray complex' is, of course, a fiction. It does express, however, some of what psychoanalysis means by 'the narcissistic defence', which is a flight from experience, from relations with people, a withdrawal into madness or fancy, often covered by charm, and apparently comfortable conventionality. As we turn to the Reagan life I am less interested in this than in what is being avoided, i.e. the core themes of experience, love and power, desire and rivalry, and their first comprehensive working out in the Oedipus complex.

Strong Leaders and their followers are ostensibly realists and pragmatists. They approach politics with the promise that they will concentrate on the basics, especially 'the realities of power', and that they will take the world as it is, not as idealists wish it to be. They do not escape ideology and faith so easily (as we saw with Mrs Thatcher), but Ronald Reagan presents us with a peculiar problem. How could he claim Strong Leadership's realism and practicality while he was so obviously a man of make-believe and of faith in the broadest sense? What could explain his ambition, ease with power, Strong Leadership ideology *and* his dependence on others, sentimentality, carelessness with ideas?

The answer takes us to biography and childhood and to the Oedious complex, where love, power and knowledge converge in a crisis whose working out is critical for the formation of character. With Reagan we have a particular interest in how passivity and detachment are combined with high achievement, his peculiar combination of 'ambition and unpretentiousness' as Wills puts it. If indeed he 'magicked' away the stresses and strains of desire and rivalry, which are surely close to the heart of politics, why then, and how, did he become leader of the free world? Can make-believe fill in for knowing experience and are the movies enough?

9
Childhood Magic

'I'd rather act than anything else. But I didn't think that anyone would go home and give their husband arsenic after seeing me, so I turned to radio as second choice.' Strong Leadership's childhood, by its own account, is always normal, all things having worked together for achievement. There are no skeletons in the cupboard and there is no crying over spilt milk. A realistic look at the Strong Leader's childhood would threaten the image of inevitable, not grabbed, leadership and cast doubt on the importance of positive thinking.

Before Wills, Americans writing about Reagan's childhood (like the British on Mrs Thatcher's) have accepted it much as Reagan presents it: charming, untroubled, even idyllic. In accord with the commonsense psychological assumption, affecting even psychoanalytical thinking in America, happy people are the product of happy homes. Reagan's 'sunny' outlook, therefore, implies a benign childhood. Huck Finn, misremembered, has been Reagan's own model, America's Peter Pan. Talk of Oedipal conflict seems out of place. Isn't Reagan's childhood a story of innocence, hard work and American good fortune? Even his father's alcoholism is but an occasion to discover the heroism of Reagan's mother, the gentleness of her nature, the time-honoured myth of a woman whose simple virtues and practicality hold a family together. What about Reagan himself: isn't his the story of a responsible boy who learned to look on his father's dereliction as a sickness, not a sin, and as a spur to behaving well?

The extract quoted above shows Reagan privy to a more exciting, and more real, world. Acting, achievement, life are condensed into winning wives from their husbands, not without violence. Reagan had his earliest stage experiences with his mother. He was her regular partner. In their repertoire were a number of what might now be called 'psychodramas', morality plays produced by Nelle Reagan to advise and correct errant couples in the church community. Her second son, Ronnie, played her husband.

CHILDHOOD — A TIME OF CHOOSING

In Mrs Thatcher's case the seamless web of family relations did not bear closer scrutiny. In Reagan's case there was no attempt to hide the clear divide between Jack and Neil, Nelle and Ronnie (or 'Dutch'). Religion was one mark of the difference. Neil was loyal to his father's Catholicism and eventually joined him in that church, while Ronnie, eagerly baptized Baptist-style at eleven, was a zealous supporter of his mother's Disciples of Christ. Drink marked the difference too: Nelle and Ronnie and the Disciples of Christ were teetotallers; Jack, Neil and the Catholic Church were not. Needless to say these particulars added up to broad differences of approach to life in the small towns the Reagans moved through. Nelle, who had changed her name from the common Nellie, had Protestant social standards and pretensions (literary, elocutionary, theatrical) while Jack was irreverent, gregarious, eager but apparently not very effective in advancing himself in retail business. The sons divided, growing up in the image of a parent each. Ronald was responsible early, tending to solitary hobbies, religious attendance and eventually steady girlfriends, horn-rimmed glasses and a pipe. One who knew him remembers him, as others would in Hollywood, as a bit of a goody-goody. It was as if the younger son, called on to partner his mother in her enthusiasms, which centred on social standing (though she seems lively and humorous with it), had to act the grown man he had not yet become. Reagan's adolescence, his days at Eureka College, have the same tone, suggesting what Erik Erikson called 'foreclosed' identity, an avoidance of the turmoil and productive regression essential to an expanded and firm identity in adulthood.

There are obvious attractions in avoiding a 'crisis of identity'. There were also rewards for a younger son in being so completely taken up by his mother: she was an attractive, energetic woman who opened the door to magic and glamour with her theatrical interests and her eagerness to have Ronald share them; the magic of a mother's attention was transmuted into the magic of performing. She also provided a way to avoid conflict. Reagan is hard on his brother throughout his autobiography, and he pressed Neil hard in adolescence, overtaking him in getting to college first. Yet there are no reports of bitter conflict, and presumably this was because the divide between mother and father had given them a sponsor each. Harmony, not conflict, is what Reagan remembers. It is as if the institutionalized divide in the family made competition redundant. In *Where's the Rest Of Me?* Reagan's tone towards his father is kindly and patronizing. There is no doubting who he casts in the leading role, or the second-lead, but he is at pains to show his mother and himself completely supportive of Jack Reagan, a drunk and a failure though he was. Indeed, the weakness of his father, contrasted with the strength of his mother, is the pivot of Reagan's interpretation of his childhood. Shiftless, impractical, unsuccessful, manifestly inferior to his wife in breadth of view and moral fortitude, Jack Reagan is an autobiographer's device for showing how the hero and his mother triumphed together, without in any way failing in their duty to husband and father. There is no complaining, no getting mad, no Oedipal challenge anywhere in sight. The only impatience Reagan allows himself is with a father who is not big enough to be a model or a help.

What seems to have been overlooked here and in other accounts of the President's happy childhood, is how precisely this fits the plot of the Oedipus complex. The Reagan story — mother refined and too good for father; father patronized, tolerated, not powerful enough to trouble his son — is precisely the bland cover-story that Freud believed hid the existence and true disposition of desire and rivalry. It is also identical to Freud's own cover-story before he penetrated to the mother and father of his unconscious fantasy. Of course we cannot know Reagan's childhood fantasies. However, using Reagan's own autobiography, I want to hypothesize another Jack Reagan, a more substantial figure, an influence that cannot be so easily dismissed. This more powerful father is denied centre stage in *Where's the Rest Of Me?* but he can be glimpsed in the wings. There is also another mother.

This Jack Reagan is a man of energy and charm, with too much of both for his son's comfort. At the première of *Knut Rockne, All American* in the forties, Pat O'Brien and Reagan's father went off drinking while the star, Ronald, rested and worried whether his father would embarrass him. At the official lunch, he worried again that his father would shame him with the presiding Mother Superior, because he saw him next to her and in full conversational flight. Later she told Reagan his father was the most charming man she had ever met. By Reagan's own account, Jack Reagan was a man of principle on race, fearlessly outspoken against the colour bar and anti-Semitism. He was a Catholic in a Protestant town, a political man and a Roosevelt supporter living amongst Republicans. He was also physical, slapping his baby too heartily and scraping him with his beard. Like his wife, he could sing and act but he made fun of her religious earnestness; Reagan calls this his father's 'cynicism'. He is impulsive and seems unfair. He drinks but he bounces back. He is endlessly hopeful of improving himself, an indefatigable salesman, an enthusiast for gimmicks (X-raying the feet of his shoe-store customers), a survivor in the Depression; and of course he got on better with Neil.

There is nothing here that is not in Reagan's published account of his father, but he (or his ghost-writer) does not put it this way. That it *can* be expressed this way is enough perhaps to cast doubt on the Reagan concept that here was a man no boy could have any fear of, or in whom there was much to love.

Reagan's mother, in his own account, found solace with her son. Again there are sidelights in *Where's the Rest Of Me?* that make us pause. Some of the singing and acting she did was with Jack Reagan, and they shared a sense of being a special family, a cut above their neighbours and somewhat *avant-garde* — they had the children call them by their first names and they believed they should interest themselves in politics and community affairs. Reagan portrays himself as her favourite, and his mother appears to have been ambitious for him to succeed in reading and writing and similar improving pursuits. We don't know if she was careless about Neil's improvement or if he didn't respond as Ronald did. To Ronald, at any rate, she appears both seductive and demanding, and one of the clearest demands she put on Ronald was that he respect, not judge, his father. Reagan ought to have been in no doubt that, for all his obedience to her and their stage-partnering, Jack was Nelle's true partner, however 'cynical' or dissolute he seemed to his earnest second son.

I have wondered at the meaning of Reagan's comment that 'people don't like to be saved', especially in light of his sentimentality about America as the country which rescues. He was referring to his life-saving days where for six summers he worked long hours alone at Dixon's pool, making more rescues than anyone else before or since. It is conceivable that the uncharacteristic bitterness has roots in the line a tantalizing, encouraging mother drew between her stage husband and the real one. That, however, is more than we can ever know. It is enough that through a straightforward re-reading of the autobiography, Reagan's childhood takes on a pattern more in line with the Oedipal promptuary, and with Strong Leadership's focus on desire and rivalry, love and power. Instead of an idyll we have real experience, not the phoney 'normality' of Strong Leader legend and Reagan's relentless optimism; an ordinary childhood traversing the usual dilemmas of growing up. The choosing between mother and father, as it was in Margaret Thatcher's family, is fraught with more complex meanings than Reagan presents, and its consequences are far greater.

GETTING WITH THE STRENGTH

Came one night when I seemed to see a street lamp and a lonely patch of sidewalk. Humphrey Bogart appeared, and we played an interminable street scene, exchanging and wearing innumerable trenchcoats, and trying to say lines to each other, always with a furtive air of danger in the surrounding darkness. Someone else can take a crack at analyzing what this Freudian delirium meant.

Reagan's autobiography has the tone of those *Reader's Digest* stories that begin 'How I did X and became a millionaire'. It is a tale of triumph, of a man's successful search for a task worthy of him. He finds the answer in politics. *Where's the Rest Of Me?* is a campaign book and of course it has a happy ending, but it is only a prologue: a mere actor is tapped for politics and he is now on his way to bigger and better things. The book ends with Reagan established as husband and father and advertising himself as a speaker in the crusade to alert Americans 'of the danger to freedom in a vast permanent structure so big and complex it virtually entraps Presidents and legislators'. The political aim is intertwined with a personal apologia. Reagan's metamorphosis is not just from actor to politician but from boy to man, from handsome shadow to 'the real stuff'. This is the meaning of the title.

Even ghost-written campaign autobiographies may tell more than they intend, and *Where's the Rest Of Me?* finally contradicts its intention. The strongest impression it leaves is of a man afraid to assert himself and an unlikely aspirant to the substantial presence he seeks. It shows Reagan's agitation, nervous worrying, insecurity and dependence on others. As Wills points out, 'father figures' abound. Reagan even managed what few better men have done, he 'stayed on good terms with his agent' and his relations with authority, with the bosses, even as a supposed union leader, were always 'cosy'. His fortune was made for him by others, his union leadership was an exercise in something close to selling out. Though it ends hopefully, *Where's the Rest Of Me?* hardly shows a man becoming his own master. I used the phrase 'tapped for politics' earlier (as one is tapped for a fraternity), because that is the nature of his new beginning — finding his legs, his strength, in a roomful of powerful men. For Reagan, making it meant joining the club of senior actors and producers and being taken up by powerful men who would promote him in his political aspirations. His escape from celluloid second-lead to leading man in a real job is only to being the 'boy' of powerful men.

There are numerous examples of Reagan's readiness to take direction from men he admired. As a B-movie actor he muttered complaints but rarely made a fuss. On one occasion he found the pain of a quarrel with Jack L. Warner so great that he rang up with profuse apologies, feeling immensely relieved when he had done so. In the autobiography he is still complaining about bigger stars, those like Errol Flynn (an early Crocodile Dundee) with sword-and-saddle roles who stole his spot in the dressing-room, and the fast talkers and sharper ad libbers who did him out of good lines. He explains his accepting to appear in many bad pictures as favours owed, or as forced on him. He boasts that 'an Irishman couldn't stay out' and that once he overdid a punch and the other actor fell, knocked out: 'Naturally I felt terrible, [but] it was nice knowing I could do it'. In similar vein, referring tangentially to a homosexual director he disliked working with, he boasts that when he, Reagan, passed through the chorus-line's wardrobe room he expected the girls to bolt.

However his tough-guy self-portrait is unconvincing. When he wins something useful for the Screen Actors Guild, he gives back the advantage; when he talks of his boss at General Electric — Reagan was 'a Boy Scout in a Boy Scout company' — his hand goes up in an 'unconscious' salute; when he pushes for the making of *Knut Rockne*, he yields the role he wanted to Pat O'Brien; boasting of his 'leading ladyitis' (i.e. falling for each of them), he sat at home alone in the years following his divorce; he speaks of 'hospitalitis' too — the comfort and pleasure in being immobilized, dependent, cared for. As we have seen, his first big campaign, for the Governorship of California, was as the most packaged candidate ever, Reagan taking direction then as docilely as he had taken it in the movies.

A reporter at the Venice trade summit in 1987 asked the President, 'Why hasn't the communique more teeth in it?'. Reagan appeared to laugh nervously, then answered, 'Because we couldn't find anyone to bite'. He has always admired great men, especially businessmen, and has 'deep and abiding respect for soldiers, policemen and anyone else who risked his neck in the right cause'. *Where's the Rest Of Me?* goes into considerable detail about Reagan's efforts to stifle his aggressiveness, to rein in any inclination to act assertively. As with the remark about scattering chorus girls, he appears to be flattering himself. As Wills says, Reagan perhaps takes defeat too well. Time and again in the autobiography we see him competitive towards other actors, judging them predatory, then, after studying hard to try to hold his own, backing off with a rueful laugh. It is meant to be a book about becoming a politician, but the training seems more fitted to monastic religion. A particularly strong example is the report of Reagan's rehearsals for the debate with President Carter in 1979. In rehearsals his remarks have a high-spiritedness, not to say wildness, about them that is not there when the occasion is real. He had joked once into an open microphone, 'We'll nuke them'. This time his aides were alarmed at the brutality of his responses to the stand-in Carter and told him so. He replied 'Don't worry. I won't behave this way on the night. I'll faint or I'll have a coughing fit'.

Reagan's other recurring theme is the effort of getting himself 'up'. In the autobiography, most of the problems of acting — and politics — are 'motivational problems'. His main strategy is detachment: although he loves to tell how getting mad worked the trick, there is more simulation than gut-feeling in this. He studies, learns lines, rehearses over and over to sound live and real: unable to ad lib radio advertisements, he had to learn them and read them, discovering that he then sounded natural and spontaneous. Like Perry Como, Reagan found contrivance was the secret route to apparent naturalness. He was lucky in having a 'photographic memory', though presumably in politics he could rely on electronic visual aids.

The picture that emerges by the end of *Where's the Rest of Me?* is not of a man finding his strength but of a man getting with the strength, of a hard-working apprentice reapprenticing himself in a more promising trade, of a protégé finding more powerful masters. It was not just in Hollywood, nor is it a fact only of his past, that Reagan cosied up to authority. As Governor and as President his work was structured to shield him and to allow him to lead without experiencing the conflicts decision-making usually involves. Margaret Thatcher, in an after-dinner speech at the White House, spoke of 'two-o'clock-in-the-morning courage', the capacity to tolerate loneliness if one was to be a leader: courage, conviction, wisdom and 'at the end of the day you have to live with the decision you've made'. Some months into the Iran/Contra imbroglio Reagan was required to make a speech 'accepting responsibility'. This speech, up-beat and smugly cheerful, only gave the impression that he thought himself uncommonly noble as he fronted up to his responsibility, as if in coming out from behind the shield of his helpers, he should have a hero's response.

'PASSIVE-POSITIVE'; LEGLESS; DEAD

One of Reagan's complaints about his fellow actors in Hollywood was that they said their lines too fast. The tempo he liked was slower. David Barber's characterization of Reagan is clearly right, up to a point. It does not distinguish sufficiently, however, between Eisenhower, for example, and Reagan. 'Laid-back' and amiable they both were, but Eisenhower's executive style appears to have been a great deal more active than Reagan's and he handled conflict, both in the war and in politics, quietly but without shrinking. Reagan's passivity goes deeper. It is not only that, even after Hollywood, he was still an actor, but that his deepest wishes were for dependency. His experience must be mediated by a woman — Nancy Reagan combined the qualities of mother and nurse, catering to both 'leading ladyitis' and 'hospitalitis' — and supportive men, younger as well as older; and a structure that gave him 'tranquillity' and plenty of sleep. Even the would-be assassin's bullet gave Reagan the opportunity to show courage — which he certainly did — in a passive, brave victim's manner. He showed no anger, revived old jokes, and, when he was down and almost out, seemed at his best.

Reagan's two favourites among his films — partly because they were 'serious' films — are *Knut Rockne, All American* and *King's Row*. Wills has shown what a mishmash of fantasy and distortion the first is, though supposedly a biodocumentary. A loutish football player, George Gipp, is made the saintly hero of a football game that is hanging in the balance. Reagan plays 'the Gipper' who returns from the dead, as it were, in a pep-talk the coach (played by Pat O'Brien) gives his team in the interval. There is significant ambiguity in the film over who is 'son', who is 'father' (Reagan appears to have wanted to play the coach but settled for the Gipper). Sport may contain a lot of ancestor worship, as Wills says, but in *Knut Rockne* the *young* man is long dead while the older man, the coach, is alive and looking to the dead boy for inspiration. At the same time, the Gipper depends on the coach to recall him, like a living player, when he judges the time to be right — and Reagan made much in his Eureka College Commencement address in 1986 of the eight-year delay between the Gipper's death and his ghostly reappearance. All in all, the story, mixing up the authority of father and the vitality of sons, fudges the conflict between them. It turns, too, on the paradox that victory comes through defeat. A man tragically cut down is nevertheless still alive and influential from the grave; and, dead, he is still in possession of his youth and vitality.

This is father–son conflict avoided, first by confusing the question of who comes first and has the authority, second by the denial of real defeat and a final death. The movie promises reconciliation and victory without admitting conflict (the football game drains off that), a painless end-run around Oedipal desire and rivalry.

King's Row is equally escapist. Reagan has consistently over-estimated his role in this film, convinced that it turns on his scene where the character he plays wakes to ask 'Where's the rest of me?'. His legs have been amputated by the sadistic doctor whose daughter Reagan's character has been wooing. The confused plot, made more so by the censorship laws of the time, is taken from a novel in which the girl and her father are involved incestuously. The role Reagan is so proud of is to be cut down, momentarily appalled, then, incredibly, becoming up-beat and 'brave': in the film he says, with a laugh, 'Did he think I lived in my legs?'. Reagan worked hard, almost method style, to prepare for this role, sensing an important experience he should try to do justice to. As it happens, his famous line is delivered off-camera; the screen is filled with his girl's horrified reaction, not with Reagan's 'denial' of the seriousness of what has happened. 'Did he think I lived in my legs?' is closer to the Reagan we know, his denial, optimism, passivity. More than 'Where's the rest of me?', it predicts his actual life-direction: not finding his legs in politics, but finding a higher optimism in make-believe and other men's support. At the very least we need both lines — one a wish for the substantiality of a grown man doing real work, the other a nonchalance that denies reality and, with jokes, avoids seriousness.

Reagan clearly admired those who are aggressive, and would wish to have been so himself. However, he needed it legitimized, ennobled, and he was drawn to the opposite wish, for everyone to be reconciled. We have seen how he boasted of his red-blooded, manly instincts in the autobiography. We also saw how readily he backed down in Hollywood and how unassertively, dependently, he conducted his political career. This is how he speaks of football, which combines aggressiveness and safety: 'This is the last frontier, the last place where you can go out and hate the next guy because he's got a different jersey on and throw yourself at him until after the last gun — and then you discover you kind of like the fellow'. He says elsewhere 'Our lives have lost a certain amount of excitement since we quit having to knock over a mastadon for the family lunch . . .' and describes his college football as 'a matter of life and death'. This seems to be how his aggressiveness was engaged — under the supervision of the coach, an older man, for immaterial goals ('different jersey'), and it all ending in love and even, as Reagan says elsewhere, in tears on the bench.

Reagan is reportedly fascinated by war movies. One of his favourites is an old news film that shows Americans being rescued: 'That's the greatest thrill'. If Richard Nixon (and others) whoop and swear through *Rambo*, Reagan reminds us that war movies, not excluding *Rambo*, are as often about love as about hate; they are rarely sadistic, often sad. Against 'calisthenics' Reagan, in Strong Leader style, put 'winning' (competitive sports) but though he ennobled aggression, the larger wish was to obviate it. If he put troops into Lebanon, he was quick to withdraw them; Grenada was a *Mouse-That-Roared* war; the bombing of Tripoli and the Gulf flag-waving were eerily indefinite. Reagan's first inaugural address invoked a real-life equivalent of the Gipper — a young soldier who went to his death in Flanders after writing in his diary that he would fight 'as if it all depended on me'. Again, aggression and power were linked to defeat, to protected arenas and eventual, tearful reconciliations, to being pulled from the fire in the nick of time or to moving martyrdom. Strong he would be, standing tall, not flinching; but, however plucky, Reagan's heroes were a 'happy few' as likely to be cut down as imperially triumphant. At best they were the cavalry, riding into the scene from which the enemy instantly fled, rescuers who brought the movie to its end when the body-count was already complete.

CHILDHOOD AND THE PURPLE ROSE

The characters in Woody Allen's *Purple Rose of Cairo* are suspended in the black and white shadows of a film that runs round and round again, condemned to the same plot, the same lines, the same poses forever. One character escapes into the real world, but only for a short time, eventually resuming his place in the celluloid make-believe he was made for. Reagan claimed to have found 'the rest of him' when he abandoned Hollywood for politics. However, the acting continued, and in Reaganism, as Stockman described it from the inside, 'Metaphor and reality were at odds from the beginning . . .'. Moreover, Reagan's passive, hesitant, hands-off style of addressing the world evoked an image of him still holding the old poses, playing parts from the movies and the rose-coloured history he believed, still reading the same lines that expressed his blend of heroism and sorrow.

There is a timelessness about Reagan's life, as if he were indeed stuck in a period of youth where nothing happens. In a sense personal dramas, played and replayed, preoccupied him in the midst of politics. In another sense he lived apart from these, staying young and staying stupid, always the 'best friend', never the leading man. His politics were a kind of shadow play, inspiring for a time, alarming, but ultimately empty, Strong Leadership in projected, escapist form.

Reagan's childhood, reconstructed above, contains some clues to the man and the Leader, why he retreated from experience and knowledge, why nevertheless he wanted to be a Strong Leader. Nostalgic worship of boyhood is common among sports fans, hobbyists, those who go huntin', ridin' and fishin', and Reagan always found refuge in these, horse-riding and stable-cleaning, football, a train-set in the California Governor's mansion. But the preference for middle-childhood, coming before the turmoil of love and hate and the unsettling new knowledge that adolescence brings, is only the tip of the iceberg. Adolescence is centrally Oedipus revisited, and it is those earlier, Oedipal years that must concern us.

Behind Reagan's 'idyllic' childhood we found Oedipus: an enticing yet frustrating mother who stimulated her son yet remained loyal to her husband; a boisterous, worldly father not very successful at work (though the family did not starve and his spirits would revive) but not a failure at home or amongst acquaintances; finally a partnership that has moments of magic in it, singing and dancing and a sense of being a bit special. There is no mystery in the Reagan response: nostalgia, reluctance to assert himself, arranging that others look after him, tears of joy and stories of heroic reconciliation (especially between fathers and sons), an image of America as a nation of loving heroes, admiration for the men who literally protect the nation and for those who, unselfishly, would promote its interests. Oedipal desire and rivalry can issue in Margaret Thatcher's fierce, defensive determination to dominate, ambivalence hidden behind an elaborate structure of firm convictions and determined acts. It can also issue in inhibition, a partial immobility, where ambivalence is covered by a haze of ambiguity. 'Some might think Reagan takes defeat almost too well', Wills writes, expressing the inhibiting outcome of Oedipal desire and rivalry; 'he seems best at deferring, as he was the hero's friend in the movies'. Reagan's childhood strategy of detachment and idealization (optimism) meant that he dared not become the villain's rival for the leading lady. Predictably, no one in Hollywood thought him capable of any such role.

Inhibited, ignorant, passive, Reagan nevertheless reached the heights of real-life politics. There is a mystery here. Part of the explanation is that make-believe, however it distorted his view of the world, was a spur and a popular advantage. The 'impossible' magic of a boy's special relationship with his mother was made over (by her) into the True Magic of self and country, where both are uniquely heroic and good. It was a distortion when Reagan saw the world in terms of individual heroes, and saw America as a kind of individual hero (Wills attributes the Star Wars proposal to this fantasy of Reagan's), but we should not discount the energizing force of even a distorted ideal, implanted in his special relationship with Nelle Reagan, his first drama teacher. This made make-believe a kind of truth.

As well, in reflecting on how so passive and dependent a man became President, we must take account of the attractiveness of sinless, open-faced youth. We know the effect Dorian Gray had on a roomful of crusty old men. Reagan appears to have had the gift of attracting the support of a long list of powerful men eager to smooth his way.

Indeed, this seems to have been the main thing Reagan had to offer. His achievements, except in overcoming his own unlikeliness for high office, do not add up to an impressive curriculum vitae. He was never a businessman, never fought a war, was barely a star. His only jobs had been in the intangible business of communication and self-presentation; he would be the most complete example of the 'unproductive' New Class Reaganites identified and excoriated in the seventies. He was an embarrassment in his first term as Governor of California, in his second he was described as 'adequate'. When he became President his incompetence and confusion become clear to all, only excused by his redefining political leadership as political popularity. Embodying certain ideals, trained to communicate them, Reagan did not have to study and work and achieve anything but to be himself.

The criteria of political achievement may be different from those in other occupations. In politics, to *be* may sometimes be enough. Certainly Reagan's promise of rejuvenation was timely in 1979. Carter made the mistake of sharing his worries about America, made it seem a lot of hard work was necessary, and confronted the uncomfortable mood of the country directly. Reagan seized on Carter's speech about Americans 'suffering from a crisis of confidence' and resoundingly announced: 'I find no national malaise . . . I find nothing wrong with the American people'. Ideals, even make-believe, were the things wanted, a tonic, not therapy. For this, of course, Reagan, in his personality, was exactly right, the medicine man in the right place at the right moment. Three Presidents had failed. The country needed, above anything else, a lift in morale.

10

Conclusion —
The Politics of Ingratitude

There is one more question. Why should Reagan choose the politics of ingratitude? Why should he go for Strong Leadership, confronting enemies, sharpening competition, getting ahead? If Reagan is, underneath, the 'soft touch' his brother says he is, if he is as dependent on the help of others, as passive, as moved by the love of heroic, peaceful deeds, as inhibited from acting aggressively as I have painted him, why then were his politics not the politics of consensus and compassion? Why was he in Margaret Thatcher's camp?

The short answer is that Strong Leadership is defined by its distrust of collective action and its wish to claim sole authorship of its achievements. It fears to lose itself in gratitude. However dependent on others in fact, in Strong Leadership's ideology the individual has earned all he owns and should own all he earns. Reagan was a phoney union man. Twice president of the Screen Actors' Guild, the deals he made always looked too favourable to the studios and he used studio-influenced unionists to break the picket lines of more radical actor unions. Reagan, writes Wills, is 'as distrustful of organized social action as he is trusting of the individual. Human natures darken only when they act in conjunction'. Reagan needs a world of individual heroes and both Communist and (Big) Government were his enemies because they threatened this world.

In Hollywood, apart from a union career apparently stooging for the bosses, he became agent T-10, helping the FBI in the fight against Communism in the entertainment business. Characteristically, the anti-Communist Reagan was a confusing mixture of hard rhetoric about sinister influence, and astonished innocence. As one blacklisted actress put it: put it:

> It isn't that he's a bad guy really . . . what is so terrible about Ronnie is his ambition to go where the power is. I don't think anything he does is original; he doesn't think it up. I never saw him have an idea in his life. I really don't even think he realises how dangerous the things he does really are.

To 'go where the power is' or 'get with the strength', Reagan's 'naturally ingratiating' personality — these are at first glance phrases that imply a lack of ambition and self-doubt. Yet they can mean that a man's ambition is for an escalator ride to the top. Collective action gets in the way of individual aspiration even if it is covert, and it threatens even the man who's strategy is staying young and staying stupid. We can understand this, I think, through a reading of Freud's *Totem and Taboo*, which extends the Oedipus complex into society and politics.

The plot is a primal father who monopolizes everything and treats his sons with disdain; the sons rebel, killing their father. They are then remorseful and afraid and establish rules of conduct to hold back any of them who might be tempted to lord it over the rest, as their father did. These rules are legitimized and sanctified by a sort of ancestor worship, love and respect paid to the absent, spiritualized father. We may think of Reagan (through 'denial' and 'idealization') keeping himself apart from this cycle of frustration, rebellion, momentary exhilaration, and finally remorse. We can think of him, again, as avoiding experience.

We can now add to this the observation that collective action implicates individuals in guilt. Collectively frustrated, the sons in *Totem and Taboo* harbour treasonable thoughts, and they are morally blemished. Collectively rebelling and committing patricide, they are comprehensively guilty, except that for the moment they do not feel it. Finally, in remorse and organized social life, they live collectively with guilt, with a sense of themselves and their kind as blemished. This is the opposite of Dorian Gray's individualism and his blamelessness.

Reagan's 'cosying' up to authority, and his faithfulness, not to mention his autobiography of childhood, deny that his father was ever frustrating. Thus there was no need for rebellion, no guilt and no reason for feeling collective responsibility for the evils in society and the world. He was relentlessly individualist, dedicated throughout his adult life to stopping Communism. He became increasingly alarmed at the growth of the federal government, seeing in it the threat that he would be implicated, that he would be made to feel responsible for what had gone wrong.

His apt and potent exploitation of the 'Vietnam syndrome' — a guilt Americans should simply refuse to accept — thus fitted with his whole personality and personal history. Carter called Americans to their knees, inviting them to plumb the depths of their demoralization and face their mistakes. Reagan, invoking America's up-beat religious tradition, asserted the Strong Leadership creed: never look back, or down, or inwards. All kinds of guilts would be lifted from American shoulders: middle-class guilt, white ethnic guilt, a slew of guilts about 'minorities', male guilt about women, guilt about the environment, and more. Society had to be a collection of individuals, who could be considered heroic, the more virtuous and heroic they were, the better the society. Thinking collectively, acting collectively, would implicate each individual in fantasies of hate and rebellion. It would bring the discomforts of remorse and life would become a constricting exercise in painful propitiation. Experience, the experience Reagan retreated from, is both collective and guilty.

If collective action is linked with guilt, that would explain the individualism of any Strong Leader and his or her followers, all of whom complain of the paralysing guilt that afflicts the Left. However, avoiding guilt is not the only motive involved. There is also the attractiveness of the 'primal father' himself. Strong Leadership builds tight structures to contain rivalry and it is strong on law and order and conventional morality. It is also inclined to keep God alive. Mrs Thatcher claims to be a Christian and Reagan was passionate about the shortcomings of humanism which, like Communism, makes men as gods; it is important to have someone above and outside men to keep them under control.

Beside this control, there is contest — in this instance, the wish to emulate the great, to be the primal father oneself. Strong Leaders are themselves testimony to the gratifications to be had in becoming outstanding and powerful, and their success is a promissory note given to their followers that they too can be above the herd. Needless to say, collective action threatens this hope. The America of a Mondale, hopelessly out of synchronization with the times in 1984 in stressing compassion and sharing, would undermine the Reagan hope: 'I want America always to be a place where a man can get rich'. Like Mrs Thatcher, he preferred a 'ladder of opportunity' to his opponents' safety net, which could entangle individuals shooting high.

We must therefore give Jack Reagan another part to play in his son's life: the role of primal father, a secretly admired, powerful man. Not that Reagan got very close to identifying with his father, though his charm and story-telling gift descend from his father's example. These characteristics partially overlap with the charm and power of their revered Roosevelt, though admittedly Nelle Reagan supplied the route map and much of the energy for Reagan's ambition. However, Reagan relied — warmly, trustingly, faithfully — on many older men, Altschuler, Cordiner, Loyal Davis and others. His love for America, though corny, centred on men working together, rescuing each other, inspiring each other, becoming reconciled. It is as if he was not content to stay his mother's son but wanted to be his father's too — the 'rest of me' meaning to become not just a politician but a man, not just someone who 'sings pretty' but an heroic figure in the fight against evil, a worthy successor to his old man.

I would not want to push this aspect of Reagan too far. The Dorian Gray Reagan is the dominant one. Whatever one thinks of a man like David Stockman — he is surely closer to Iago than to Dorian Gray — his blatant ambivalence certainly implicates him in the experience of frustration, rebellion and perhaps, one day, remorse. He reports being astonished at Reagan's attitude to the famous betrayal. When Stockman publicly admitted the illusoriness of

Reagan's economic policy with its limp reliance on the 'trickle down' idea, the President showed no anger and made no prudent moves to protect himself from the younger man. He turned the blame on to the press. (In return, Stockman noticed and published how old Reagan looked, his age showing in his hands.) It was as if Reagan did not find the role of indignant father within his range, as he had not, much earlier, found it in him to openly challenge and freely admire Jack Reagan.

Reagan blurs the line between fathers and sons, which makes either part hard to play, or even to grasp; evading men, fathers cannot be played by actors who are unable to empathise with universal guilt, with hate where there is also love. Or, if they are played, they can only appear as sentimental and unreal, like a Santa Claus performing miracles of forgiveness on 34th Street.

THE GREAT COMMUNICATOR

'You are the type of what the age is looking for, and what is afraid it has found' (Lord Henry to Dorian Gray). Inevitably the showman is suspected of shallowness. Reagan's early lessons, building on his father's charm, salesmanship and story-telling, were from Franklin Delano Roosevelt. FDR was not shallow but in the early days of his career Mencken and others distrusted his brilliance. FDR had ideas and read widely, was worldly and knew politics and he had little need to idealize men or ask the men and women around him to filter his experience. FDR was wily where Reagan prided himself on his All-American naivety. Despite his physical disability, FDR had energy to spare and an arrogance of class, whereas Reagan was home-town humble and, as the autobiography repeatedly shows, had to work at getting himself going. FDR's fireside radio chats were only one prong in his rhetorical attack, of which the other was wit and his command over a hard-bitten press corps. Reagan had only the one, soft, tone and performed better 'canned' or closely cued. FDR was a shrewd propagandist and he certainly rehearsed, but Reagan tells us he discovered that sincerity and spontaneity were only possible if they were false, when he learned his lines to sound as if he were talking spontaneously. He also discovered that making speeches, or the one speech over and over, convinced him of the ideas, not the other way round.

What did Reagan communicate? The short answer is a magical self and a magical America. Magic, because of the heroic deeds Americans have done in the past and can do again. Magic, because they have not been sullied by the ordinary realities. This is Strong Leadership but studio-lit. Purposefulness became 'Go for it America'; sacrifice dissolved into the legerdemain of painless supply-side economics; realism turned into NASA's faith in 'looking good'.

More profoundly, Reagan communicated ambiguity and with that, ambivalence. As leader he was part-man/part-boy, part-father/part-son. All 'great communicators' in democratic societies may have to convey the delicately blended message of command and sympathy, experience and innocence. Mrs Thatcher is called a great communicator too, but she communicates little sympathy while her 'innocence', unlike Reagan's, is better rendered as 'integrity' — in other words, she is tipped towards the side of experience and command. Reagan leant the other way, toward the pathetic and the naive, towards playing the part of the son merely acting the father, sympathizing but not daring to act definitively, though he would have liked to and pretended to do so.

For a time this was enough to hold him in the public's affections. It hardly secured him the standing of a man in command. Reagan believed great men matter, not programmes, but he himself seemed closer to the dead soldier, to the ghostly Gipper, to a small-town Rousseau in tears over his lost boyhood. I have always been puzzled by a supposed conservative quoting Taine so often and so stirringly: 'We can begin the world anew'. Now I think Reagan meant we can go Back to the Future to magic innocence and heroic boyhood.

MALCOLM FRASER

11
The Politics of Contest-and-Control

Henry Kissinger calls Malcolm Fraser 'a distinguished statesman' and claims him as a friend. Valéry Giscard d'Estaing, former President of France, writes that he and Fraser 'have developed a true friendship' and he describes the former Prime Minister of Australia as 'a man of conviction' — though 'fidelity to his principles does not prevent him from having a decidedly pragmatic approach to international problems'. Margaret Thatcher, whose doctrine of small government Fraser had been preaching years before she took office, looked to him for advice during the run up to her election in 1979 (Fraser had been elected in 1975 and again in 1977). Each has expressed satisfaction at the others' successes, though on the issue of applying full sanctions against South Africa they are sharply at odds. In Carter's day, Fraser was inclined to be critical towards the US, hinting at a lack of leadership and resolve. (Carter got his own back at a White House 'photo opportunity' when he called Fraser 'My good friend John', Fraser's first and unused name!) Fraser, like Thatcher, was fulsome in his praise for the newly-elected Reagan in 1980.

Fraser's political achievements have been dogged by doubts about their legitimacy. A very tall and powerfully-built man, his stony 'Easter Island' expression, his dour manner, his carping and sometimes hectoring rhetoric gave him a small man's reputation for narrowness and insensitive moralizing. Fraser unseated two of his (Liberal) Party's leaders, becoming Prime Minister in the extraordinary circumstances of 1975 in which the Governor-General sacked Whitlam (1972–5) for being unable to guarantee the money bills. The Supply legislation had been blocked in the Senate by Fraser's coalition of Liberals and the National Country Party. The Governor-General's action was unprecedented in Australian federal history and Fraser's actions took him to the outer limits of Australian political practice. After a month as caretaker Prime Minister, Fraser was elected with a near-record majority. In 1977 he was again elected, this time with a majority that *was* a record (Whitlam was still leader of the Labor opposition) and in 1980 he was narrowly returned (Hayden was Labor leader). Then in 1983, Fraser was defeated by Hawke and a Labour Party now safely distanced from the Whitlam years. Fraser immediately resigned, from the parliament as well as from the leadership, and has become — though he is a year younger than Hawke — something of an elder statesman who likes to make public comment on the Australian economic crisis, international affairs (particularly, now, the Pacific region) and, above all, South Africa. He has declared himself interested in the job of Commonwealth Secretary.

There was a good deal of residual bitterness when Fraser resigned, though it was tempered by some last-minute displays of his 'humanity' He spoke in the last week of the election campaign about some childhood anxieties and he went close to tears in his concession speech. Fraser had always said he preferred to be respected rather than loved and it appeared that people had indeed withheld their sympathies from him, a man most thought 'cold', 'aloof', 'arrogant'. Since his involvement against apartheid, many formerly unsympathetic to him have found themselves in the surprising position of cheering him on. The Australian Prime Minister, Hawke, was among a group at the (British) Commonwealth Heads of Government Meeting in Nassau in late 1985 who proposed an Eminent Persons Group to visit and report on South Africa's progress towards racial equality. Fraser became the Australian representative and has been perhaps the Group's most trenchant and effective spokesman.

Even as a 'statesman' and 'Eminent Person' Fraser continues to be controversial: many in his own Party are appalled by his 'anti-white' stance and he has been an outspoken critic of his Party's direction since he left the leadership. He has always had an astonishing capacity to throw oil on burning oil. The 'confrontationism' of his years as Prime Minister was rejected in 1983 in Hawke's appeal for 'reconciliation, consensus and accord'. Since then Labor has perfected a strategy of inclusion and negotiation involving both unions and business, which Fraser, though half of him might have wanted it, had found to be beyond him. He would structure things to promote reasonable co-operation, then would suddenly undo the good work with warnings and threats. He is a man who even when he makes a sincere attempt at unity carries a cheese wire in his hand.

For example, in 1987 he gave an address on the need for 'balance' in politics, for not going too far to the right, for not over-doing the 'small government', 'privatizing' trend in the right-of-centre parties. However, he gave his address amidst the tensions of a national election campaign when it could only reflect badly on Howard, his successor in the leadership of the Party. The statesman sounded more like a saboteur. Even his biography, launched later in the same year, which might have placed him among those whose work is complete and ready for calm, historical assessment, again opened wounds in the Liberal Party, and embarrassed its leader once more. Moreover, as a would-be statesman who acts as a politician still, Fraser cannot be surprised if some people see him as attempting to get back into the political world. Such uncertainty and suspicion of motives have always been associated with the man.

D'Estaing's shrewd observation that Fraser's principles do not prevent him being pragmatic is echoed by Kissinger's parenthetical note: 'True, he has had a highly developed sense for the realities of power . . .'. This double-visioned view of Fraser takes us to the heart of what makes him an interesting example of the Strong Leader.

The theory has alerted us to the balancing act Strong Leaders and their followers must perform: they propose a structure in which individual will can be freely exercised while at the same time individuals are restrained and channelled by the rules of the game; they promise power and success *plus* good order and social virtue. In Thatcher's case the reconciliation of these opposites is very convincing (though it may be that only a fraction of the people receive either freedom or security). In Reagan's case, the contradiction was hidden behind a fog of imaginary successes and (until recently) ignored or forgotten failures. In the case of Fraser the strain is patently clear: he was once described as 'patrician and pugilist' and throughout his career variations on this have been tried in an attempt to pin down the double-sidedness which seems to be the very essence of the man. Lofty ideals — lofty not because they are particularly ennobling or inspiring but because they are painfully exacting — have performed cartwheels with breathtaking opportunism and apparently ruthless ambition.

The 'balance' Fraser now speaks of was always an agitated hopping from one foot to the other. Fraser would enunciate 'principle' from the highest moral ground, then point to the fine print which legitimated, legalistically, a change of position. Self-restraint would be displayed with all the pride of a Pharisee, then 'extraordinary circumstances' would license a surprise political attack. Fraser would call for loyalty, while time and again he signalled the limits of his own, and a comfortable, flexible unity — as opposed to division patched over with 'discipline' and under threat — always escaped him. Even his biographer admits that 'one of the most significant . . . qualities' Fraser lacked was 'the ability to inspire in the people a feeling of identity with the leader'.

Some years ago I described Fraser and Fraserism as embodying a politics of contest-and-control. This applies to Strong Leaders and their followers as a whole: one aim is effective individual will, or power; the other aim is social control, on the assumption that all men and women are self-interested to the point of lethal anarchy, and need governing. I intend to take this so-called 'realistic' view of human nature and social order very seriously here.

In particular, I will approach Malcolm Fraser with a seriousness appropriate to his own, deep convictions about the dangers of spontaneity, unstructured loyalty (trust), frankness, creative thinking and open administration, etc., and his belief in Strong Leadership, and that society can only survive if it is what I call 'structured'. We should be clear, too, that a Strong Leader is no less one because he is deeply sincere, and a moralist who applies his psychological and social taxes most strictly to himself. We are not interested in buccaneers and small-time hoods. The profound inner division Fraser reveals — one foot on the accelerator, one on the brake — and its political consequences belong to Strong Leadership as a whole, to all Leaders and their followers whose myth is that human ambivalence has been overcome in singleness of mind and wholeness of character.

CONTEST-AND-CONTROL

Thus the ego, driven by the id, confined by the super-ego, repulsed by reality, struggles to master its economic task of bringing about harmony among the forces and influences working in and upon it: and we can understand how it is that we cannot suppress a cry: 'Life is not easy'.

Freud, *New Introductory Lectures* (1933).

Arnold Toynbee once wrote twelve volumes to demonstrate and analyse the cause of the rise and fall of nations. His thesis can be condensed to a sentence and is simply stated: that through history nations are confronted by a series of challenges and whether they survive or whether they fall by the wayside, depends on the manner and character of their response. Simple, and perhaps one of the few things that is self-evident. It involves a conclusion about the past that life has not been easy for people or for nations, and an assumption for the future that that condition will not alter. There is within me some part of the metaphysic, and thus I would add that life is not meant to be easy.

Fraser, *Deakin Lecture* (20 July 1971)

Freud published his famous image of the embattled ego shortly after Malcolm Fraser was born. Fraser's 'life is not meant to be easy' will pursue him to the obituary pages. At different times he has denied that he ever said it, claimed that it, or something like it, was only a throwaway line to a young reporter, and finally traced it back to Shaw, so that it could be softened with Shaw's 'but it is often delightful'.

When Fraser was Prime Minister there cannot have been an Australian who thought the phrase uncharacteristic of the man. However, an important point is not emphasized enough: Fraser did not say life is not easy but that it is not *meant* to be easy; he is importing the church, as it were, into politics, implying a system of oughts, not simply describing how things are. This is exactly what the 'super-ego' does to thinking and rationality. Freud's discovery that 'morality' might not always be the fruit of people's highest thinking but, on the contrary, an expression of irrationality (of the 'id' which is the unconscious at its most inhuman and amoral). 'Life is not easy' provokes a sympathetic response: we identify with each other as struggling human beings; 'life was not meant to be easy' is a rebuke. It disowns the needy and embarrasses reformers who try to help them. Fraser, though subsequently he worked hard to undo the impression he had made, was telling us to stop complaining.

A Strong Leader need not be a man or woman who lacks sympathy. What Strong Leadership fears is the *constituency* of the needy, a concerted wave of people who would threaten enterprise ('wealth creation') and pull everyone else down. Hence the refinement and the oft-used refrain 'the genuinely needy'. This fear of institutionalized dependence combines with the other message in his remark, an attack on expectations, on the sort of political 'progressivism' that sees government making improvements across the whole range of social ills. Fraser's ideological orientation — summed up in 'small government' (and very similar in its application to the ideas outlined earlier as 'Thatcherism') — was radical and eccentric when he first began propounding it in the 1970s. Since the 'New Right' has taken it further, making Fraser seem moderate and in his own estimation 'balanced', this can be overlooked. The main point is not how 'dry' or 'wet' his views are but the profound and personal pessimism — fatalism, even — from which they stem.

It is common enough among Strong Leaders, whose *raison d'être* is crisis, to adopt a Toynbean or similar belief in dire challenge and the need for sacrificial response. However, not all are quite so daunted. The future can present opportunities as well as perils, and the past can be more than a catalogue of disasters only narrowly averted. Compared to Fraser, Reagan radiated hope and encouragement and even Thatcher approaches the future with zest, and both the

American and British leaders have made much of their country's glorious past. Fraser's thinking is so heavily moralized, so lugubrious, that it suggests a man in whom the clear-sightedness and inventiveness of the 'ego' are burdened by the unconscious pieties and fears of the 'super-ego', the 'over-I'. We see in Fraser great ambition severely restrained, a self set against itself, at best a precarious balance and at worst a permanent discord that undermines credibility and turns away sympathy. The politics that result are quintessentially contest-and-control, now loftily principled and restrained, now wilful, opportunistic and confrontationist to the point of overkill.

A CAUTIONARY TALE

Fraser's biographer reports Fraser's admiration for John F. Kennedy's inaugural speech, particularly its stress on social responsibility: 'Ask not what your country can do for you but what you can do for your country'. On the same page Ayres also writes that Fraser 'has always been an admirer of what he calls the "earthy pragmatism" of Machiavelli . . .'. The point of Freud's discoveries about the 'super-ego' is not the well-known fact that practice does not always match principle; and no one would begrudge Fraser or any Strong Leader their realism about political affairs. The point is that the pursuit of principle itself can be corrupt and that the freedom to act intelligently and helpfully can be undermined by the high 'standards' the 'super-ego' proudly claims. To explain this I can think of no better story than R. L. Stevenson's *Strange Case of Dr Jekyll and Mr Hyde.*

In an older view, Hyde would be man's brutal nature, Jekyll his civilized and even altruistic better self, gradually pulled down by the importunities of selfish desire. This is not the story. In his confession Dr Jekyll writes that as a youth, 'imperious' for social standing, he hid his pleasures behind 'a more than commonly grave countenance' (shades of Fraser's Easter Island mien). He was desperate, in other words, for getting on and for being conventionally approved. Then as a grown man he discovered himself committed to a profound duplicity. Hyde is not the cause of this duplicity;

on the contrary, he is its effect, for the story takes off from an urge for social achievement, not for personal pleasure, so that the division in Jekyll is not between a higher and lower nature, each beginning life at the same time, but a division born of exaggerated social propriety. The eminently respectable, anxious-to-do-good Dr Jekyll himself creates Mr Hyde.

It was thus rather the exacting nature of my aspirations than any particular degradation in my faults, that made me what I was and, with even a deeper trench than in the majority of men, served in me those provinces of good and ill which divide and compound men's nature.

The sin is one of pride and resides in the loftiness, the social urge, not the 'animal nature', in the 'super-ego' not the 'id'. The warning given as the story proceeds is that the 'ego' that is under too much pressure from social demands may by degrees — or in sudden lunges or spasms — shift allegiance from its stressful ideals (for example, to serve its country) to its impulses to serve, with one mind, itself.

Like the rest of us, Strong Leaders and their followers see the world in their own likeness. What they see is continually raging conflict (crisis), its containment a job, not primarily for sentiment or ideas, but for structure, including Strong Leadership. As Fraser put it:

People are essentially imperfect. We're always going to have a society that is capable of improvement, and rules and laws that are capable of improvement, because the essential — you know, the raw material of society is itself so imperfect . . . people could not live together in the most primitive tribes without rules and they cannot live together in a modern State without them.

However, the exclusiveness and intensity with which one relies on structuring social life depends on one's attitude to Jekyll and Hyde. Strong Leaders and their followers are profoundly dualistic, convinced that the evil Hyde is part of creation, and they are continually anxious that he is about to take over the world. The latter explains their wish for urgency and force while the former explains their blindness to the evil that structure itself creates, the rage, resentment and despair a legal, well-oiled but implacable social system can cause. In South Africa, Malcolm Fraser has seen this very clearly and spoken about it very courageously, allowing that illegal, even violent, opposition is understandable. Yet this empathy with desperation has not been part of his general philosophy. In matters of race he sees that 'Hyde' is the creation of an immoral system and the system must be changed. In other matters, the emphasis is on restraining and channelling human imperfection in the name of social order and civilization.

FRASERISM

Like Thatcherism, 'Fraserism' is a tribute to something in the Leader whose name comes to stand for a political era. I am not convinced, though, that the 'something' is a set of ideas, a philosophy. More likely it is the combination of political timeliness combined with personality, political skill and certain key themes repeatedly enunciated in speeches and occasionally expressed in policy. Fraser, like Thatcher, has a reputation for 'conviction' politics but I take issue with the view that 'philosophy' has been Fraser's main suit and that Fraserism brought to Australian politics a depth of thought and far-sightedness it normally lacks.

First, an outline of Fraser's Strong Leader ideology. We have already seen the interest in Toynbean challenge, the survival of nations. This orientation to crisis and threat has been present throughout Fraser's career. 'I was very happy to see in His Excellency's speech that adequate mention was made of defence', he said in his maiden address to parliament as a new member in 1956. 'The free world', 'sacrifice', 'challenge', 'national emergency', and a mention of those 'I owe a debt of gratitude to' who fought in the world wars, are also there in his speech, which is primarily about building Australia's population to 25 million in the year 2000 by means of vigorous public and private works. Thirty years later, in a preface to a book of his speeches, Fraser peppers his one and a half pages with 'challenge'. This time the emphasis is on Australia avoiding economic decline and loss of status and strength, particularly in Pacific affairs. He says:

There are enormous challenges ahead of us. I do not want to see an Australia which will celebrate the year 2000 by recognition that a dozen countries in Asia have passed us by in living standards, by recognition of the fact that we have made ourselves irrelevant to our own region.

Even our democratic neighbours, he continues, are 'more disciplined than we, more hard-working than we, more determined to achieve their place in the galaxy'. Unlike us, 'they have not yet arrived and grown soft'.

The Strong Leader's fear that the troops have lost their taste for battle (because they've had so much peace) was a major theme of Fraserism as it crystallized in the Liberals' three years of Opposition when Whitlam Labor was in power. 'Every group or individual who gets a handout from the Government', Fraser wrote, 'decreases the capacity of some section of the community to cope with its problems. This madness has got to stop'. In an interview, he looked back to the 'big government' of Menzies's days, explaining that it was different then, 'because up to that time [1965] we had the apparent stimulus on our tail of recurrent balance of payments crises . . . you had something to point to and that was the discipline'. (That image, 'stimulus on the tail' is somehow characteristic of Fraser.) Menzies's days were also Fraser's own, and he had shared the belief in a massive public/private partnership in development, but by the early 1970s, when the Liberals were staggering to their first electoral defeat for almost a quarter of a century, Fraser was turning towards small government: 'the demands [on government] often appear to be unending, the requirements unlimited, and they tend to obscure the fact that a continued strength in the productive sector is a prerequisite for nearly, all the objectives we wish to achieve in other areas'.

When Australians elected Malcolm Fraser in 1975, it was not for his philosophy of small government but for the alternative to Whitlam, whose government was then in great disarray. The small government message only gradually became clear. Even then some people confused small government with weak government, a semi-populist belief that everything would come right if governments got out of the way. Like Thatcher and Reagan, Fraser was an activist and an interventionist eager to use government for some and against others.

Those to be encouraged were the productive. They were to be helped in their struggle against the organized voraciousness of the needy and against those, primarily the public service, whose productivity was, at the very least, in doubt. (Ironically, it is the Hawke Labor government which succeeded Fraser that has brought 'privatization' into public consciousness.) One academic commentator suggested that the invidious distinction between the productive and the unproductive (which is at the heart of Strong Leadership) was the core of Malcolm Fraser's philosophy as Prime Minister: 'He believes a government should preserve and enhance the position of manufacturers, rural producers, miners, the professions whom he sees as being the economic and social basis of society. The rest of society . . . must always be subject to the interests of this group'. In Reagan's America, thanks to David Stockman, this became known as the 'trickle-down' theory.

One strand in the view of Fraser as some sort of visionary was his persistent appeal to moral values. Indeed those who support him still, in opposition to the 'new moneyed' New Right espousing 'market forces' and nothing more, seem mostly to have this in mind. Moralizing he certainly did, though no one would argue that Fraser succeeded in uplifting Australians the way Kennedy uplifted Americans (and many others). Fraser's calls to sacrifice and to 'stand on your own two feet' were frequent, usually uttered in warning tones and often with a hint of menace. Most importantly, the call for lowered expectations of government, while received enthusiastically by the 'productive' and rarely contradicted in theory, was never accepted as the honest, fair, moral thing Fraser hoped it would be.

In other words, though often directed at essentially irrelevant things such as Fraser's personal wealth, aloofness, exclusive background, etc., the public attitude to Fraser always retained a touch of cynicism. The 'life wasn't meant to be easy' tag stuck to Fraser and, given that he seemed so alien amongst his own people, his constant lecturing (that money does not grow on trees, that there are no free lunches, etc.) only reduced his credibility. No one identified enough with Fraser to be sure that he wasn't favouring some over others, especially whilst calling for national unity, sacrifice and lowered expectations. While speaking to the electorate as if they were naughty children, he was also emphatically contrasting the productive good guys with the unproductive bad.

Fraser would say 'We need a climate of national responsibility', but, rather pathetically, he was left to lament over his inability to inspire unity: 'It isn't easy to inspire people to idealism, to inspire a country to believe that there is some great objective ahead of them that they've all got to aspire to and work for . . .' Even when he was trying hard, Fraser's vagueness ('some great objective') and his hint of constraint ('they've all got to') betray him. Strong Leadership's efforts to establish unity are undermined by its determination to rank some ahead of the rest. It hopes to inspire while — priding itself on its knowledge of human nature — expecting to have to coerce. These are built-in contradictions and they lie behind Fraser's failure to unite people behind painful policy measures which Bob Hawke could later introduce with widespread support.

Through the 1960s, and then again in the Nixon-Kissinger and Carter days, Fraser built for himself the reputation of a foreign policy hawk. Ayres counsels us not to forget 'how multifarious the threats to stability seemed' at that time and that this 'context of instability' justified Fraser's being 'out of tune with the permissiveness of the sixties'. However, it is not certain that he *was* out of tune. The ruling Liberal-Country Party coalition, supported by the Democratic Labor Party (a hawkish splinter party), was several years behind the US — not to mention Whitlam's Labour Party — in loosening up its foreign policy postures. 'All the way with LBJ', the enthusiastic Vietnam rallying call given by the Liberal Prime Minister Holt, climaxed the 1960s under the team of which Fraser was a part.

Moreover, Fraser has always sounded as if he had a special mission to raise alarms. In the troubled South-East Asia of 1965, following a visit to Indonesia as chairman of the government's defence committee, he warned 'I'm afraid we might have passed the stage where personal knowledge and friendship can be of much help'. He recommended that the Malaysian government 'must either hit at Indonesian bases [over the border] or lose the confidence of its people'.

Indonesia, he said, planned to rule the Pacific, perhaps in partnership with China. That same year he compared Vietnam to Berlin and Cuba, adding that it was more sinister still since 'China uses a different tactic — subversion'. This was harder to deal with because electorates did not see the danger: 'it is not always easy to persuade people to use new and drastic tactics to overcome the long-term problems'. Fraser accepted the 'domino theory' enthusiastically, welcomed the introduction of American ground forces to Vietnam and later the bombing of the North, when he expressed relief that the rules 'which tied the hands of the United States forces and the South Vietnamese have at long last been broken'.

At all times Fraser insisted that Australians recognize the interconnectedness of threatening events. They should see the Vietnam war and Indonesia's confrontation with Malaysia as part of the same danger of Chinese-inspired subversion, which in turn contained the threat that, seeing the success of subversion, Russia would take 'a new interest in the tactic'.

By 1970 Fraser had retreated on Vietnam just so far as to say that the case for the war effort should be better argued. His concern at that time, following Nixon in the US, was with the lawlessness of dissent which 'attacked the foundations of our democracy' and amounted to propaganda subversion at home. He suggested that critics of the war must in their heart of hearts want Communism to succeed. This led him to the general theme of counter-subversion programmes. The West too often delayed its response too long; 'what we must learn from' the war in Vietnam, what we must study, is the subversive process in its early stages. 'We must identify the indicators of insurgency while our enemy is in the early stages of phase one of the Maoist three-stage programme.'

In 1971, as Minister for Defence, Fraser gave an important lecture, the Deakin lecture. It was largely concerned with international matters (to an extent that seemed like poaching to McMahon, then Minister for External Affairs). His main point was to warn against *détente*: there was 'a feeling of relief. We are being told the world has changed. Concern, the possibility of fear, are to belong to some distance past. Our naivety hurts. Visits to Peking alone do not alter the facts of politics'. Elsewhere, Fraser admitted *détente* had, for him, 'connotations of weakness'. In the lecture he seemed to be concerned that hospitality (Nixon's, and earlier, Whitlam's visit to Peking) meant thought would be swayed by feeling (visits are 'no substitute for proper negotiation and agreement') and he was anxious that nothing Australia did should weaken the bargaining power of its strong ally and that the US should keep its wits about it.

Regarding American resolve he became maudlin. Should the US weaken on Taiwan 'then the world would have to change in a manner that would make me fear for my children'. Summing up, Fraser said he wanted regional solidarity and confidence ('without confidence we are nothing'), a collective refusal to 'appease' China and, above all, agreement that the time ahead was one of the greatest danger. Certainly Australia should make efforts on its own behalf, but it shouldn't exaggerate its own powers; let us show we were doing our best, then the US would help. Finally he warned us that the enemy was strong. The Chinese had immense strength, patience, dedication, commitment, purpose and disciplined concern, and, to contain China, Australia and the US should cultivate the same strengths.

In 1973 the China threat was put more sensationally and tied to subversion within the Australian government which was now Labor, led by Whitlam. Fraser castigated the government for risking the trust of the US by being too sympathetic, as he saw it, to the view that the US was the aggressor in Vietnam. In his opinion Australian politics were now run by left-wing trade unionists and extremists and Australia was soon going to find itself allied with Peking rather than Washington. Fraser's reaction to Watergate was subdued. President Nixon had some things to answer for, but 'where the evidence indicated that he acted with a sense of dedication, he should have credit for it'. The important thing is who's side you are on: Whitlam, in chastising Nixon for the alert ordered in the Middle East that year, was simply copying the Russians, and encouraging them.

As Prime Minister, according to Ayres, Fraser had two broad objectives in international affairs: 'to exclude the Soviet Union from gaining a dominant position in the South

Pacific and the Indian Ocean' and 'to heighten Western awareness of the strategic risks of neglecting Third World economic weakness and political conflicts'.

> These two objectives, involving a fresh and original equation of 'north/south' and 'east/west' issues pervaded his diplomacy with China and the United States, and to a lesser extent with Japan and Europe. The Commonwealth in Fraser's eyes came to be a significant mechanism for pursuing these objectives'.

He began early, in 1976, with an attack on *détente* and the Soviet Union, his views 'close to the dominant thinking in NATO at the time' and 'anticipating some of the central attitudes of the Reagan Administration by several years'. He was critical of the wrangles between President and Congress, warning that the Soviets were 'profiting from a weakness in American self-confidence, . . . undermined by the loss of Vietnam and by Watergate'. China, however, was increasingly a likely ally, because of her disputes with the Russians. Australia and China would both want the US as 'an effective presence in the Pacific' to 'balance' Soviet power there.

President Carter himself became disillusioned with *détente*, and after Reagan won office in 1980 Fraser could feel he had seen off the optimists and appeasers he had long warned against. His reaction to the Russian invasion of Afghanistan was a combination of 'I told you so' and sheer alarm. In the days immediately following the news he called it 'the greatest threat to world peace and stability since World War 2' and drew a parallel with Czechoslovakia in 1938, predicting a rapidly spreading conflagration. Then he knuckled down to a sustained campaign to have Australian athletes boycott the forthcoming Olympic games in Moscow, putting immense pressure on (and, allegedly, offering some temptations to) individual athletes and officials of the athletic union. When he failed to deliver the boycott, he did not restrain himself from a little bitterness as he expressed the hope that the athletes would not be treading the same path as their forebears who went to Berlin in 1936.

'There could not have been a more enthusiastic response to the election of Ronald Reagan . . . than Fraser's', writes Ayres. Fraser made his enthusiasm clear to the President himself when he visited Washington in mid-1981, praising him for leading 'a popular revolt against past attitudes'. 'In recent years our societies have simultaneously suffered from comforting illusions about our enemies, and from doubt and uncertainty about themselves.' This was the role he had been preparing for, the role of Goliath's second, his East/West role. At a subsequent meeting with the President, and with Al Haig (then Secretary of Defense), Fraser introduced his other role: he put forward the idea that 'progress on North/South issues was critical to the East/West position. It was important to show the developing countries the advantages of a market economy . . .'; moreover, we must practise as well as preach liberal trading values, a message that must reach the Europeans in particular, whose protectionist wall Fraser had unsuccessfully tried to breach in the past. Fraser also told the Americans that the developed countries needed to understand and give more weight to the political complexities in the Third World.

The link between East/West and North/South issues is Strong Leadership's link between being (first) strong and then fair. The stiffening, under Reagan, of American resolve towards the Soviet was an important condition for Fraser's commitment to including North/South issues in the broad strategic thinking of the developed countries. He was often explicit in his warnings that the Soviet was set to take advantage of the West's increasingly neglectful attitude to Third World miseries. Even the crudest Strong Leader can see potential danger in massive, festering discontent, especially if there is a powerful rival in the field.

Fraser is not a crude Strong Leader, and in a speech which his biographer calls the *locus classicus* of his thinking on international affairs, Fraser displays his wish to add something nobler to strategic considerations: 'Like the working classes in the domestic politics of the nineteenth century, they [citizens of the South] want to have full citizen rights in the world, to be subjects who act rather than objects who are acted on'. However prudential or strategic it is to 'structure in' potential dissent, and though Fraser is an unlikely champion of the working class, there is no doubting his moral interest here. The Third World has meant for Fraser mainly Africa, and his reputation for opposing racial exploitation is secure. As well, I think, one hears in the phrase 'to be subjects who act rather than objects who are acted on' an echo of the ego's predicament when, pressed from two sides — by those who moralize about self-restraint and due process and by desire frustrated until it becomes enraged and unthinking — it cries out 'Life is not easy'. South Africa appears like a morality play in which, in public and *in extremis*, Fraser's inner predicament is vividly projected.

History will undoubtedly give due weight to the signs of sympathetic understanding — empathy — in Fraser's championing of North/South issues, and the even stronger evidence in his Eminent Person role on South Africa. However, the overwhelming impression of Fraserism, despite Fraser's support for 'multiculturalism', his environmental concern (for example, in saving Fraser Island in the Great Barrier Reef), his celebrated decision to pay family allowances to mothers rather than fathers, and several other liberal reforms, is of *empathy withheld*. The early years of his governments were marked by blaming the victim. 'Dole bludging' was the official explanation for levels of unemployment which are now admitted around the world to be the symptom of economic changes no one properly understands. This rain of blame was a continuation of Fraser's long-standing belief that positive government ('big government') had made people soft, a polite, or politic, way of saying that, left to themselves, people naturally shirk and demand that things be done for them.

Hence, in a newspaper article, Fraser argued that small government would encourage people to solve their own problems; many seeking help were not genuinely needy; there were plenty of jobs for those willing to work; Labor's big government and egalitarian refusal to distinguish between the willing and the lazy had sapped Australians of their idealism, had fostered selfishness and cynicism, etc. Fraser's small government, by contrast, would revive idealism by leaving wealth in the hands of those who had made it; would not 'replace the decisions of individuals with the decisions of politicians and public servants'; freedom to spend one's own income would be 'just as important as freedom of speech, of religion and association'. In other words, Labor's Robin Hood principle would be inverted, becoming Strong Leadership's facilitation and protection of the strong.

Individualism appeared in the resounding finish to Fraser's maiden speech more than thirty years ago. All the great prospects he saw for Australia 'will mean nothing if one thing is ever forgotten — that the individual happiness of each citizen is, and must remain for ever, the first thought of our national leaders'. In 1986 he wrote of the 'need to unleash the motivation, the talent, the initiative and vigour of ordinary Australians' — though he went on to scold Australians for having 'the world's highest wage costs' (paying themselves too much), and being 'the most strike-prone nation in history'. This evocation of talent and initiative (though notice that 'motivation', or will, comes first and notice the sting in the tail) is set in a piece largely concerned with the nation's standing among other nations in the Pacific region. This is an example of Strong Leadership's concern with the overall structure, the regiment not the soldier, the arriving wagon-train more than the struggling settler.

In another statement about individualism, 'Courage, foresight and initiative' are linked to 'the basic will to work, to achieve, to be successful', suggesting that Strong Leadership's version of freedom is the freedom to climb the conventional ladder. Ending with 'to advance in his own cause' the statement suggests, not so much the cultivation of individual virtue, as Strong Leadership's celebration of privately-held advantage. This is Strong Leadership's idealism, an invidious idealism: the nation should be 'strong, relevant, participating, and appreciated' — Fraser's aim for Australia in its region. To that end its citizens must be 'more disciplined', 'more hard-working, more determined to achieve their place in the galaxy' than their rivals. The aim is national greatness, the means contest-and-control.

Finally, to clinch the point that Fraser's individualism is Strong Leadership's combination of 'responsibility' and will to succeed, we have his statements about what citizens must do for their country. Formally, Fraser puts himself in the liberal tradition against what one supporter calls 'the Rousseau-Marx-Whitlam tradition'. Government, in that tradition, is seen as 'embodying some higher wisdom, as the authentic voice of the community . . . distinct from the individuals who make up that community'. However, 'Government is not the embodiment of the community. It is a set of institutions within a wider society'. This is why 'the liberal tradition of political thought had sought to keep government limited because its power always threatened individuals and community groups'. Among the policy announcements and stated aims of the Fraser programmes for 1980 and beyond, the Governor-General's speech included philosophical statements such as this: the Government 'believes that the only legitimate yardstick for assessing any policy is not conformity to an ideology, not the strengthening of the state, but the effectiveness of that policy in enhancing the lives of people'.

This fundamental creed of the Liberal Party is a deeply-held belief of Fraser's. Moreover, it is not hypocrisy or thoughtlessness that underlies Fraser's equally strong belief in the opposite, that the highest good is to serve your country, as in Kennedy's 'idealism'. Strong Leaders, and the parties of Strong Leadership, are unavoidably suspended between their celebration of the contestant, the enterprising individual, and their 'responsibility' to see that the rules of the game are obeyed and that the future of the game itself — the structure within which individual competitions are played — is assured.

A PHILOSOPHER-LEADER?

Strong Leadership bristles with beliefs but it is suspicious of ideas. Ideas are secondary to will or resolve, they are tools for furthering Strong Leadership's programme of decisive action and for building a stable, controlling structure. They are also weapons, wielded in defence of orthodoxy and for controlling dissent, or wielded offensively against the ruling authority by commanding the higher ground of 'philosophy'. As we saw with Margaret Thatcher, the 'conviction' politician whose ideas are fundamentalist and strongly and repeatedly presented, can get the reputation of a thinker just because ideas are in the political arena. However, perceptivity and imagination, not to mention complexity and incompleteness, which are essential to thinking philosophically, have no place in preaching and power-play. Indeed they are ruled out there, where the ubiquity of crisis, partisanship and enmities, and the need to get results, require instead Strong Leadership's combination of implacable determination and pragmatic flexibility.

Malcolm Fraser thanks White and Kemp in his preface to their edited collection of his speeches and addresses, *Malcolm Fraser On Australia*, for making it plain 'that my main interest has been in ideas'. He tells us that, since leaving office 'I have spent a good deal of time with major policy institutes in the United States, . . . thinking about the future of Australia within the Pacific region'. White and Kemp, who were among his leading advisers, intended to show the quality and range of Fraser's thinking. They describe him as 'always prepared to listen to a good argument', as a believer in 'the power of rational argument and debate' and 'rational leadership'. In office, they say, he was 'a powerhouse of imaginative policy ideas'. Like Margaret Thatcher, he liked people who were 'prepared to give him a good argument', he 'probed the advice he received for weaknesses', and 'insisted on absolute accuracy and honesty from his advisers'.

In regard to substance, White and Kemp credit Fraser with having 'almost single-handedly altered the agenda of Australian political debate', administering 'a crushing intellectual defeat to "democratic socialism" and its objective of bigger government'. There were 'very few domestic policy areas in which he failed to develop a perspective of enduring interest', while internationally he 'pursued a policy securely based not in ideology but in enlightened self-interest'.

However, the book of Fraser's speeches does little for his reputation as a philosopher-leader. 'Ideas' for the most part means 'policies', that is they are tied closely to particular issues — crises actual or anticipated, for example in the Pacific region — and make Fraser seem more like a zealous and able administrator than a theorist. In fact, under portentous headings that testify to the editors' professorial skills, something like 185 thematic 'statements' are taken from about eighty 'speeches'. One important speech, with liberal use of scissors and paste, accounts for eleven extracts and appears under eleven different headings. Many of the original speeches were brief, given virtually on the run as busy

Prime Ministers have to do, and were not infrequently delivered to the clatter of knife and fork. There is proof here of Fraser's involvement in many issues, and a sense of his wishing to take the long view (which of course in three or four speeches he did). Yet this penchant for the portentous is not the same thing as imagination and vision.

'Ideas' had another meaning in the Fraser years. To call Fraser a philosopher-leader was to refer to his public high-mindedness, his statements on principles and probity, his sombre warnings and rebukes. 'Ideas' in this form suggested anxious brooding more than intellectual openness, obsessional worrying (like a dog with a bone), more than freely operating intelligence. Edwards's book *Life Wasn't Meant To Be Easy* takes Fraser the philosopher very seriously, but contains two profound criticisms: first, his 'philosophy' was *parti pris* and served Fraser's personal ambitions; second, what was called his 'philosophy' was a naturally anachronistic view of the world strategically cultivated and enhanced for the electorate. A politician who sent people to their philosophical dictionaries to look up 'physiocrat' had to be remarkable in Australian politics, and at first glance it seemed he and his political ambitions were governed by pro found thinking. This was before the strain between ideas — ideological and moral — and political success became apparent, and before (as I would put it) the profoundly divided Malcolm Fraser could be seen as the true Malcolm Fraser.

There was nothing in Fraser's background or upbringing which prepared him for philosophical leadership. By Fraser's own account, politics and social philosophies were not discussed at home, though there was a great deal of anxious worrying over family affairs. His secondary school years at Melbourne Grammar were undistinguished: 'work didn't come all that hard. I was seldom . . . top of the class. I would have been in the top half-dozen I suppose . . . or between third and sixth or seventh in a class of thirty-five'. There is an air here of scrupulousness or some oddly continuing worry. Fraser goes on to defend himself against other men's (or boys') brilliance: 'I think it's dangerous in kids — this is probably, I suppose, justification — when things come too easy at school. They very often don't succeed later on . . .'

Brilliance, though, sometimes goes with rising interest in the world, interests of a religious, psychological, technological, cultural and political kind. Indeed this is expected of any able student from fifteen or sixteen years on. In Fraser's case no such personal renaissance showed at school, nor, and this seems very significant, at Oxford University. In later years Fraser recalled how hard his undergraduate years had been, how intellectually unprepared he was, and regretted not going (as was already common then) to an Australian university first.

His biographer, Ayres, to whom he told this, gives substantial space to several of Fraser's undergraduate essays, working to undermine the supposed view of an Oxford tutor that Fraser was 'the biggest colonial drongo of them all' (a view passed on by a political opponent after the tutor's death). Fraser is shown to favour, in broad terms, a progressive Toryism, a conservatism that can accommodate change, and in one essay he argued boldly for a no-party system, a kind of plebiscitery democracy, where talented individuals would not have to submerge themselves in party disciplines. This is every Strong Leader's secret wish. Fraser's concept of the individual is characteristically double-sided. On the one hand, 'a party label on this or that candidate only blinds electors as to his true ability'; on the other hand, the change to a no-party system would cause uncertainty in society at large, though Fraser hoped 'it would not place an undue strain on the national character'.

The important thing, however, is the impression of a serious youth applying himself manfully to his lessons. There are people who think of education as 'equipping yourself for life', a half-truth that misleads them into reducing childhood and youth to a kind of apprenticeship. This turns the drama of experience into a programmed text. The young Malcolm's tutors apparently tried to loosen his thinking but his kindly recollections centre on their lack of political bias, their virtue not their wit. He worked solidly but there was plenty of social life, which the wealthy young squatter was in a position to participate in expensively and generously. What is missing are signs of intellectual flowering; if not the 'red rebellion' of well-brought-up youth, then some extra-mural intellectual interests and play with alternatives (intellectual, cultural, political and so on) that speak of real thinking and rethinking. In fact, Fraser was simply bewildered by undergraduate intellectualism:

> I didn't take part in the Conservative or Labour or Liberal party politics at Oxford. I thought the Oxford Union atmosphere was fabricated and phoney . . . people devoted an enormous amount of time to it and they took it terribly seriously — which is almost some sort of contradiction when you . . . note the subjects they debated.

Even within his courses he judged some subjects serious and others rarefied and unserious. The PPE course (Philosophy, Politics and Economics) seems to have been mainly Politics for Fraser. Ayres shows us no Economics essays, and the suggestion is that Fraser felt his lack of preparation most in this subject. He took exception to Philosophy, even Political Philosophy, when it seemed impractical:

> Locke's theory of Primary and Secondary Qualities . . . seems to solve no problems but opens up many new ones such as what do we see and how? I would suggest that the distinction and the question arising out of it are bogus — an intellectual playground, but what do they tell us?

The impatience here is surely that of the man of power and action: practical-minded, combative, committed to the 'objectivity' of his world, a Strong Leader scorns unnecessary questioning.

In effect, Fraser's seriousness and studiousness meant he was unphilosophical. University made him 'more aware' but what he was aware of was either vague — he says he learned 'what was happening, and what issues there were in the world and within countries' — or precisely what he had been brought up to believe. This was the threat to 'our way of life' by foreign powers and creeping socialism (Britain's National Health Service is one example he remembers worrying about). Fraser's learning at Oxford was mostly a relearning of what he had absorbed at home, an interval for brooding about the defence of his world against its enemies and how he could be part of it. Edwards has said Fraser's ideas at Oxford were 'banal and pathetic', but even the sympathetic Ayres sums up with: 'by the time he left Oxford Fraser had developed a strong set of political convictions not particularly idiosyncratic or out of character with his background . . .'. They were, says Ayres, 'distinctive nonetheless' — their distinctiveness in the charge of 'idealism' they contained, an intensity that came from Toynbee, an idealism which was more fatalistic than creative.

'Strategic' thinking

A tough attitude in relation to the Soviet Union is necessary . . . in the West's interests. But rather than partnering that with an unsympathetic attitude to the Third World, we should be sympathetic and accommodating where we can be . . . A tough attitude to the Soviet bloc and an accommodating view toward the Third World . . . represents the best way of advancing . . . the Western systems of values . . . the way to defeat communist influences is to see that a society is governed freely and well, and fairly . . . if a country is governed that way, the better it is for Western interests . . . Mr Reagan or Mrs Thatcher would say that the National Party government is anti-communist and in strategic terms they think it is a good thing if that government survives. I think it is a bad thing . . . its very policies will encourage people to extreme solutions . . . [the Botha government is both] a strategic advantage to the West [and] a strategic impediment . . .

A general is no less a good warrior for taking advice, studying his options closely, winning his battles with the minimum of bravado and bullying display. Fraser aspires to be a Strong Leader of this type, cool and considered. The best account of him will not underestimate his interest in the broad picture, his deliberativeness, the sophisticated pursuit of his will within the structures of reasoned debate, legality and even moral principle. It is true that he was not the leader he aspired to be: sudden lunges for power, an often excitable rhetoric, and a predilection for working by 'applying pressure' show another side of him. However, all Strong Leaders must continue to play host to the rough beast of raw combat and the ultimate crunch of 'him or me'. Fraser is interesting precisely because the conflict between principle (including deliberation and rational-legal processes) and applying 'pressure' is so sharp, the sophistications of Strong Leadership so tensely juxtaposed with its crudities.

Fraser's thinking, then, is not that of a philosopher-leader, but that of a strategist. 'Strategic' thinking is thinking attuned to and shaped by Strong Leadership's world of contest-and-control, so that political thinking must necessarily calculate advantage. Not to do so in the permanent crisis of human affairs would be absurd. This kind of thinking can be crude and parochial, it may mean a watchful, or over-watchful, eye on colleagues/rivals, or unsettlingly lethal judgements of electoral opportunity, and so on. On the other hand it can lead to Fraser's moderator role in Africa and to his East-West/North-South linkage; these too are the result of sophisticated strategic thinking.

Note how blurred becomes the line between principle and practical effect. 'Strategic' thinking — a cast of mind, a set of intellectual skills and habits, a store of selected knowledge — aims at this, a harmony between values and practical advantage, between virtue and profit. Thus, surprising as it may seem, at the heart of Strong Leadership's 'realistic' response to the world is a religious-like belief that principle and power can be reconciled. There is a balanced strategy somewhere that will let us hold up our heads as moral people *and* simultaneously protect us — pragmatically, opportunistically, no holds barred, if necessary — from our enemies. Fraser's East-West/North-South linkage encapsulates such a dream, and it is irrelevant to ask if he is cynical (pro-African to keep the Soviets out) or idealistic. His motives are mixed, only in this case the mixture of high principle and 'realist' practice appears wiser than Thatcher's and Reagan's obduracy. Admittedly, it is just a formula and it would be too abstruse for the great majority of people it would benefit, nor is it at the heart of the things for which Australia carries responsibility. It is nevertheless an example of how strategic thinking can project, on the distant horizon, a kind of vision.

Ideas and contest

Fraser began his climb to the leadership of his Party with the claim to be shaped by ideas: 'I've always had a strong viewpoint about what I think right and what I think wrong, I'll always go back and check the first premise of an argument'. This was part of the image of 'philosopher' but its main consequence, given the in-built rigidity, is not intellectual but moral. It is a promise of self-control and disinterestedness. This is control by ideas. There is also control (and contest) *by way of* ideas. Fraser, remarking that 'policies must be related to a theme, a view of life, without which all actions become *ad hoc* and piecemeal', argues that ideas ought to have command. In particular, they should enhance the position of the leader: leaders 'express the general approach and philosophy of his party . . . the sense of direction. That's a leader. He has got to be an interpreter for the party. No one else can do that'.

The note of challenge in Fraser's remarks is not hard to explain. Between late 1972 and early 1975 the Liberals were in Opposition under Snedden, of whom there was a good deal of criticism. Fraser unseated him in early 1975 following an unsuccessful attempt six months before. In this struggle for leadership Snedden was called 'directionless', and his attempts to share the political middle-ground with the Whitlam government, like his courting of the new, middle-way Australia Party, were taken, not as part of a rethinking of Liberal ideas, but as weakness. Fraser, the man of conviction, came to seem a Strong Leader. 'Philosophy' or ideology was essential, in his view, to whet the edge of political combat: any blurring of the differences between Liberals and Labor would 'destroy our capability to be a cohesive force which alone enables us to form a government'. In other words, parties need ideas the way armies need rallying cries (not to say different uniforms) ultimately to build a strong fighting force.

The ideas-weapon had to be deployed first in the Party. Fraser's reputation as a philosopher-politician rested partly on a confusion between 'super-ego' insistence on fundamentalist tenets with thought and genuine review. It rested also on simply not knowing that Fraser began very early to move against the too-accommodating Snedden. A few months into Whitlam's term Fraser, describing himself as a Liberal Advocate, wrote a series of articles in the popular press. His sub-editor called it a 'call to arms'. Fraser seemed to be part of the Liberals' rethinking, but in truth he was substituting regrouping for rethinking, keeping the adversary position in the forefront and implicitly recommending himself as a leader who would bring unity — 'cohesiveness' — through political belligerence.

A good indication of Fraser's attitude to the supposed rethinking is the attitude he expressed in an interview towards heterodox views:

> It's always pretty dangerous for . . . a party's unity when a group of people make up their minds they're going to try and act in certain ways, to lead or force the party in directions it doesn't want to go. Especially if their ideas about where they want to go are themselves pretty hazy.

The sneer is against woolly-mindedness. Fraser's ideas would always be fully worked out, or made to seem so, whether they were to be used to fend off criticism of his authority or to legitimize his own grabs for it.

We will look at the recurring patterns of 'disloyalty' in Fraser's career, a pattern in which self-advancement is canopied by tight reasoning and high principle. A more general point should be briefly noted here. This is Strong Leadership's profound anxiety about uncontrolled, unstructured activity of any kind, including thinking. In Strong Leadership knowledge is power if it is hard, organized, massive. The intrinsic power of an idea — its enlightening, inspiring, qualities — is not the thing. What counts is the confusion it produces in the adversary, the power and range it has that sends the other party out of the room to 'do more work' on his proposals. Knowledge, in other words, is valuable to the extent that it is powerful, secret (available only to your side), and effective. Strong Leadership thus has a special affinity with espionage and a great horror of leaks, as well as a great cunning in arranging and deploying them. Even in routine administration, control is enhanced by the sheer command of professional advice, coupled with demands that complaints be 'properly documented', proposals 'fully costed', etc. Reasonable as it is to administer 'rationally' and 'legally', these are versions of political suppression, too. They are also ways of being deaf to disorganized, nascent, inarticulate needs that may simply go unmet, or have to grow to such a pitch that they become a force of which Strong Leadership has no early warning and cannot contain in the ordinary way.

12
Fraser at Work

Early in 1979, halfway through Fraser's seven years as Prime Minister, a sympathetic journalist had an informal chat with him. The journalist came away 'remembering that Malcolm Fraser sought power with greater determination than any other man in Australian history'; 'You know he would work very hard, play any card to hold power' and he was 'more confident and more relaxed about his power, and more willing to use it than ever before'. This is the other side of Fraser, widely recognized throughout his career as a puzzling contrast to the side that moralized about citizens' responsibility, probity in government and the disinterestedness of his own motives.

Fraser inherited Nareen, a valuable property in the rich Western District of Victoria, and represented the rural/provincial seat of Wannon, which includes Nareen. Fraser is said to have always involved himself closely in the management of the property, which runs cattle and sheep, and he is described officially as a farmer in the two or three years before he was elected to federal parliament in 1955 (taking a seat in February 1956). However, politics has been his only career. His mother described him as 'homesick' for Australia at Oxford. He also had his ear to the ground and wrote home to local Liberals in a way that signalled his political ambitions, though he had barely finished his studies. He was quick to seize his opportunity when the Liberal candidate retired and, at his second try, with Labor split and the Liberals supported by Democratic Labor Party preferences, he began a career as a responsible, hard-working, though still young, local member.

Fraser rose slowly, despite the personal resources he could use for research assistance, secretarial help and travel, resources not available to the typical back-bencher. He became chairman of the Government Members' Defence Committee in 1963 and at about the same time a member of the Joint Parliamentary Committee on Foreign Affairs. He became a junior minister (Army) only in 1966 and Minister of State for Education and Science two years later. In 1969 he became Minister of State for Defence, a post he resigned amidst considerable turmoil in the government in 1971. When the Liberals were in Opposition from 1972 to 1975 Fraser had Shadow Cabinet rank. In early 1975 he unseated Snedden as leader of the Party. Then, on 11 November 1975, he was appointed Caretaker Prime Minister by the Governor-General until, a month later, the Liberals in coalition with the National Country Party were elected to government and Fraser became Prime Minister in his own right. He won again at a general election in 1977 and in 1980. In 1983, calling a snap election for March of that year, Fraser was surprised by the Labor Party's switch of leader — from Hayden to Hawke — and was defeated at the election he had called. He held the Prime Ministership longer than anyone except Robert Menzies.

AUTHORITY AND LOYALTY

You cannot commit yourself to somebody else, to a party absolutely. You can't give a blank cheque . . . I'm just not made that way . . . Harold Holt was the example of somebody who was, if anything, over-loyal to his subordinates. He often took their own problems on his shoulders; whereas somebody else might have washed his hands and said 'Well, sorry. You made that mess, you get yourself out of it' . . .

A constant in the assessment of Fraser as a boss, in ministerial positions and then as Prime Minister, is that he was autocratic. In the assessment of Fraser's attitude to *his* leaders, the constant is the charge of disloyalty. Fraser himself suggests a third theme in the extract quoted above, that a leader must know when to cut the painter on his struggling subordinates.

Fraser couched his attack on Prime Minister Gorton in a characteristic blend of political and moral terms. The Prime Minister had been disloyal to his Minister (Fraser then had charge of Defence), the Prime Minister 'was not fit for his office': he was 'impetuous and emotional', self-aggrandizing, lacked principles. Fraser told the press that he was glad to be leaving a Cabinet where there were 'too many wrong ways of doing things'. Some time later Fraser told an interviewer 'I get very concerned about the way things are done. I am just as concerned about the *way* things are done, as *what* is done'. By 1975 this had become the central attack on the failing Whitlam government as Fraser called repeatedly for 'propriety in government'. In March 1971, Gorton went on to use his casting vote to sack himself and six months later Fraser returned to the Ministry under McMahon.

Strong Leaders walk a fine line between loyalty and initiative and between standing for order and standing for self-interest. Fraser explained his dilemma in precipitating a crisis in his party: on the one hand there was the principle of subordination to the team, on the other hand there was his duty to the country, which was not being well governed. (The same argument of principle vs. principle, as he put it, would serve for the constitutional crisis Fraser was to precipitate by withholding Supply in 1975.) He did not mention his deteriorating relations with Gorton over the previous year, there was no hint of the plotting that went on and, of course, no suggestion that his own behaviour — allegedly involving newspaper leaks against his own department's head — was a contributing factor.

In the moves against Whitlam, Fraser claimed once more to be motivated only by principle, while he laid siege to the Whitlam government using his powers in the Senate, and hung a Damocles sword over its head while saying he was in favour of a government running its full term and wanted Whitlam's government to feel sufficiently free of the Senate threat to govern the country well. When they were first announced these sounded like assurances, promising a respite in which the Labor government could pull itself together. Indeed, people who listened to Fraser heard over and over again from him how strongly he desired 'stable government'. However, explosive charges were laid in the fine print of his first press conference as Liberal leader. Fraser's most-quoted phrase said that the Senate would block Supply only in the most 'extraordinary and reprehensible circumstances' which, of course, he later claimed had occurred; the power to judge them so was his. As well, cheek by jowl with principle, was simple politicking: declining to say more, Fraser said he would want 'to catch Whitlam with his pants down'.

Fraser cultivated the Governor-General, Sir John Kerr, shrewdly, giving him the respectful attention Whitlam did not; it was widely said Kerr smarted under Whitlam's taking him too much for granted. Fraser had had experience with Governor-Generals before — as a young man; with Sir William Slim, and when he resigned from Gorton's Cabinet he tendered his resignation directly to the Governor-General, a correct though unusual procedure that was a slap in the face to Gorton.

On that occasion, Fraser's 'Good-night Boss — have a good sleep' the night before he catapulted the party into crisis is justly famous. Looking back, Fraser thinks he was justified in his duplicity: 'if a Minister's resigning he's not going to give his Prime Minister prior notice so that he gets sacked . . .' He calls this a 'little bit of self-preservation' and believes it was Kerr's right too, though the constitution requires a Governor-General to take the advice of the Prime Minister. Fraser, writes Ayres, 'has no doubt' that Whitlam would have sacked Kerr before Kerr sacked him, 'and a total stooge would have been put in his place . . .'. (As recently as 1987 Fraser was inclining towards saying that he knew what was in Kerr's mind while Kerr, feeling this sullies his statesmanlike role in Australia's major constitutional crisis, denies it.) Thus enabled by the powers of the Senate and his reading of the Governor-General's attitude, Fraser could pursue the twin policies of disruption in the parliament, (which exacerbated the government's disorder), whilst calling, in the country, for the return of good, stable government.

'Loyal coups' — against Gorton and Snedden (leaders of his own Party), and via vice-regal intervention, against his country's Prime Minister — are the milestones in Fraser's ascension to office. In office, ambition could be expressed mainly through control. As Minister for Defence, he began by 'showing he was boss' and he was soon being called in the press 'abrasive' and 'autocratic'. He had 'vision, and energy, and some other characteristics', says his Public Service Head, 'to say "that is not good enough", and to begin "a process of interrogation" Defence was not accustomed to'. The sympathetic Ayres adds: 'occasional brusqueness, what sometimes seemed unreasonable demands regarding timetables, and his tendency to question the advice he was receiving' explain 'a psychological atmosphere that could be quite sharp at times'. Intolerance of delay was a sore point in any job he held. One department head 'told Fraser in mid-1972 that it would help considerably if he would use the word "urgent" more selectively in future'. Fraser is described as 'impatiently phoning junior officers', making 'a blitz on delays in correspondence', 'being very "inquisitive", "compulsive", always maintaining the pressure to get things done, to achieve, willing to exchange views with trusted officers and work closely with them, and displaying a great command of detail'. He appreciated 'being told he was wrong' and wanted people 'to argue with me'.

Unfortunately — as I suspected in the discussion of Mrs Thatcher's supposed pleasure in being opposed — Fraser's adversarial style led in the direction of deteriorating work as initiative was withdrawn from subordinates to the leader. Strong Leaders pursue 'room to move' and then fill up other people's working space. Sir Arthur Tange (later described by Fraser as 'a great Public Servant') had to write 'I would like to talk, Minister, about the pressures that you're imposing, and the number of crises that are being created, it seems to me quite unnecessarily'. As well, Tange told Ayres, Fraser had to be warned against being 'overly distrustful of the motives behind written advice . . .'; Tange grew tired of defending submissions in which Fraser suspected 'ill motive'.

As Prime Minister the style of working was the same. 'It seemed to be Fraser's policy to keep officials under pressure

— perhaps sometimes mistaking activity for achievement', writes Ayres. However, distrust is reason enough for pressuring people and for interfering closely. The reference here to officials (in the Department of Prime Minister and Cabinet) could be extended to include Cabinet and other colleagues. Disappointingly, Ayres, though privy to Cabinet papers, does not venture into an analysis of Fraser's leadership there. By all outside accounts he continued to work in a highly interventionist manner, to the extent that a Minister once joked 'When Malcolm's ill, and we're left alone, that's when we get work done!'.

Fraser was often questioned in the press about rumours that he was an autocrat in Cabinet. He would reply in these terms: 'I think that there might be a difference between being a hard taskmaster and running a tight ship but there is no doubt that there has got to be discipline within a team'. He had made much of the looseness of discipline in the Whitlam Cabinet and came into office vowing that he would 'not comment on individual Ministers' and did not expect to change ministerial portfolios often. He liked to give an impression of Cabinet as a stable but vigorous structure:

> People have to feel able to express their views strongly on one side or another (and they are no use if they don't) but then, once a decision is made, that's got to be it for all of us. Whoever is on the winning side or whoever is on the losing side has to accept the decision as it comes out.

In Fraser's Cabinet (as he idealized it) there would be no power-plays, no bruised egos, no revenge-seeking, no leader-flattering cabals, none of the sort of pressure from the boss that unbalanced the game — in short, no politics. Like Strong Leadership in general he promised individual vigour and orderly social processes equally and simultaneously.

In fact, a flood of leaks flowed from the Fraser Cabinet and a plethora of reshufflings and resignations. In addition, journalists eventually became aware that to Fraser 'consultation' had a particular (Strong Leader's) meaning. It became a way to reach agreement by 'locking-in' support ahead of time in individual, separate treaties. Recently a political scientist, given access to the Fraser Cabinet papers, has been impressed with how a Prime Minister can manufacture support through manipulating the Cabinet agenda and its debates. Moreover, Fraser was always clear about the hierarchical nature of Cabinet: 'The PM retains the clear prerogative of selection and dismissal . . . You cannot make decisions with 24 people around the table. The junior portfolios [ministers outside cabinet] are necessary for ministers to learn. But the inner cabinet makes the decisions'.

Press charges that he was a one-man-band always brought a response about the 'team' from Fraser. Many awkwardly handled issues and an *ad hoc* element in government seemed due to him and one paper editorialized: 'The concentration of power in his own hands reflects his patrician view of rule. It also stems from his wish to keep options open for sudden shifts, his so-called "flexible" style of government'. As a result, the function of Fraser's Cabinet — it sat more often in Fraser's day, and longer than ever before — was to legitimize Fraser's decisions and to lock-in support, making sure that work done would not be undermined by Ministerial criticism.

When that failed, Fraser could still play his trump. Following the resignation of Withers, a senior Minister and very senior Liberal, Fraser made one of his more blatantly self-serving appeals to order — specifically to an order which gave him the vital role:

> Countries look to Australia not only as a nation with a sound economy but as a country with continuing political stability . . . to an Australia with a stable, united and determined government. This I say in no sense other than fact. In terms of what happens in countries overseas, whether one likes it or not, and because of the personalisation of politics (which the media does so much to promote), the reputation of this country and its economic policies overseas is Malcolm Fraser's reputation overseas. . .

Fraser's aim in these remarks was to hoist himself above the criticism directed at Withers for interference in electoral matters, to make himself essential. Characteristically he found someone else to blame — the media — as if they had created a state of affairs he reluctantly gained advantage from.

The more direct truth, though, is that Strong Leaders finally identify the general good with what is good for them. Cabinet government, under Strong Leadership, is only nominally 'collegial'; its main features — especially in the hands of a man who likes to 'apply pressure', 'drive' subordinates, and distrusts advice (except from chosen allies) — are managerial. There is hierarchy, an appearance of consultation and contest, but finally a leader who retains flexibility and initiative in his own hands.

The unity Strong Leadership builds — in Cabinet, as anywhere else — is always calculated. It is not surprising that Fraser's frequent attempts to 'listen more' to backbenchers, to 'free up Cabinet debates' and so on failed to convince anyone. Many Ministers, feeling confined and compromised, resigned or were dropped, making the Fraser years as stormy a period within government as anything in the Whitlam years. Profoundly committed to stability and order but wilful, distrustful and over-controlling, Fraser installed the forms of solidarity but missed the spirit. As one leader writer put it, 'In a time of crisis, Mr Fraser has little personal loyalty to fall back upon. Not a man to give unqualified loyalty himself, neither can he command it'.

PARLIAMENT: DEFENSIVE OFFENCE

Fraser claimed that he did not want to centralize power in his own hands. A leader has 'got to want to do the right thing' but that 'is quite different from wanting to get his own way. I think he ought not to want to get his own way'. He should 'be prepared to modify and change and abandon' his views 'depending on what's put to him. In other words, he ought to be able to run a team'. His aim should be not to 'get round the team' but to 'use the team to get a sensible type of judgement'. The problem is that the Strong Leader can only ever be ambivalent in his 'constitutionalism', his rule-bound beholding to others; as a contestor he must play to win and dominate where he can. In Fraser this tension was particularly evident. He was a powerfully self-centralizing leader, his ideology notwithstanding, at the same time as he wanted to see his motives and ideals in the most disinterested, moral terms.

Defensiveness is the clue to the tension in Fraser. His agitated manner, the tone of his voice, often the content of his speeches make this a leading characteristic, as if — like Dr Jekyll — he felt always under attack from people who were claiming to be more politically virtuous than he. (The unrelenting pressure of self-criticism from the 'super-ego' anticipates and amplifies ordinary political opposition.)

An illuminating study of Fraser in parliamentary question time shows how defensive he was. Question time, though frequently staged, at times lives up to its promise of unfettered challenge to the executive, an occasion for the parliament to prick the self-absorption of the leaders. Brereton and Walter took a sample of Fraser's responses to questions without notice — relatively unbriefed, relatively extemporaneous — in his first year of office (1975–6), and compared them with a sample taken from the three-year term of his Labor predecessor, Whitlam. It is important to remember that, objectively speaking, for much of the time Whitlam's government was in dire threat: his majority was small, and the Upper House was able to force him to the polls after eighteen months, and force his sacking eighteen months later. Fraser, by contrast, had a huge majority and consequently a small and discredited Opposition to contend with; also, his replies are all from the first, honeymoon year, though it is true that smoke from the constitutional crisis still hung in the air.

The analysis of responses to questions without notice reveals 'four distinctive' things about Fraser: 'The first and, perhaps, most distinctive of these is the theme of defensiveness'. Fraser apparently needed 'to justify his and his government's actions frequently even where the question [did] not demand it'. Brereton and Walter suggest that Fraser's alleged arrogance 'is underlain by considerable sensitivity . . . not only to actual but to "suspected" criticisms'. Fraser had a marked tendency to deal with attacks on his government by attacking back, defending his side by excoriating the previous government. (He was to continue this strategy into and beyond the campaign of 1977.) This aggressiveness — and the authors throughout are comparing Fraser with Whitlam — is the second thing in the Fraser responses. 'It is significant that Fraser relies [on the strategy of attack] so consistently and employs it in such a diffuse way . . . when the Opposition . . . offered little threat to his position.' Moreover, 'these attacks are often imbued with a moralistic tone . . .'. The third theme is over-control. Fraser's responses are short on 'information, praise, and even to some extent reassurance' (i.e. of his own side). 'This wariness suggests a general distrustfulness and a tendency to see as threatening what others would let pass.' Finally, seriousness. Political leadership is 'hardly a job that encourages light-heartedness'. Nevertheless, Fraser is distinctly lugubrious, presenting himself as a victim of duty.

The counting procedures used by Brereton and Walter clearly yield the Fraser we know — a man under pressure to defend himself, a man who acts as if embattled even when he is in a commanding position. The suggestion of internal division and strain, and *self*-criticism, is strong.

WORKING THE ELECTORATE: REMONSTRATION AS RHETORIC

In the Fraser years, as if 'small government' left a gap that needed to be filled, the Prime Minister was big on rhetoric. The rhetoric was moralistic — a climate of threats and scorn, of blaming and shaming. Fraser, in the view of two former advisers, was 'No silky orator'. In fact, his voice was grating and his speeches hectoring. Though he extolled enterprise and even talent, and promised freedom from 'excessive direction', rhetorically he demanded the hair shirt. These were 'super-ego' years when the lid was put on the tumult of the Whitlam years, when high, supposedly naive expectations were dampened down, when the rampant adventurism (individualism?) in government and the public service, and among the general public, was reined in. Fraser was elected to quell the excitement of the Whitlam years, as he explained (with a startling oxymoron) to the BBC: 'People want . . . a government that can be . . . exciting in a way that's predictable'.

So there was a call to order ('we need a climate of national responsibility') and a demand that citizens grow up ('People are still expecting more than they are prepared to work for . . .'). The crisis Australia faced, 'and that's not too strong a word', was that people had not worked out what they 'are prepared to do for Australia' and 'what they expect or demand governments do for them'. There was need for discipline and for unity, for people to realize that 'there are objectives, policies and attitudes that all Australians have in common'. Indeed ordinary interest politics, pluralism, was a luxury crisis did not allow:

> I think what we have to do is to try and get underneath the particular interests of groups and try to bring to the surface the true national interest . . . it's only if you can have a common objective that is widely recognized that you are then going to get the overwhelming majority of the people working for it.

Nor was the crisis something that would quickly pass, so that people could soon be demobilized and go back to their private pursuits: the 'idealism, the sense of direction that Australia needs, [should last] not for six months or twelve months but for twenty years, to the year 2000 and beyond'.

Fraser, as quoted before, lamented that 'It's not easy to . . . inspire a country to believe that there's some great objective ahead of them that they've all got to aspire to and work for'. Typically, however, coercion and threat are wound into his rhetoric, undermining the inspiring he hopes to do. The rhetorical figures he uses — mainly that the electorate is juvenile, soft, needing to grow up and wake up, and sporting images — have an illiberal, uninspiring ring. In the following, for example, what is the meaning for an Australian citizen in his own society of being dropped from the team?:

> People are still expecting more than they are prepared to work for . . . They also have expectations of what they want governments to do for them . . . If you take successful football teams, they have to show a great capacity for training, a great degree of mental determination, they have to share a commitment and a dedication . . . anyone who doesn't perform properly — doesn't conform with the coach's rules — is going to get dropped from the side . . . Unfortunately at their normal work many Australians don't show the sort of commitment or dedication footballers do.

That Fraser's calls to unity were internally contradictory is one thing. That they were combined with attempts to undermine and delegitimate rival centres of power — 'rival' in Strong Leadership's eyes — made division all but certain. Fraser's calls were zealous in pursuing the Liberal Party's hostility to the union movement and its conviction that the media (particularly the non-commercial Australian Broadcasting Commission) had a social democrat bias; in attacking the Arbitration Commission; in gloating at victories over State Premiers (despite his New Federalism and antipathy to Canberra centralization); in generally castigating all who opposed him or who were a threat to him, including the unfortunate 'dole bludger'. This may have been only the public face of Fraserism, but it gave the Fraser years an unparalleled reputation for 'confrontation'.

The trouble seems to have been the Strong Leader's inability to negotiate without keeping a 'big stick' in reserve. Immediately after the 1982 budget, a senior political commentator asked Fraser to expand on his hint about the 'other measures' he would use if the unions did not moderate wage claims in a trade-off with the government's concessions. Fraser's reply, if not disingenuous, at least suggested that he would not take too many of the risks that necessarily accompany genuine co-operation: 'Let me go into that because that looks like trying to establish a basis in which you can work by co-operation, on the one hand, but if that doesn't work you can take out a club. I don't want to be in that position'. The ambiguity in Fraser's attitude to unions dated from his days in Opposition, when he made himself a reputation for enlightenment and commonsense, then included in his final proposals a provision for a kind of industrial police. In effect he did not succeed in moving against the unions as, for example, Reagan did against air-traffic controllers. However, many commentators saw in the shift from a conciliating Minister (Street) to a man more in Fraser's mould (Viner) a policy of deliberate stirring, and the rhetoric seemed designed to mobilize public opinion into forcing unions to yield to government demands. These are just three examples:

> A number of these disputes were quite deliberately designed to demolish any possibility of orderly settlement of dispute and the orderly determination of wages in Australia . . . can anyone deny that certain extreme elements in the union movement are seeking to destroy economic recovery in Australia?

Men engineering the industrial disputation are leaders of unions with close affiliations with the Labor party. Yet we need to understand that a number of these men are avowed enemies of democracy and the Australian way of life.

The statistics of the time lost through strikes are way down . . . but . . . some elements of the union movement are becoming more and more adept at disrupting operations with fewer and fewer people . . .

These are examples of a rhetoric that had McCarthyist tones, but the main strategy was to divide the union membership from its 'extremist' leaders: 'It is worth remembering that union officials who initiate strikes often go on getting paid'. The success of this strategy of divide-and-conquer was essential to Fraser's version of national unity: 'what is damaging our country more than anything else [is] the utterly selfish pursuit of advantage regardless of its cost to other members of the community'. One man's pay rise is another's job. Happily — and Fraser had opinion poll support for attacking union leaders while appealing to their members — 'An increasing number of people are prepared to stand up and say no, they will not strike without good reason, and they will not go along with those who urge disruption and conflict'. Striking workers, were not in fact, true Australians. They were confronting the people of Australia 'and can't be allowed to be successful in that'.

The point here is not whether tough legislation was used or not, nor is it the case that Fraser relied on threats alone. In fact, he negotiated a 'wages pause' near the end of his term, which was widely acclaimed. The point is the Strong Leader's belief that threat and division are a necessary part of negotiating, his belief that bringing-them-to-their-knees or firing-a-few-shots-across-their-bows is essential to diplomacy. Later, of course, like Margaret Thatcher in her dealings with the Soviet Union, the Strong Leader claims that the credit for successful negotiation should go to the big stick, claims that peace was brought about through belligerence.

A slightly different approach begins softly and hardens towards the end, or is menacing between the lines. Throughout his career Fraser appears to have used calculated leaks to some effect, and he has used the 'set piece' to announce his alternative policies and leadership (against

Snedden) and, through press features on his family life, to soften criticism of his allegedly autocratic style of leadership. As well, it is said he would often approach newspaper proprieters directly. Clearly, Fraser saw the media as powerful, though he complained that their criticism was not always 'constructive'.

Speaking in 1976 to the 50th anniversary of the *Canberra Times*, Fraser began flatteringly: 'In many ways a newspaper is the single most important institution in a community . . . Newspapers are vehicles that inform, enlighten, entertain, sometimes annoy, and often act as a social and political conscience'. But, he goes on,

> Today more than ever the role of the press and the politicians are interwoven . . . This role gives the press great power — although perhaps not quite as much as it thinks — and power carries with it a great responsibility . . . People in a democracy acknowledge the need for a free press. But there is no such animal as absolute freedom any more for the press than for the citizen. The limits of one freedom always clash with the limits of another freedom — so boundaries have to be drawn.

Two comments may be interposed here: is the sentence about 'acknowledge the need' setting it a little low, despite the flattering remarks of the previous paragraph? Also, does the existence of clashes of freedom necessarily mean that boundaries must be set? Is it not a liberal position that freedoms should compete rather than come under control? Fraser then explains what he means by drawing boundaries: 'Information may be untimely, comment may be premature and judgement may be incomplete — so there may well be a case for judicious delay or a case for maintaining confidentiality'. Fraser admits that this could simply serve politicians' interests, and that there is no absolute answer. The question he does not address is why not have competition between press and politician? The answer, I think, is that Strong Leaders are not eager for free markets in power. They preach free-market individualism in the economy but favour monopoly for the polity, particularly in regard to information.

Fraser's later remarks do not dispel the impression that he wants to structure press/politician relations. He is in favour of reducing governmental secrecy, but hopes the process won't go as far as in the US. He wants his Ministers to help the press with an 'unhindered flow of information . . . *factual* information' to the media — but makes the point just as strongly that

> The democratic system is not exempt from the hard realities of practical day-by-day administration which demands that some reticence at least must inevitably be applied to when and how the information is supplied . . . policy . . . could well be jeopardised if published prematurely . . .

This is the formula for a managed press that waits for handouts and permission to print. It bears no resemblance to his earlier description of the press as a government's conscience. Two years later, when Fraser told the International Press Institute 'It is the ability to fuse criticism with the equally important sense of responsibility', the *Australian Financial Review* (no fierce critic of conservative governments) wrote in an editorial: 'Mr Fraser is the most practised manipulator and massager of the Australian press since the days of R.G. Menzies. His latest call to enlist the press in some sort of national front . . . is a calculated step along the route to greater news management . . .'.

Managing the press was an egregious feature of the Fraser governments. Tight control over Cabinet and the public service, and frequent and intense action over leaks, had some impact in limiting public scrutiny. In addition, especially in election campaigns, tactics were used which supplement mere management: stonewalling, the exclusion of the print and Canberra journalists (the best informed) in favour of TV journalists, and so on. A more complicated set of rules for off-the-record/on-the-record briefing also hamstrung journalists. There was talk of unofficial blacklists; certainly on more than one occasion Fraser bitterly attacked particular pressmen (Negus, Carleton, Willesee), attributing political bias to them, and he walked out of TV or radio interviews complaining that an agreement had been breached. For the most part, the issue was one of Fraser's wish to sell his policies or records and his belief that the press was obstructing him in a biased way.

At various times Fraser has spoken off the cuff about the media, usually in a low key but always critically. A major theme was that ordinary people wanted a more orderly, civilized media, i.e. he set the people and media at odds. In late 1979 a journalist wrote that the Prime Minister 'dislikes the way interviews are conducted on Australian television'. Fraser was quoted: 'People didn't want brawls brought into their sitting rooms. An interview shouldn't be about winning'. In one tame interview he put this in his most patrician way:

> To an extent Australians are a nation of knockers . . . When you look at the political scene . . . you see a much greater preponderance of criticism than you do of constructive efforts. I suppose it is not much fun writing what good work so and so did . . . it is more important to be credible — to expose that which is wrong . . . But . . .

Presumably Fraser's attempt to show the press in a bad light by insinuating that it is juvenile ('fun') and unpatriotic, is directed to the people at large. The strategy is Strong Leadership's. When it holds the reins of power, it stresses orderly management. Its message becomes that we should all be mature, judicious and competently informed (all these are in the address on the press quoted above) which is an effective way to pull the teeth of critics without power, whose only resource may be straining the rules of decorum. Strong Leadership turns against strife when its opponents have the more to gain from its use. In addition it must be remembered that Strong Leadership believes more in administration than in ideas, in executive action more than consultation, in leadership more than in participation. Its idea of freedom requires that knowledge be in constructive hands, and that the clash of ideas be stilled if it threatens a responsible executive. Its Nirvana is a structured world, where power is in the right hands and everyone else behaves 'constructively'.

NEGOTIATING: HOT AND COOL

> I think the most enjoyable part of it is when you have a victory — and it might be a victory for something in your own electorate, it might be a victory in getting your colleagues in government to accept a new policy . . . Everyone likes to be on top, in relation to a policy or winning a point. Not for yourself but for what you think that policy will achieve . . . it's the most stimulating part, anyway.

Fraser's 'confrontationism' carried over into some aspects of foreign affairs, particularly in trade matters where Australia has had long-running differences with the European Economic Community. In mid-1978 a headline read 'EEC baffled by Australia's "wild buffalo" diplomacy' and the story in the *Australian Financial Review* was that 'Officials have bestowed on Mr Fraser a unique title: the most hostile Head of State encountered over the past twenty years'. Alan Renouf, head of foreign affairs under Whitlam and appointed ambassador to the US by Fraser, wrote in Fraser's early years:

> We started off by confronting the Soviet Union in the PM's speech in June 1976. I have no illusions about the Soviet Union. On the other hand, why take them on unnecessarily? Then we turned to confront the European community over trade issues . . . Then we turned to confronting the ASEAN countries . . . Then we confronted Vietnam with our decision to withdraw aid . . . we were regarded as quite a good friend of Vietnam . . . we turned ourselves into an enemy for no good purpose whatsoever . . . we have confronted the United States . . .

I am less interested here in this 'hot' style of negotiating than another way Strong Leadership can work: through ingratiating itself, albeit in a dignified way, with its powerful allies. In the big league the Strong Leader comes across less as a wielder of the big stick than as a small boy with spirit.

Fraser, telling the story to his biographer, seems immensely proud of his negotiating achievement over the FIII fighter to be supplied by the US. He was then Minister for Defence and drew the lesson, often pointed out to Whitlam (when the latter would publicly criticize the Americans), that support in public and tough bargaining in private was the way to handle our great and powerful friend:

> We thought we had a point which the Americans ought to concede . . . I had a team of eight or nine people with me — we were negotiating against about fifty or sixty. We would negotiate all day and then plan the next day's tactics, and the Americans [would] just feed in a new team. It was funny because we were only due to be there three or four days, and their Secretary of Defence said 'Well, you're off tomorrow?' I said 'No' . . . 'we haven't got anywhere, have we?'. He said, 'Do you think we can in the next couple of days?'. I said, 'Well, I hope so' . . . and then over the next couple of days [he repeated his question]. I said 'No'. [Eventually] he said, 'Do you intend to stay here till we've resolved this?'. I said 'Yes'. He said, 'All right, well, we'd better!'. After that we made progress.

Ayres gives this episode a substantial airing and quotes the head of the American team, Lieutenant-General Glasser, as finding Fraser

> a fierce adversary, a real fighter. He knew what he was after and was determined to get for Australia the very best deal that was available. You can't call him unfair, though he grabbed every opportunity for himself. That's your privilege when you're negotiating . . . we certainly felt we had been taken to the cleaners.

This may be Strong Leadership at its best, but note the conditions: a friendly Goliath, a plucky David; a clear and tangible goal; no fundamentally divisive issues involved. These are the parameters appropriate to a sporting contest, the game hard fought but not finally deadly, the goals set and, in the underdog's case, much to be gained in personal satisfaction and prestige with the friendly, powerful adversary if one does better than expected. No wonder Fraser was pleased. This was an important saving to Australia and a political boost for Fraser at home, but above all it had a personal charge — these 'cool' victories have a Kipling-like manliness attached to them.

Recent publications about Fraser, written by supporters, have emphasized his ability to talk with the great and impress them. Ayres quotes President Ford, whom Fraser met in 1976: the President called Fraser 'very forthright. I don't think Malcolm would be a subtle, deceiving, negotiator' (subtlety was not part of Ford's image either). D'Estaing says, 'He has a very strong presence . . . he speaks to persuade his audience. He has a set of values which are very clear and he tries to convey these values in a very forceful and direct way'. One gets the impression — as one did with Mrs Thatcher — that negotiating with foreign leaders (tête-à-tête as it were) is the best part of their job, perhaps the thing they had aimed at all along: to be calmly, firmly influencing major world events in the company of other great men or women, the undisputed head-person of their own tribe. This is almost beyond politics, beyond at least its pinpricking criticisms and muddied achievements. Hence the calm, as if politics had become 'public service' raised to a heroic level. An election campaign at home is the very opposite, a different story and a ruder one, where calm is the last thing a leader intent on gaining or holding power can hope for, and dignity is easily lost.

ON THE HUSTINGS AND OVER THE TOP

There is a careful balance Strong Leaders must aim for between capitalizing on their reputation for being men or women of determination, putting themselves 'above the crowd', and being knowable, one-of-us and reassuring. In the contest for leadership of the Liberal Party, Fraser used to deny that he had bought himself public relations assistance to tone down his ultra-conservative image (the models surrounding him in a famous photograph were presumably surprised passers-by). His biographer has since let us into the secret, showing how Fraser's image as 'austere' and 'arrogant' was professionally softened at the edges. Still, Fraser had much to gain from his reputation for being aloof, even anachronistic. Strong Leaders are meant to be the 'strong, silent type' and a bit above politics. 'Strength' lies in a reputation for saying 'no' — 'no' to compromise, 'no' to the need to be liked, 'no' to being sociable when there is work to be done — and Fraser's leader Snedden, neither implacable nor withdrawn, was made to appear weak.

Fraser's electoral victories against the Whitlam-led Labor, in 1975 and 1977, emphasized his Strong Leader qualities, especially his hard-headedness, but at the same time offered reassurances and, crucially, hand-outs. In 1975 little more was necessary than to assert the return of the stability and plenty that Labor had squandered. The tactic was for Fraser to look determined but say nothing. In 1977 a Liberal advertisement offered a fistful of dollars — the benefit of small government — while Fraser warned:

> That same disastrous Labor Party, with its same unwanted and unloved leader, now has the gall to suggest that it has the solution to high unemployment and should be trusted to implement it. In the same breath it is mouthing policies of reckless spending, unleashed wages and industrial anarchy identical to those which caused the original disaster.

At this time, the reassuring leader was the leader who promised hard times. Steadiness, continuity, not new policies, was the reassurance given (sweetened by the hand-out) and this was enough to outweigh the growing view in the press that Fraser — a master of inspired leaks, hints and the fine print — had first spread anxiety about an early election, and then called one, by popular demand as it were, to bring stability back into government:

> A situation in which a government is constantly concerned with the holding of elections is not conducive to sound government and hence is not in the public interest. A fundamental requirement [for the success of his policies] is an atmosphere of certainty and confidence in the community.

By going to the polls a year early, Fraser had the advantage that Whitlam was still Labor's leader. And leadership, figured greatly in all his calculations of electoral success.

Fraser's steady-as-you-go theme was not quite the appeal to asceticism it seemed. Apart from the tax cuts there were other promises: for example, unemployment would fall 'in a strong, steady and sustained manner'; 'recovery is now under way', 'a new period of stability and fuller [*sic*] employment is within our grasp'. Gloomy economic forecasts, some from the major banks, were scoffingly dismissed. However, employment did not fall, recovery did not occur and the tax cuts were taken back, and the 1977 election did more than anything before his late 1979 back-track to Keynesian pump-priming (when Fraser abandoned all his Friedmanite, proto-New Right ideology in an effort to hold on to power) to open up the issue of the Fraser government's credibility. Moreover, for all the theme of responsibility and steadiness, it became clear that a Strong Leadership government had no qualms about baiting its hook. By 1979 a columnist could wrote of 'Mr Fraser's tendency to promise and predict rashly for the sake of the electoral needs of the moment'. To hear the Prime Minister at the time, a spectacular minerals boom was about to solve all the nation's economic problems, like Mrs Thatcher's North Sea oil. In other words, Strong Leadership does not make the mistake of promising *only* blood, sweat and tears. Condescending to the electorate, looking beyond the economic *cogniscenti* (whom it might privately reassure that tough measures will be instituted after the return to power), it turns to placating fears and dangling bribes. Characteristically, when the tax-cut promise was broken, Fraser called the resulting opprobrium 'a cross we must bear'. Whitlam had stuck to a promise not to raise taxes in his first term, and that had damaged his government's economic prospects; Fraser was saying that suiting himself was his cross, an inversion that ennobled opportunism.

It is impossible to say whether the campaign distortions — 'the worst collection of half-truths . . . I can remember in a Prime Minister's policy speech', said the Melbourne *Age* — were worse under Fraser than under anyone else. Problems of credibility dogged his whole time in office perhaps because, under Fraser, the political cynicism *showed.* He, after all, was the loudest exponent of probity in public affairs and of moral discipline as the means of national salvation.

Leadership — 'a policy in itself' as Edwards wrote in his mid-term profile of Fraser — played an important part in Fraser's next two elections, though his and his Labor opponent's roles were to be reversed. In 1980, Labor's Hayden was portrayed as a weak leader. In Labor publicity Hayden was flanked by popular Labor leaders from State governments and the union movement. This only enhanced Fraser's image as the Strong Leader, standing out in front, alone. In fact, Hayden went close to an upset win at the election and in the weeks before polling day Fraser appeared to panic. Quickly, he too appeared as part of a team, his strong, solitary leadership suddenly an embarrassment because Fraser had begun to symbolize an 'over-the-top' raucousness and bullying that the electorate did not want. Wherever Fraser went in public, his stridency and sneering left a trail of anger and protest. In the event Fraser won narrowly, but increasingly Liberal voices would be heard doubting his confrontationist style and wondering if Fraser was now an electoral liability.

Hayden was not a Strong Leader (in the special sense used here), though a man of intelligence and sincerity. There were moves during 1982 to replace him with Hawke, former leader of the union movement and the most popular man in the country, who had recently entered parliament. Fraser calculated that if Hawke became Labor's leader, Hawke would defeat him in an election. He calculated further that his best chance of a further term in government required an early election that would catch Labor with Hayden still its leader. Labor upset Fraser's plan by a few hours. While he was in the process of gaining the Governor-General's consent, Hayden was resigning in favour of Hawke. A month later, Hawke was Prime Minister.

Under pressure of losing, the Strong Leader became more strident and raucous than ever. However graceful under pressure in private, in public Fraser appeared thoroughly rattled. I suppose all Strong Leaders know an unbeatable opponent when they see one, and Hawke had the capacity — as no one else in Australian politics had — to convey strength while also carrying the Labor message of an end to confrontation and division, a new era of reconciliation and renewal. This was the fatal combination. Fraser had spent his career preaching one or the other: strength or co-operation, shape up or ship out, respect or love. Unfortunately, as Fraser went from one disaster to another — threatening, cajoling, alarming people with a ridiculous suggestion that a Labor victory would cause a run on the banks (a remark which almost *did* cause a run) — Hawke completely undermined Fraser's anxious and angry dichotomies.

Fraser is the only one of our three Strong Leaders to have completed the political cycle. He left, looking more human in public than he ever had, tearful, disappointed. In the last week of the campaign he had begun to talk of his childhood, particularly his anxieties as a child, which gave him a fillip in the polls. There were many who held back their sympathy as Fraser announced he was retiring from politics completely, but others warmed a little to him, undermining as they did so the Strong Leader's core myth — the myth that he is fitted to lead because he is beyond love and sympathy, not concerned with his personal fate and without regrets.

13
People and the Self

An anxious, worrying man, Fraser has never been thought good at unstructured leisure, small-talk, affable companionship, the loose ensemble of personal relations. Edwards thinks he is comfortable only with older people or with subordinates, a structuring of authority which reduces surprise and allays competition. In reply, Ayres (Fraser's biographer) gives examples of equals who were Fraser's friends but they are National Country Party members who were not only juniors in the Liberal-NCP coalition but men rather inclined to combine 'macho' politics with the sort of letting off steam that Strong Leaders call recreation and sociability. Strong Leadership values leisure when it is 'structured in', that is relaxes the tensions for a time without endangering commitment to work and achievement; like sportsmen and medical students, they come back on Monday morning readier than ever to fulfil their allotted tasks. Of Fraser's more solitary pursuits, fast motor bikes and cars, fishing and photography, the first and last are similar — both simple distraction and a continuing reminder of the need to keep one's 'eye on the ball'.

Fraser reacted defensively and competitively to charges that he was unfriendly and unable to appreciate social occasions: 'Maybe those critics should come on a pub crawl with me one day, if they could stand the pace'. Similarly, he explained that he seemed dull on TV only because his jokes would be 'a bit rough'. At the same time, he seemed sometimes to get over-excited and to go too far, becoming, like a sports fan, more over the top than the players. Turning to the manager of his team, which that year had just won the football premiership, Fraser shouted 'I'm going to have your arse if we don't win the next five'. For the most part controlled, when he 'relaxes' he becomes a caricature of spiritedness — or mischievousness. One former Liberal Minister claims to have nearly come to blows with Malcolm who persisted in the (aggressive) practical joke of putting olives and pickles into people's pockets at a cocktail party.

For the most part, though, Fraser is not 'one of the boys'. This hardly matters in a leader, and Strong Leaders gain from their aloofness. What does matter is if the leader, lacking the skills of informal sociability (outside the work structure, his authority subdued), cannot hear the subtle messages it can convey. Fraser's 'reserve' is a form of social and political deafness; he has a tin ear, and the knowledge which equal, easy and empathetic communications convey does not reach him. The adversarial, formal, negotiated communications that are his forte must be considered inadequate for not being supplemented by subtler, nuanced, more 'human' interchanges. As well, structured exchange, as a kind of prosthesis, can make the user unsure of himself, defensive, overly suspicious and never able to be fully in tune either with his allies or with negotiating partners less eagerly 'macho' or competitive.

Replying to a question about the people in public life he has admired, Fraser was prolific but hardly forthcoming. Apart from the elder statesmen of his party, particularly Menzies, he named Curtin and Chifley from the Labor governments of the 1940s. The international leaders he listed were Churchill, de Gaulle, Lee Kuan Yu (names which were predictable), and also Roosevelt, Mao and even Kennedy (though he repeated the cliché that Kennedy might not have delivered what he promised). He discussed none of these at length, none was enjoyed, as it were, by being talked about, and no clue was given as to what their significance was for

Fraser. One suspects that their being venerable was part of it. Fraser spoke with nostalgia of the great men, particularly the returned soldiers, who made the parliament of Menzies's day a place of great vigour and equally great idealism; in those days men were men, fighting hard, stopping when the whistle blew and in his opinion parliament, the people in it, had gone downhill since then.

Fraser's public comments on personalities, in politics or not, are therefore rare. When he does express an attitude to his political opponents, it is not generous. Whitlam bewildered and incensed Fraser, who could see the man's ability but could not understand his hubris, the freedom or licence of a wit, his frank self-enjoyment. Whitlam was 'a vigorous person with a powerful intellect' but he lacked 'honour and dignity', he was 'a bit like the Mad Hatter', he had a 'disregard for reality', and had an 'irrational dislike for business'. Whitlam, Fraser told an interviewer, 'seemed to like an almost constant state of unrest, as though he was the centre of a storm. Most people like a more settled atmosphere'. When Whitlam retired Fraser described him as 'a strange man on the scene of Australian politics'; he 'left his mark' but, 'we're still too close to him to be able to make a judgement of what he's done . . .'.

Jim Cairns did not bewilder Fraser. Cairns had led the anti-Vietnam war movement before becoming Deputy Prime Minister in the Whitlam government. He was always identified with the 'conscience' of the Labor movement, was a leader of youth and later became a guru of the 'alternative life styles' movement. Fraser knew exactly what he didn't like about Cairns: 'he's trying to be all things to all men . . . trying to be everyone's friend . . . cutting his sails to the wind'. In Fraser's eyes Cairns's 'extreme socialist ambitions for Australia' came down, I think, to this: Strong Leadership's profound distrust of people and ideologies insufficiently distrustful, naively trusting of natural — unstructured and lightly led — solidarities.

By contrast, Richard Nixon was spoken of rather warmly, as was the infamous Governor Bligh of the *Bounty*. Bligh, thought Fraser, had been given a raw deal by the historians. He had to deal as best he could with 'discontented people who didn't know what to be or what [was] best for them'.

Fraser, then Prime Minister, added: 'I think that description could be used for a lot of people at the present time'.

THE BI-CAMERAL SELF

How does Fraser view himself? The corny newspaper and television set-pieces that show the leader a family man, and 'just like us' have the important function of mitigating the Strong Leader's image of ambition and determination. Fraser was often advised to take friendly reporters and photographers to his farm, Nareen, where he would be seen riding, discussing stock with the hands, relaxing in a chintz armchair. There was concern over his health, that he drove himself (and others) too hard, and he quietly boasted 'I've learned to pace myself'. (Needless to say he added, invidiously, 'you do see some politicians, of all parties, get too tired, too tense . . . and you sometimes worry about them . . .'). 'Familywise', he said in 1977, 'this year has been better. I've been able to spend more time with my wife . . . I think it's terribly important to just slam the public door occasionally, make sure you spend some time with the family, going fishing or camping or whatever'. Fraser, characteristically, went a little far for this sort of article when he told the reporter that he was concerned to hear that his son's schoolmaster wore a Shame Fraser Shame badge in class: had he known earlier, he said, 'there would have been one form master less'.

This is self-presentation, the Strong Leader's denial of ambition and dominance. We can go beyond planned presentation by asking how Fraser reacts to criticism. Consider these three quotations from interviews he gave in the press:

> No government can ever be loved . . . The best that any politician can hope for, and . . . should hope for . . . is to be respected for the decisions that he takes, for the policies that he seeks to implement . . . Australians want a government that they believe will do what it thinks is right, no matter how much flak you're going to get as a result of those decisions in the short-term.

> [Is he aloof etc?] Well, look, I think other people can judge that. If I made a judgement other people wouldn't agree with it, and it wouldn't change their views anyway. It sometimes amuses me how somebody can write one

week that I'm a Tsar, a dictator . . . the next week they write that Fraser just accepts what the last person to speak to him said. So the only point I make in that is that judgements often differ very wildly.

You know, whatever people think of you, they think of you. What I say won't alter it.

Arranged in a series, Fraser's remarks suggest that other people are irrelevant in the short term, perhaps because they have not organized themselves into a real, political, danger; they are just noises off-stage. Then, they're stupid, the sum of their criticisms is zero because they all cancel out. Finally, they are implacable: it's useless trying to appease them, a man cannot hope for an understanding ear. Ultimately, then, just as Strong Leadership must govern against the tide of public opinion — which is irrelevant, stupid, not able to be influenced — so individuals ought to measure their progress by the fear ('respect') and opposition they provoke. About his alleged arrogance and aloofness Fraser says 'I think it would be much worse if people said I was weak and inept. That would be a condemnation . . . I wouldn't like'.

It may be that Fraser's hide was never as thick as he pretended. He was often off sick and usually looked strained, his skin blotchy, a sign of the pressure he felt. (By contrast Whitlam bloomed like a baby and Hawke shines like a centrefold.) My emphasis, however, is not on Fraser's sensitivity to what others thought of him but on what he thought of himself. No one pressured Fraser-the-contesting-politician as much as Fraser-the-moralist did. There is a very revealing story he tells, the point of which is the need to restrain ambition:

I can remember a conversation I had with Sir William Slim. He was visiting a property in the Northern Territory which I was staying at. Well, he was Governor-General, I wasn't yet a member of parliament, although it was the interregnum between the two elections. And he was talking about how he got up to be Field Marshall, and how it was an enormous incentive on somebody who had been a private soldier to cease being a private soldier, and this was a spur on your tail. And started talking about politics. And I said, 'Well, you know, I can't imagine anyone wanting to go into politics if they thought people were' — I've forgotten the word that was used, um, but it meant people were unthinking individuals, that um didn't have independence and character of their own — and I was saying 'What's the point of politics unless you've got a certain view of people?'.

> And I can remember he just looked at me and, again not the precise words, said 'Well, you know, that's a fine view for you to have'. But to a lot of people who seek power it wouldn't make any difference what their view of people is, it's just what you have to do to gain power. If everyone was a zombie and everyone was a robot, what would be the point of trying to achieve something in that sort of society? It wouldn't be a society anyway, it would be some sort of mechanical structure . . . I don't know that that explains the point very well. Somewhere in there, there is a point.

Slim, with the candour of a self-assured and successful man, apparently explains the origins of ambition, and its aims, without frills. The young Fraser — though he is sensitive to his and Slim's relative standing — cannot take his meat so raw; his motives must be purer, his ideals higher. His will be a career in which the voice saying 'rule or be ruled' is counter-balanced by the voice of ideals. He will reassure himself that he, and his party, are for individuals, that it's the socialists who make men zombies, and that he, Fraser, can restrain and channel his individualist ambition in a way that ultimately benefits all men.

It is interesting that Fraser cannot quite locate his own point. The confusion became the storm-centre of Fraserism and the Fraser years, a grating contradiction between the promise of stability and the fact of raucous disorder which may have demoralized his own party as much as it enraged much of the Australian community. Even in this anecdotal recollection Fraser cannot integrate ambition (contest) and ideals (control), and he shows the depth of his fear of himself — his personal ambition turning everyone else into zombies — should the 'lower house' not be countermanded by the lofty 'upper house'.

CHILDHOOD AND FAMILY

On a television children's show during the 1983 campaign Malcolm Fraser, answering a child's question, smilingly told his favourite dream: his mother is riding in an Irish gig; the gig hits a stone and topples over, his mother is up-ended and thrown out; a young Malcolm is looking on, doubled up with laughter. At the launch of his biography in 1987 Fraser began his remarks with a story about his father's Delage, a car Neville Fraser imported in the twenties, which was so fast it could outrun the police. Later he sold it, and eventually it found its way into the hands of Squizzy Taylor, Australia's most notorious criminal, who wrecked and abandoned it in an abortive getaway. The police came to interview Fraser's father who, of course, had no difficulty proving his innocence. At the launch we were all amused — with Fraser — at the coincidence which linked a man of distinction with a man who was notorious.

These two stories are against the grain of the accepted version of Fraser's childhood which, besides accentuating the rigours of Australian country life and Scottish-Presbyterian severity, is built around the preponderance of a bond with his mother and the insignificance of his father. They suggest an ironic side to the man, and some acceptance, if at a safe distance, of seamy, colourful exploits that do not accord with his Easter Island grimness and insistence on proper behaviour. Apart from illustrating the split in him, they also redirect our attention from an image of mother as everything while father is unimpressive and untroubling, to a boy's resisting his 'correct' mother and taking fugitive pleasure in his father's almost improper vitality. As with Reagan, though there is a great deal to be learned from understanding Fraser's special link with his mother, there is also much to be learned from a less visible tie to his often absent, never properly successful, and apparently impulsive and colourful father.

Both biographers, Edwards and Ayres, fix on the amount of time Fraser spent alone with his mother. Una Fraser, thirteen years younger than Neville, gave birth to Lorraine in 1927 and Malcolm in 1930. A good deal of their life was spent in remote country and the young Malcolm, who had frequent health problems (particularly respiratory ailments), missed some school. He was late in going to boarding-school and when he reached secondary school age he reverted to being a day boy. Edwards and Ayres look to this boyhood loneliness to explain Fraser's later difficulties in establishing close personal relations and in conveying warmth to the electorate; and they consider it the source of his Strong Leader's ability to make difficult, unpopular decisions. To this special relationship with his mother they attribute Fraser's self-assurance. Of this self-assurance, both writers are very convinced: it explains Fraser's independence of action, his tolerance for not being liked, and so on. It derived from a home filled with 'affection and security' (Ayres), from parents who 'indulged their son' so that he could grow up 'gratifying in the idea of himself' that they had created, and from his isolation 'and the great gift of a secure childhood with deeply implanted values [which] sustained Fraser's confidence and direction in circumstances which would have rattled others' (Edwards).

It will be obvious from the rest of this profile of Fraser that where others see self-confidence I see internal division and chronic self-doubt, his contest side tending to desperate lunges, his 'philosophizing' and moralizing a straitjacket designed first for himself. Moreover the Fraser I see could not have come from the sort of secure and affectionate childhood in which the child is encouraged to think well of himself and to pursue his own tastes and interests; on the contrary. In my reading of it, Fraser's childhood experience, like that of Thatcher and Reagan, and like that of all Strong Leaders, was a good deal more fraught than the conventional view suggests. It was more about fear and division, about struggles against being controlled and feeling inferior, and struggling for a sense of self-worth and for the right to please himself.

Listening to Fraser one is introduced not to a family of country-kitchen warmth nor to a family of shared social and cultural interests, but to a family divided, restless and anxious. Ayres begins his biography with the three-and-a-half-year-old Malcolm watching the destruction of his celebrated grandfather's mansion, the family's most obvious claim to wealth and standing forced under the wrecker's hammer. Fraser told Ayres this was his earliest memory. He also claims to remember the terrible floods that cut off the family property in 1931. Even if he doesn't remember this, there is abundant evidence in both biographies that the young Malcolm was not spared the family's worries as they battled a terrible decade in their remote region. His letters home from boarding-school show him worrying about the prices his father will get for lambs and show him trying not to ask too much or be a burden. 'Sometimes his parents talked in his presence of how the property was draining their resources, so even as a small child Malcolm was aware of their worries and the threat of collapse', writes Ayres. The looming war was an additional threat, one his father, a veteran of the First World War and a desk recruit in the Second World War, was particularly attuned to:

> I think I didn't know enough of the detail. I was fourteen when the war ended . . . We were aware at some stages that there was a good deal of concern, or even fear, in the Australian community . . . the prospects were very real and many people thought that Australia might be invaded. I can vaguely remember conversations: where was the safest place to try and be, if we were.

Each morning he would get up and open the paper 'to see if the lines' (the allied lines) 'had gone forwards or back'.

The previous extract begins with his not knowing enough, with the child permitted to share the worries but not given the intellectual means to master them. (This is Strong Leadership's expectation that we, especially children, participate through our work, not through being part of the decision-making.) Fraser says 'Politics isn't something that we talked about at home very much', that 'neither of my parents tried to teach any particular philosophy of life or social attitudes'. So the following extract has great poignancy in its portrayal of a child set to worry but not offered the intellectual and communal means to control his anxieties. Note the last sentence:

> I was aware of the depression. People out of work and things being tough, and this was brought home at home with our own employees. We were in it as much as anywhere else. [What else?] Certainly aware of politics during the war. We had a German at home that used to listen to the broadcasts from Hitler in German. I tried to get him to explain what was happening. He never would. It's understandable why . . . But what was happening in Europe, what was happening during the war — my memories aren't bright but I had got to the stage of just about reading the newspapers I think . . . I suppose a lot of it was kept away from a kid of that age, but enough of it seeped through . . .

When an interviewer asked Fraser how he could say 'Life isn't meant to be easy' since he was so wealthy, and followed up with 'But money helps, doesn't it?', Fraser replied 'Does it?'. He might have said the same to anyone who thought him fortunate at boarding-school when (in the forties) he came and went by plane, had tea with the State Governor on outings to Sydney, saw his headmaster put up his father on a visit, and so on. He was fortunate to have a family that could send him to Tudor House to escape the feared invasion and the threat of a polio epidemic in Melbourne; fortunate in that, though Balpool (where they farmed) was remote, the family would usually spend three months of the year in Melbourne or Sydney and in society at seaside Portsea; fortunate in that though droughts and floods drained his resources, Neville Fraser could use the proceeds from selling Balpool for a property in the rich country of the Western District in Victoria. One could go on listing Fraser's advantages, including getting into Magdalen College at Oxford through his father's connections, the luxury of smart cars while still a young man. The fact remains, however, that his early memories are few and they are all gloomy. His childhood is an overcast land, painted in greys. There is no glamour and excitement, despite his parents' social connections. There are no enthusiasms or interests — cricket is talked about in his letters home from school, but agonizingly, as he struggled to make the team; he seemed more confident in shooting and cadets but, instead of warmth and security, the main feature is the young boy's worrying over matters he could not directly control or change.

Fraser's mother once remarked, 'he has always been wise beyond his years'. Wise or resigned? Speaking of his going to boarding-school, which his ill-health had delayed, Fraser says 'it would have been common then. It was not an unusual occurrence'. He then goes on to speak 'philosophically' about childhood:

> you know kids accept things probably much better than their parents understand. The war was on, there was no alternative, so you just had to accept it. I think with a lot of children there's a reasonable degree of fatalism — you know, what's going to happen happens, you can't really do very much about it. I would only have been nine when the war began, and not many children of eight or nine are masters of their own destiny or really can contribute enormously to . . . the sort of choices that might be available . . . The war was on, this was the way it was going to be, that was the way it had to be.

There is an implicit politics in the Fraser family glimpsed in these extracts. It is simply this: parents command and — if they do not flee the battle as Lorraine, Malcolm's older sister did — children obey.

This is true of all Strong Leader families. Authority is life's central, immutable truth and the Strong Leader's call to action and independence as well as law-and-order protection from the worst consequences of defeat, is fuelled by his impotence and humiliation in childhood. In these families there is limited scope for ideas, for fantasy, for creative alternatives; and achievement must not be undermined by too much 'molly-coddling' affection. The child has to be prepared for a hostile world, has to be trained, ideally to give orders but at any rate to do well for himself while conforming to the ruling social expectations.

The family that specializes in authority and achievement narrows the Strong Leader as much as it enables him or her, making it hard either to be creative or to establish co-operation. There are other features of the Fraser family which we have to go back to: in particular, division. I have mentioned the leader/led division between the parents and the children; there is also a hinted difference between father and mother. Una Fraser says 'My husband Neville had a very strong character. He was brought up in the Victorian era. He was very Victorian in his outlook on life, with the idea that children should be seen and not heard'. Elsewhere, she describes Neville — who was considerably older and spent a great deal of time away from their property, in the city — as 'a law unto himself'. Her daughter, Malcolm's older sister, says her father 'decided practically everything'.

If there is a hint of difference here it is not on 'basic values'. Mrs Fraser goes on, 'Both the children got their determination from him and their perseverance. I think half the battle is perseverance'. She speaks warmly of how hard Malcolm would work: 'He used to come in from school and sit straight down and do his homework; he wouldn't stop until he'd done it all'. The difference between Neville and Una is perhaps the pleasure she took in Malcolm, the wish to have him around her. Like her husband, Una Fraser wanted their son to succeed: 'when he was little I was afraid he was not a fighter . . . A disappointment would show in his face, but there was always an acceptance of a verdict'; but she also wanted his quiet companionship: he usually 'fell in happily with any arrangement at all', was 'a very easy child to live with and tremendously loving and affectionate'. A 'very good son', she recalls. He was 'perfectly happy and contented' to live among his family and the farming household.

The mother in families that shape Strong Leaders and their followers is inevitably involved in both push and pull. She must see that the authority of the patriarch, which is necessary for training the children to succeed, is not undermined; she believes in it herself. Yet it cannot be surprising that — especially if she is often alone — a son's company is desirable in itself. If they are to be close he must be biddable in addition to being a fighter, high-spirited and determined towards the world, 'loving and affectionate' towards her. This can be confusing for a child (be a fighter but do what you're told; go out and master the world but stay with me), a confusion that sends down deep roots until it can be considered ambivalence. Resentment burns alongside love for mother, achievement is desired but felt as a burden too. As well, an internal division of opinion about oneself becomes established: as too biddable; as unduly, selfishly, ambitious. There can be considerable strain in trying to combine these opposite attitudes, both in regard to mothers whose position is typically ambiguous, both unassailably good and owed everything and yet (for men) to be repudiated and left behind, and in regard to oneself.

Neville Fraser may have put his own strain on the boy. He was frequently absent but when he appeared he acted, if not autocratically, without carefully preparing the ground. Father, says Fraser, 'was away a good deal'. He does not criticize him for this. Instead he excuses him:

> After the war [1914–18] some different sort of, you know, quite a lot of people took a while to settle down. And then the depression hit, and for most people it was just a question of struggling to stay alive during the depression. And that ended with another war. So that . . . probably left its mark on my father.

Elsewhere, he speaks of his father's generation being made restless by the war, never quite able to take hold of their destinies. Ayres notes that Fraser for some years let stand a *Who's Who* entry that devoted considerably more space to his grandfather's achievements — which included membership of the first federal government — than to his father's. Edwards reports friends describing Neville Fraser as 'an able businessman and a pleasant fellow but not a powerful personality'. He was whimsical, short, and known as 'Pinocchio', 'an "easy going, busy little man"; "small irrascible . . . with a good sense of humour"'.

The suggestion is of a man not quite serious enough, nor present enough, for a full partnership in the rearing of his son. 'My mother', says Fraser, 'was a good deal more placid, calmer than my father . . . more philosophical . . . quieter' or 'less excitable than my father'. (In the same set of remarks he interpolates 'My father's dead, my mother isn't'.) Father did the disciplining — though 'my mother's influence would have been quite significant' — and it 'probably says something about him' that, though unavailable for small things, 'if things were important he was always there'. However, Neville Fraser was not rock-like. It is perhaps his 'excitability', and an illustration of how he would assume final authority (made a touch arbitrary by his absences), that Fraser referred to in his last election campaign. He told of being taught bushcraft as a boy by being rowed out across a flooded river to a snake-infested island, then left by his father to find his own way back.

Though never a rebel, and even now not complaining or judging, Fraser paints a picture of a man who combined Victorian strictness, long absences and sudden, demanding appearances with a more relaxed attitude to his own pleasures and duties, even while the family's circumstances deteriorated. There is no question that Malcolm Fraser ranks excitability — he saw it in Whitlam — well below his mother's placidity and the patrician calm and statesmanship he tried to embody in his political career and now propounds from the sidelines.

The Fraser childhood is hardly, then, the paradise of ease and high hopes Edwards and Ayres suggest. There was the push-and-pull of a very attached and determined mother, a loyal wife whose partner was often absent. (Una Fraser's admired father had run for parliament unsuccessfully when she was a child.) There was a father who could be very demanding but was not very attentive; a father whose worries 'seeped through' to his son; a father who nevertheless thought children should be seen but not heard; a father who could seem arbitrary, unimpressive and, in his own lack of sustained achievement, small encouragement to gaining a hopeful and self-confident view of the world.

There is yet a further burden, though it might have seemed pure benefit. This was the distinction drawn between Malcolm and his older sister, Lorraine. Mrs Fraser says Malcolm and Lorraine 'were very close to each other'. Lorraine was sent to boarding-school at the age of six; Malcolm went at eleven, and was at home again in his teenage years. Soon after graduating from Arts College Lorraine left for Europe, where she has lived ever since. The pattern of division we saw in the Roberts (Thatcher) family and in Reagan's, occurred in the Fraser family too. Neville's attitude is unknown, but certainly Una found Lorraine, three years Malcolm's senior, hard to understand. 'Malcolm was very easy to get along with as a child. Lorrie was more temperamental. I didn't realise then that she had an artistic temperament.' (A woman who had early theatrical interests could apparently miss this quality in her daughter.) Ayres reports Mrs Fraser's frustration over arranging some social occasions for her then college-age daughter — 'at least I tried. She's an artist and I was not allowing for the artistic temperament, which I should have done . . . She was so determined'. Malcolm was not sociable either but he is described as 'self-conscious . . . and desperately shy'.

Edwards writes that the Frasers 'indulged their son so lavishly that his older sister felt excluded from their affection. Where Malcolm grew up gratifying in the idea of himself his parents created, his sister rebelled early and permanently'. When Lorraine went to boarding-school the only consequence Edwards allows is that Malcolm was deprived of a companion. How comfortably could Malcolm 'gratify' himself in his parents' favour? Parents who give arbitrarily and pointedly can as easily take away, and to be favoured in this way is likely to be inhibiting as well as gratifying. We must add this to Fraser's childhood burdens: the worry that his 'specialness' was at another's expense, that his pleasures might be undeserved, illegitimate, and they could be removed at will. In a letter from school the small boy worries that he is asking 'too much' wanting a new bike while the war is on; he then says he's changed his mind and he'll refurbish the old bike, 'to make it fair for Lorrie'.

There is an insurmountable crisis of legitimacy in every Strong Leader's childhood, not because he has a uniquely powerful 'patricidal' impulse (the crisis of legitimacy affects followers too), but because the structure of the family encourages it. Families that accentuate difference — between parent and child, older and younger, boy and girl — induce conflict, failure to integrate and division, first between the participants then within each person. This is because the family demands achievement (without which love might be jeopardized) and expects obedience at the same time, driving disappointment and rage underground. Such a double demand — especially when the only escape is to solitude unimproved by creative activities — allows only rebellion, extreme submissiveness, or a tense combination of the two. The last permits achievement but narrows it, and exacts considerable emotional cost.

Tense, narrow, emotionally costly achievement appears to have been Fraser's solution. The uneasy balance of 'patrician and pugilist', of principle and pragmatism, of control and contest reflects a family — not in anyway 'abnormal' — which accentuated power, achievement leading to power of one's own, and a conventionality (rather than creativity) that made the question of the legitimacy of a child's own desires a loaded and difficult one. Fraser grew up knowing he should win, and yet win virtuously. Moreover, any space he had was restricted to the literal space of his family's properties and their travels from place to place. Psychological 'space' — such as a less attentive mother might have granted, and a more encouraging father; or that which derives from a family that masters its anxieties with spacious ideas and warm tolerance — was not so lavishly available. It was not solitariness that shaped Fraser's political career but, on the contrary, a crowded psyche which felt an urgency but could see very little room to move in the heavily 'politicized' but not political family he had to internalize.

Rather aptly, Ayres conveys the cost of a childhood too

fraught for play, as if Fraser had enough on his plate (or in his mind) without adding other people or complicated emotions and disturbing ideas. At his boarding-school, the eleven-year-old 'would not seek or give to those around him at the school much "warmth", but he would enjoy a full social role'. This exactly catches the kind of limited community — Fraser was 'successful in team games' and took 'a leading role in the Scouts' — that Strong Leaders and their followers can achieve in what I have called 'structure'. There are 'frequent references to friends' in his letters home. Here is one contemporary's view of Malcolm: 'I remember him as being serious and studious, very conventional and frowning upon those who may have appeared slightly eccentric, like myself'. This man was a loner too, but it appears that, in his case, being his own man led him to experiment, to find his own way to the point of seeming eccentric. Not so in Fraser's case, where keeping himself to himself implied, not freedom, but duty proudly pursued.

At his secondary school, Fraser was officially noted for angrily demanding why a club secretary had not done a better job, and for securing through his connections a private court for the tennis club to practise on. The headmaster described the chilling effects of a boy nicknamed 'Freezer': 'When I had him in my study, I felt as if I had to be on my best behaviour'. The 'super-ego', of course, begins in self-condemnation but it becomes an implicit censoriousness of others, carrying the weight of resentments stored up and ambitions nursed in secret. 'He was very different from his father, who was a natural extrovert', the headmaster went on.

Earlier, I spoke of Fraser's complaint that at Oxford student debates in the Union and epistemology both seemed childish and irresponsible, mere intellectual playgrounds unlike the serious, studious activities he was comfortable in. I have also written about Fraser's studies in the light of the claim that he was a political visionary, a 'philosopher'; his biographer admits that Fraser's youthful, university ideas turned out 'not particularly idiosyncratic or out of character with his background'. This tense, tight seriousness, maintained rather than undermined by conventional ways of letting off steam, is of a piece with the picture of his childhood we have been considering. Now I want to look briefly through two windows the young Malcolm opened on his childhood. These are a poem and a story.

A poem and a story

Both are published in full in Ayres's biography. The poem is called 'Those I have Loved' and was written when he was eleven. It speaks of a return to the bush — 'once more' — and is a catalogue of its pleasures, ending with 'Last of all, wind rustling through the tree tops, and swaying the branches in its arms'. In its fifteen lines the poem is virtually a delineation, as in early realist paintings, of what a country boy remembers and regrets, but this last line is genuinely pathetic. Much more so is the story. A boy dies, his parents depart his bedside 'leaving behind one who would never speak again, in our world'. 'A strange spirit' carries the boy away over 'a land no mortal eye had ever seen'. The spirit, his grip loosened by a 'devastating storm', lets the boy fall but as he does so, and to the sound of 'a mighty thunder-clap', a sparrow escapes from the boy's body. After a long journey and many dangers, the sparrow, 'as if led by an unseen hand', flies to the boy's house. 'Now each morning he wakes the household with his cheerful chirping'.

All children dream of escaping and flying above the storm and of turning troubling nights into sunny days. In Fraser's tale, the gloomy riddles of human life are escaped as the child throws down its arms, in death; when he returns he is no longer a troubled thirteen-year-old but an innocent creature doing good, not evil, to his father and mother. Bettelhein, in *The Uses of Enchantment*, links birds with the super-ego:

> Birds which fly high into the sky symbolize [a certain kind of] freedom — that of the soul to soar, to rise seemingly free from what binds us to our earthly existence . . . Birds stand for the superego, with its investment in high goals and ideals, its soaring flights of fancy and imagined perfection.

Both poem and story speak of stasis, of development aborted, even of a longing to go backwards to a mother's cradling arms, and sleep; to a time when in ostensibly innocent boyhood one's only wish was to lighten father's and mother's load if one could. The story's solution is the magical recovery of innocence through passivity to the point of self-sacrifice. All will be well again if the boy — who dies, presumably, because he is to blame — makes himself insentient, unsexual, totally unambitious, becoming once more a true and faithful son.

There is little that is remarkable, in either a literary or a psychological sense, in Fraser's youthful poem and story. They only confirm the 'normality' of his experience, the cry of the ego 'life is not easy', and are significant largely because others have suggested Fraser could not know the dangers and unease which, in politics, he so frequently invoked (and evoked). Moreover, his metaphysical gloom is only part of the story. There is also his contesting side, his ambition. I shall finish this chapter attending to this, the origins of Fraser's ambitiousness, his striving to be in charge, his 'pugilism'.

I can do this only with allegory. We haven't the data, nor perhaps an unfettered right, to 'psychologize' his intimate ties, and, moreover, the allegory is a venerable one. It comes from Plato who is pondering the relation between constitutions — types of society and politics — and character, or types of men. (Women are not considered as political actors or leaders.)

Constitutions and children

Plato describes how character and the constitution are linked through the kind of leaders a family cultivates. Against the benchmark of the 'best', or aristocratic, constitution, where leaders are philosopher-kings, Plato lists the inferior constitutions that are the consequence of leaders who 'beget children wrongly'. The first, midway between aristocracy and oligarchy, he calls *timocracy.* In this system people prefer, instead of wise, balanced leaders, i.e. the guardians, leaders who are 'spirited and more straight-forward men, made more for war than peace', who model their politics on 'military tricks and strategems'. These timocrat leaders are avaricious, on the side, but their dominant feature, 'which arises from the prevalence of the spirited element' (i.e. contest) is 'rivalry and ambition'. In their education 'compulsion and not persuasion has been used, and [as in almost any modern public school] reason and philosophy have been neglected for gymnastics' (or sports).

The *oligarchic* constitution, Plato's second deviant type, is one step further away from the politics of the common good. It is frankly materialistic, its main activity is commerce. Oligarchy 'rests on property valuation, where the rich rule'. Virtue is slighted, money is honoured above all else and in political leadership merit is put aside, even that based on the military model: 'He seemed to be a ruler but was nothing but a spender'. Oligarchic leadership is thus less about political competence and success in political competition, where there is at least some question of who is the better man, than about money and class. Happily, says Plato, pure oligarchy will not last because it neglects to nurture, educate or govern. It collapses under the weight of its preoccupation with the superficial and the short-run.

As always, the theories of the ancients have a contemporary ring. Since Malcolm Fraser was defeated in 1983 there has been a boom in 'entrepreneurialism' and the businessman has become a cultural hero. Fraser's own party, the Liberal Party, has become increasingly divided between 'wets' and 'dries', the latter making the running. Alongside, or intertwined with this conflict, has been a conflict between business heroes who back the Party, and the Party's political leadership. This conflict crystallized when a leading businessman, John Elliott, became president of the Party and immediately showed his discomfort in submitting to the political leader, the parliamentary wing, the politically shaped Party rules. Battles over pre-selection — should they be left to the party-political process or changed to allow businessmen and others quick entry into politics? — have reflected the same issue.

The timocrat is political, even if more self-interested and privately materialistic than the guardians. The oligarchic leader reduces politics to business, has no time for autonomous political aims and political skills independent of managerial skills and commercial criteria of success. Malcolm Fraser, re-entering political debate in Australia, takes the timocrat position against Howard, the Liberal leader, and against businessmen, who would use the Party for an extension of their predominantly commercial ends. This battle is not so much 'wet' vs. 'dry', or liberal vs. conservative, as a battle between politics and business, a battle between long-term allies over who will lead the other.

Our interest, however, is in the 'man corresponding to the constitution', and in his development. The leading characteristic of the timocrat is that he is 'emulous', rivalrous. He is also hard (proud of his taste for 'the hard decisions'?), and less musical (or harmonious) and less of an orator (less uplifting?) than the guardian. In line with structure and Strong Leadership's emphasis on hierarchy in social life, he is tough on inferiors (Plato speaks of slaves), and only civil to, rather than intimate with, equals, while towards superiors he is zealously obedient. He is also combative. Others (like Hawke) may want to be honoured for their skills at reconciling warring factions, but the timocrat leader 'Loving rule and honour . . . will claim [honour] . . . for warlike deeds and warrior qualities'. Others (like Whitlam) may delight in displaying their wit, culture or aesthetic sense but the timocrat leader is 'a lover of gymnastics and hunting' — or football, shooting and fast cars.

How is he raised? The timocrat, says Plato, 'arises in some such way as this': there is a good father who is rather too good, too uncompetitive, for the political world he lives in. He is a man 'content to be got the better of if only he is not bothered'. Then, and this is crucial, the son hears unfavourable interpretations of his father's reasonableness: he learns from servants, from men of the world, and above all from his mother that his father is a weak man.

> He hears his mother complaining that her husband is not one of the rulers, and that in consequence other women are set above her. Then she sees that her husband does not trouble himself about money, and does not fight and wrangle in lawsuits or in the assembly . . . and she perceives that he is always attending to himself, treating her neither with marked reverence nor marked disrespect. All these things make her angry and she tells her son that his father is unmanly and utterly casual and treats him to all the many varied complaints which women love to make on such matters.

As a result the son grows up pulled in two ways. 'His father waters and makes to grow the reasoning element in his soul, while the others nourish the desiring and spirited elements'. He becomes 'contentious and spirited'. He also becomes divided: 'a lofty-minded ambitious man'.

Before we reflect on this theory of the timocrat's development, we must look at the oligarchic leaders. A father's failure (as it seems to the son) is again the pivot. At first the boy is 'zealous for his father and follows in his footsteps' but then he sees him financially reduced, which leads to loss of standing in the community. His father then abandons higher, political, aims and turns 'greedily to money-making'. The son then rejects idealism too, the larger view, and learns how to appear hard-working and socially concerned while he nurtures his self-interest. Self-sufficiency is all he cares about. He is, it is true, self-constraining, which is 'virtuous after a fashion', but this has a hidden motive and is not an authentic, chosen value; on the contrary, the oligarch holds himself back because of 'necessity and fear'. He is afraid to lose what he has already, as his father did. The upshot is that he is restless and divided: 'he would not be one man but two'. Nevertheless such a man would, by self-constraint, 'be more respectable than many men, but the true virtue of a simple and harmonious life would be far beyond him.'

In Plato's portraits of timocrat and oligarch, the outstanding feature is a personality divided, and a constitution threatened as a result. As to Plato's theory of what makes the humanly ordinary leaders what they are (their childhood), we must first distance ourselves from the psychological equivalent of *cherchez la femme* common in our time, *cherchez la mère*. The essential point is a father not used, or not available for use, or not willing to be used as the main enabling model. This leaves the son to a special relationship with his mother — but one that is not only stimulating but dangerous. It is dangerous because it provokes in the son a sort of hubris, on the one hand, and on the other a continuing doubt about his legitimacy. Fathers who are away frequently and then quick to reassert their authority when they return, must provoke in the boy a self-estimate that swings from feeling very special indeed, with great prospects, and feeling suddenly dumped, humiliated, of small account. This is all the worse when father is neither successful nor naturally impressive, i.e. when, in Plato's terms, the father fails economically or politically.

Now it appears true, from hints Fraser gives himself about his father's 'excitability' and his mother's 'placidity', from comments quoted in Edwards by Neville Fraser's acquaintances, and from the seemingly reliable evidence that Fraser's father was often not present and that his financial success was only indifferent, that there are parallels between Plato's character types and Fraser's experience of growing up. However, to Plato we must add Freud. Plato's is an external, objective explanation, making personality rest on a boy being forced to choose between his parents, on a real division between them. Since Freud we give more weight to the subjective in a child's experience, and to what is virtually inevitable even if exacerbated in Strong Leader's families, that is the Oedipus complex.

From Plato to Freud

It seems virtually universal that a boy will depreciate, internally at least, his father and idealize his mother. Any ambivalence towards her is buried deep while coolness towards a father misleads us into thinking that fathers are dispensable, neither particularly admirable and desired nor a serious hindrance to the boy's ambitions. However, as we saw in Ronald Reagan's case, it is fruitful to restore even apparently inconsequential fathers, social or objective 'failures', to their full status in their son's childhood eyes — which means to being ambivalently desired and competed with. It is glib to explain anything by Neville Fraser's alleged shortcomings without first allowing for the small boy's view of the man who, from the boy's earliest awareness, seems to command mother and the world. Subjectively, fathers begin powerful and are both desirable (as helpers) and troubling as rivals. In other words, though not ignoring the particulars of a family, and holding to the view that there are families that make for Strong Leaders and followers by narrowly and emphatically focusing on desire and rivalry, we must take account of the fact that the same story is repeated over and over: an unimpressive father, a wonderful mother. Hence, against Plato's emphasis on a shrewish wife, and loosening the tie to specific observations common to the families that make for Strong Leaders, we must weigh the willed misperception of the disposition of family forces and values common to all children.

The young Malcolm, the humanly ambivalent Fraser, was formed essentially in the opportunity afforded him by his mother's special interest in him — which stimulated his ambition — combined with her insistence that he please her with his obedience and virtue — which fuelled the moral pressures with which he restrains himself (and would restrain us). The space for this special relationship was the outcome of Neville's attitudes and behaviour: his comparative absence, his flickering example, and his sudden, perhaps ominous reappearances and insistence on his authority. The last factor, the authority who might at any time return and interfere, is the root of the fatalism that runs through Fraser's view of the world. In addition, if the 'third party' in the Oedipal drama continues to live on, the son's legitimacy remains continually in doubt in his own mind.

Unfortunately, I cannot say much about the side of Malcolm Fraser that reflects a boy's love for his father. An indirect way of expressing rivalry with father is to admire *his* father, as in Fraser's *Who's Who* entry on Sir Simon. Though that can be considered a criticism, it can also be the opposite, a way of linking up with father. Fraser has tried to be an attentive father himself. Again this can be a rebuke to his own father but also a sign of what, as a boy, he hoped for. He has shown an inclination to appeal to higher authority (like Governor-Generals) expecting or demanding assistance and he has shown both great respect for, as well as calculating insight into, men in this position. Finally, I've suggested that there is a larrikin streak in Fraser. It shows in practical jokes, escapades (most publicly in Memphis, Tennesee, where he had his trousers stolen from his room in a surprisingly ordinary hotel), sports cars and powerful bikes, and (as I mentioned at the beginning of this section) some pleasure in the shadier side of his father's past. I have always been intrigued by Fraser's choice in the debate over the national anthem. He wanted 'Waltzing Mathilda', a song which is as decently far from the pompous 'Advance Australia Fair' as it is possible to get, and a song in which a sheep-stealer outwits a rich squatter. Son defeats father. Yet, in its good humour, it is not just pulling father down; it is a triumph all men can enjoy, the colourful fathers as well as their usually obedient, restrained sons, where the figure of authority could stand for mother.

Still, this is the minor theme. Being good and being successful weigh heavily on Fraser. In Strong Leadership's form of life and society, where recreation is either a rerun of the main tasks (sport is the leading example) or a catharsis that gets rid of rebellious feelings as if they were waste products, the 'humanity' of the Strong Leader is not in his or her capacity for intermittent boisterousness. It lies rather in the ambivalence that has driven them to an ideology of exactly the opposite — an ideology of 'unambivalence' that depends on the illusion that good and evil are distinct, that there are good men and bad ones, that they can be dealt with externally by structures and processes that are unambiguous, unreflectingly technological, and controllable by people who can maintain a constant and undivided will. This is the crippling demand Strong Leaders put on themselves — to be inhumanly distant from their own complexity. Enemies do not believe they can do it. Supporters are desperate to believe that they can.

14
Conclusion — The Myth of Balance

At the election count in March 1983 Fraser conceded defeat to Hawke's Labor and announced his retirement from the Liberal Party leadership and from parliament. He left parliament, he said, so that the new bloke 'wouldn't have Fraser breathing down his neck'. For a time it almost seemed he was happy to be back farming and going fishing. He reappeared on the margins of politics, first in letters to the editor, then as an occasional columnist, the latter more often as he saw economic events providing 'unmistakable similarities between today's circumstances and the years leading to 1929'. His columns typically carry warnings of this kind, and carry the suggestion that they are the views of a man who is still an 'insider' but free to pass on what he has been told ('On my last visit to the United States . . .'). Two other roles stand out in Fraser's activities since he left office: in one he is still the controversial, disruptive, 'political' figure he was in office; in the other he is a statesman interested in writing and being chairman of the organizational wing of the Party, an international eminence who could play a key role in easing tensions in South Africa. Some years after his retirement, Malcolm Fraser still divides himself between the roles of pugilist and patrician.

In July 1987 Fraser gave a memorial lecture which he

subtitled 'In Search of Balance'. He ought, perhaps, to have directed the lecture more at himself, though space does not permit me to show how awkward Fraser's grip on the idea of balance is. He uses the Liberal Party's legendary leader of the past, Menzies, as a stick with which to beat the present leadership and to scold the Party for its move to the right. Yet all he can offer is an impossible combination of 'on the one hand', and 'on the other', a hopping from foot to foot that bears little resemblance to the trapeze artist's poise. Fraser even attempts to find common ground between the Irish-Catholic Archbishop Mannix (after whom the lecture is named), who had fought off conscription in the First World War, and his own Scottish Orangemen forefathers.

Fraser was active at this time in stirring the pot of Liberal factionalism in the name of 'breadth' and 'balance'. 'Balance' he defines, idiosyncratically, as 'strength and a sense of direction and purpose'. Balance is not ecological or egalitarian: a party pursuing balance will be one that gives 'full loyalty' to its leader, in which 'habitual dissidents' are dealt with forthrightly, even if that requires changes to the Party's constitution. The tendency is to centralize, finally placing power in the hands of the leader, whose party is his well-maintained tool. The Liberal Party must appeal over the heads of 'powerful pressure groups' to 'the Forgotten People' (a famous image used by Menzies), the 'great majority in Australia', because interest groups 'do not seek balanced policies . . . A rounded, balanced set of policies supported by an organization loyal to itself and loyal to its leadership is needed . . . As the leadership comes more and more to demonstrate that it sees the way ahead, then other problems will start to fall by the wayside.'

At this time Fraser was embarrassing his Party, drawing from Howard, a former protégé and present Liberal Leader, angry advice to 'butt out'. (Even Fraser's official biography does not leave current issues alone. The author 'restores' Fraser's small-government reputation by trying to destroy Howard's.) The exasperating irony for Fraser's opponents is in his ideas themselves. Balance turns out to mean putting a man like himself in charge, obsessively attending to every possible threat of disorder or disunity by locking in support and pushing out opposition; balance in fact equals Strong

Leadership and hierarchical discipline, exactly the Fraser recipe in 1974. Moreover, Fraser the ultra-contestant is here recommending the methods of Fraser the arch-controller. The extracts quoted in the previous paragraph show the Strong Leader attempting to moderate and counsel while showing himself unrepentant, unimproved and still divisive. He still confuses balance subtly 'there' in human affairs with a constructed 'unity' under a leader like himself, which is suffocating and builds resentment. It is no wonder he has come out against 'too much reliance on market forces' — in a pure form they would do away with the need for a Strong Leader.

In South Africa, Fraser had the opportunity to establish some conditions on which others could begin negotiating. His commitment to stamping out racialism anywhere is well established and it was widely appreciated that the forces against him and the other Eminent Persons, Britain and the United States, were immense. He has rightly gained stature and respect for his work towards ending apartheid, however disappointing the results. Ayres (Fraser's biographer) ends his book with an eloquent account of Fraser's efforts, giving a diary-like account of Fraser's whirlwind visits to unexpected places, his meetings with Mandela (whom Fraser speaks of admiringly), his patient attempts to deal with representatives of the South African government. It is a heart-warming account of the man and it shows a Strong Leader at his best: tough, demanding, persistent, patient where necessary, impatient if need be, physically energetic. 'What used to be perceived in Australia as Fraser's aloofness and arrogance came across in South Africa as natural authority' writes Ayres. Fraser's calm belligerence stood the Eminent Persons Group 'in good stead'. Confronted by obstructive whites, 'Fraser reduced them to deference'.

In a newspaper article, but not in the biography, Ayres adds 'Crisis and confrontation were everywhere here and, in dealing with them, [Fraser] was in his element'. As with other types of leaders, Strong Leaders have their time and their place, their 'finest hour' and their 'supreme task', when what is best in their leadership meets its occasion. For Strong Leadership, this is likely to be when the issues verge on being physical, are morally clear cut and give room for acting heroically so that, for a moment at least, it seems true that evil can be defeated, and by one person's resolve.

Balance nevertheless escapes Fraser. In his new Elder Statesman role he preaches to his domestic allies an impossible balance which consists in obsessive calculation followed by monolithic leadership and discipline, and he does so by unbalancing the political debate. On South Africa, his achievements depend on being unbalanced: the sense of potency he conveys is due to his being on the side of absolute virtue. Taken together, contradiction — now balance, now unbalance — is the way to political success. Fraser remains divided.

CONCLUSION

15
Political Criticism — Judging Leaders

In the profession of political science, the political leader is a shadowy figure beside the parliament or congress, the party and the electoral process, which in terms of numbers can claim to be the main focuses of interest. I have a preference for the term 'political criticism' instead of political science. It may be that political science is progressing step by step, apparently as some 'real' sciences do, to exposing the laws of society, but I am not sure; 'political scientist' is a term useful for telling people what one's job is, that one is not a politician, and 'science' in the broadest sense means knowledge openly pursued. However, here is A. F. Davies on the literary or political critic:

> His fundamental purpose is to build for the practitioners [authors, politicians] a body of living, discerning response . . . He sets out to show us what to attend to — and how; he selects the admirable, and explains why it is admirable. He relates past and present, preserving a continuity, or re-creating one where it has been broken. He relates a cultural present to other cultures . . . [but] commitment is first to the national literature [or politics] . . . And judging *contemporary* productions is a special responsibility of criticism — this is where the public is most engaged . . .

Political criticism is less likely than modern political science to shoulder aside the psychology of politics. For one thing, like literary criticism and the reviewing of films, plays and television, like sports writing above all, political criticism will care for politics and respect it. That is not to say that the judgements need to be kind; politics, like any good-enough literary text, is resilient to criticism (interference, like censorship and military coups, is another matter), and our problem is rather how to have an intellectual impact at all. Judging leaders is a particularly delicate task. It still puzzles me how political men and women handle criticisms that lay siege to their whole outlook and *raison d'être* and my approach to studying political leadership is in contrast with other approaches which see leadership as a 'function' detachable from personalities and whole lives, so it could be in danger of being offensively personal, judging where there is no right to judge because the insight into politics is small or non-existent. Freud warned against 'wild' psychoanalyzing — though, when it came to political leadership, Woodrow Wilson and the League, he seems to have ignored his own strictures.

The critic's job is not only to make us more discerning but to ensure a 'living response'. In other words, if the critic sees politics as an empty machine, a complex of fixed norms comprising our political culture, of institutions, ideologies and legally expressed policies, how are citizens to see it any differently? These, of course, are not the whole story: on the contrary, I see them as a kind of shorthand, a diagram for understanding the human arrangement of human arrangements, which is politics. Without attending to 'the human element', political science would be a profession for mechanics whereas I would want to see its teachers, with journalists, penetrate the political 'system' and the obviously 'political' issues of the day to show the human actions and passions behind them, linking the politics of 'up there' to the familiar difficulties and dramas of ordinary experience. Political psychology helps in this, particularly where, as in psychoanalysis, the psychology used is hospitable to drama, irony, fantasy and feeling.

Politics, though it may not be the ultimate in human achievement, fascinates because it is the place where things come to a head. It is a sort of drain or sump to which the tensions and defeats of social life finally flow. Of course, political leaders must be held to the highest standards, but we need not let the pettiness and farce, even the childishness, of public life surprise us. Politics takes on what the rest of us give up on, or are making a mess of; it is where the buck rests and the bun fight begins. Political leaders, for their sins, are right there in the middle.

Political psychology, mistakenly I believe, is confined by many to the role of psychiatric fireman, something called on to explain outbreaks of irrationality in political life. Certainly it has the intellectual tools for this, but I hold the view that rational and irrational are not so distinct and that the important job for political psychology is to trace the interplay between these, to chart the convoluted path from child to adult, adult to group, group to institution and culture and the veering back and forth.

The three profiles are an attempt to capture this; their length is both necessary and insufficient. They are a blend of theorizing — the Strong Leader as a type is always aimed at, a framework for understanding the fragmentary data of a life is always in mind — and story-telling, a dual approach to the singularity of the individuals concerned and the patternings we all contend with.

Notice in particular how the Oedipal promptuary informs the stories. It holds that the triangular drama of desire and rivalry in the family is a critical determinant of the Strong Leader's character and politics. Our three leaders (all of them the younger of two children) establish a special relationship with the opposite-sex parent, and at the same time, make an enemy of the other. With what results? A spur to ambition, because they achieve favour and believe themselves something special. A twist towards aggressiveness, wariness, competitive individualism, because their gain in the politics of the family was at others' expense (or so it seems to them). Above all, they created an enemy who might at any time challenge their legitimacy, so they must keep up their guard. Finally, there is a pattern, a way of working in life and politics, as consort; as Boy Scout and fantasist; as moralist-cum-upstart. In the whole tenor of their Strong Leadership, Thatcher, Reagan and Fraser are refining a response to a world they constructed in childhood, a world of sharp desires and rivalries, of coups and feared countercoups, of choice and division.

At the same time, we must see that they avoided being tamed, dutiful, content to follow. The Oedipal promptuary cannot prescribe for human life, as political psychology cannot legislate for politics. It only indicates what has been passed through, the response a child shaped, how the adult continues to play variations on that original theme. With those observations, of course, comes the possibility of criticism which will point to the strengths and weaknesses, the range of application and its limits, the truths and distortions the individual or the type, Strong Leader, brings to adult politics.

This means that the study of character or personality has an important place in political criticism. Not the 'odd' or 'irrational' characters (though those exist and need study too) but the whole range of character types that inhabit politics and, for good or ill, shape many lives according to their lights. Perhaps the most general political lesson of the three profiles is that leaders come in largely sealed units. We hope they will learn, and perhaps they do, extending their personal boundaries to encompass ideas and sympathies their character routinely screens out or misperceives. However, personal histories and the personality structure they construct appear to have a tight grip; in fact, leaders are chosen and supported for the very reason that their 'prejudices' are also their strengths. As a commentary on this, there is the leader who tries to be everything at once, all things to all men and up with every changing mood. Australians have experienced something of this since 1983: in his first few years as Prime Minister, elected as a man whose speciality was being at home with all the parties to the political debate and a man for all seasons, Bob Hawke later appeared to many to lack roots, to be thought of as shallow, hollow and, increasingly fatefully, without vision.

The character of the Strong Leader is not a new one. To a large extent, what I have done in this book is to continue the critique of modern society that focuses on 'alienation'. Freud's sociological and political significance was to show the tyranny of the 'super-ego' over the rational, constructive 'ego', a tyranny not suspected by moralists and psychologists who thought only of the opposition between reason and passion. The individual, Freud argued, is set against himself, within himself, since the 'super-ego' is other people, taboo, society installed in a psychological upper house with wide powers of veto. In part, then, all I have done is to remind us of this fundamental insight — at a time when the fashion for Strong Leadership is likely to install a new psychological Dark Age.

The entailments I spoke of in Chapter 1 (what goes with Strong Leadership) can be summarized as follows. In return for action, greatness, personal reward, a feeling of purpose and meaning, citizens are asked to join the Strong Leader's team. ('Team spirit' is again extolled, in tandem with leadership itself.) Behind the look of practicality and simple materialism lies a myth, and the myth — a not uninspiring or useless one in certain limited circumstances — is that we come alive when we turn our backs on complexity, including the complexity of ourselves, and face forward as in the forties song:

> Accentuate the positive
> Eliminate the negative
> Latch on to the affirmative
> And don't mix with Mr In-Between

There appears always to have been those who 'externalize' — projecting their internal dilemmas and conflicts outwards so that they seem realities of the world and should be handled there — and those who 'internalize', taking the problems of the world to be merely the reflected troubles of the psyche. Both tendencies are part of the human experience, but the first seems to make for more enthusiastic and determined, if not 'nicer' politics. Complexity, a loose description of ambivalence, suggests that our motives are mixed and, as is clear to Strong Leadership which favours externalizing, this slows us up; it is better for action if we treat the rival as evil and unworthy and ourselves as completely pure and wholly deserving.

Typically, the writer, professing the inner world, points the other way. Goethe wrote:

> For every man who has not wit
> To rule his inner self will be most apt to rule
> His neighbour's will, according to his own proud
> whim.

In political criticism, though, one has more respect for the man or woman whose genius is for 'getting things done' — for acting 'as if' the problems are external, objective and will yield to determined action. Nevertheless, we cannot lose sight of Strong Leadership's compulsive bias in that direction, a bias that is rooted in a character-type built around externalizing and a panicky flight from the negative and the indeterminacy of 'Mr In-Between'.

There are other important entailments. The latest outbreak of Strong Leadership brings with it a curiously double-visioned attitude to guilt. For the most buccaneering of the new Strong Leaders (mostly in business, I think, where the realities of broad social responsibility have not been understood and sporting contests, where responsibility is one-sided, are taken as the analogue of social life) guilt is to be dispensed with. Guilt, a sense of responsibility for the suffering and evils of the world, only handicaps enterprise and paralyzes action. Both Thatcher and Reagan say this explicitly. On the other hand, others, like the half-patrician Fraser, want more guilt. These morally conservative Strong Leaders emphasize control more than contest, a 'sense of responsibility', the structure within which enterprise should operate. Either way, what I am calling (for simplicity) the 'ego' — roughly speaking the humanist ideal of an unafraid, rational but feeling and constructive individual — is slighted. From the one side, it is assaulted by an impulsive, unreflecting amoralism to the market while, from the other, it is constrained by returning taboos, fear, and self-distrust. Not surprisingly, the era of Strong Leadership is also an era of revived religiosity, including a return (for example, in regard to assisting conception and death) to attacks on science.

Entailed in Strong Leadership, too, is restoring the male to a superior position. There is evidence everywhere that sexual differentiation is not now the embarrassment it was ten or fifteen years ago, and there is some good in this. But Strong Leadership never differentiates without ranking; any 'split' it makes (to use a psychological term) is invidious, and ultimately political, derived as it is from Strong Leadership's traumatic reading of the mother/child separation, and the divide-and-rule experience of the Oedipal conflict. To be separate and different is to be unequal, and there can be no doubting, though some feminist or women's gains will persist, who is in charge of whom.

Moreover, and here we come closer to what is conventionally a political matter, the Strong Leadership era marks the emphatic return of inequality. 'Excellence' is the nice word for a fundamental redrafting of the political consensus established about 1945 in Britain, Australia and even (thinking of Truman, Kennedy and Johnson) in the USA. I don't know if there is anything more important about Strong Leadership than this — a model of society, of human existence, derived from the Strong Leader's conviction that unless there is command nothing will happen, all will be drift and eventual collapse. Unless they are in command, they will be enslaved, or inferior at least. This is a more fundamental meaning of 'self-interest' than mere money-grabbing. It implies a life lived under the signs of fear, pride and contempt: only clear winners are worth anything, only they escape humiliation, only they are safe. I would not want to minimize the seriousness with which money is pursued in our day; I would put the emphasis, though, on Strong Leadership's search for advantage over other people its life of crisis-management in which not to be number 1 is to be condemned to lifelong anxiety. The message Strong Leadership gives about character is this: gratitude is dangerous, luck comes to the prepared, what you are is what you can claim for yourself. In this view of human experience there can be very little room for social justice and welfare politics, for the long haul of equalizing opportunities, for the practice and furtherance of friendly co-operation.

I have wondered what single observation of the lives of our three Strong Leaders sums them up best. Oddly enough, I found the clue in in the fact that not one of them has known what profound friendship is. There is much that is invigorating in the Strong Leadership myth but, finally, it is hard to overlook our Strong Leaders' failure of nerve when it comes to exposing themselves to equal, self-communicating relationships. Ultimately, the anti-democratic, or sub-democratic, character of Strong Leadership reflects the failure of a Thatcher, a Reagan or a Fraser to attempt to define themselves in tandem with other men and women, beyond the confines of their familiar class, their country. They remain tribal and familial, Capulets or Montagues, little Liberals or little Conservatives. Admittedly, given the mood of the times, and if I were advising a political leader, I would suggest a large dose of tribalism, of stressing that, in the crunch, the leader show him- or herself 'one of us'. 'Tribalism-plus', however, would have to be the longer-term goal: not on Esperanto-style universalism, but a recognition that, though we love and respect 'our own', others are more like us than unlike and that the attempt to cultivate empathy (the approach to the stranger) is leadership's noblest task.

Thatcher, Reagan, Fraser — not one of them defined themselves in the sort of friendship Aristotle defined as the essential foundation of good politics: the communion of alter egos. Nye Bevan, long before they were formulated, lived Erik Erikson's prescriptions for establishing a self (or 'identity') over and above one's tribal roots and social role as he walked the mountains of Wales as a young man, reading, talking, debating with a friend, and he continued defining and detailing his views, and himself, in the company of friends throughout his life. Not our Strong Leaders. Of course, I imagine they had friends, but these were friends in the sense of neighbours, colleagues, helpers in times of trouble; and they certainly had supporters, assistants, comrades-in-arms. These are friendships which reproduce the life of a child in the family — challenging to do well, protective, supportive, helping to revive and reroute the man or woman temporarily disabled or discouraged in the pursuit of their own people's expectations. The friendship Aristotle and others speak of is post-family. It is, above all, self-defining and the parties to it are equal. Families and many friendly relations are modelled on family relationships, are essentially unequal, however warm and helpful. Our Strong Leaders never ventured beyond these, were never brave enough or lucky enough to experience the unstructured, equal relations that are the essence of friendship. All three — Thatcher and Reagan in their lower-middle-class pretensions, Fraser in his rural and apparently social isolation — had their eyes fixed on the road ahead, the ladder stretching upwards, and on fitting in with the expectations of their own familiar world, which they would come to defend and preach as the right and proper world for us all.

Freud taught us to cultivate our eye for childhood's 'local' politics as they are entangled in adult affairs. Certainly our profiles show the influence of 'the politics of the family' in the lives of our three leaders, and to this we can add a further entailment of Strong Leadership: the return of the patriarchal family. Religion and the 'super-ego', guilt and inequality, a social order stripped down to contest and control, require a structure that prepares for and sustains this kind of world. The 'family' Strong Leadership protects and advances is one ruled over by a domestic Strong Leader; it is conscience-strengthening, clearly unequal and aimed at individual achievement that remains conventional. Strong Leadership, in other words, makes Freud's warning — to look out for childhood enmities and loves, its rigidities, in ostensibly grown-up life — more apt than it might always be. While claiming to be rational, practical, independent, 'positive' and forward-looking, Strong Leaders pull us away from equal, loosely co-operative, thoughtful relations with one another as adults to soap-opera dramas whose hyper-intensity is drawn from childhood and the last-ditch structures set up to restrain it. The ostensibly realist and materialist Strong Leaders, oddly enough, reinforce Freud's mythic scepticism about the adulthood of politics and the extent of political rationality.

Irony becomes palpable when we consider the absence of family life in our three leaders' lives, though Fraser is a partial exception. Where are the children, and their children? Where are the grandparents, uncles, aunts and cousins? I think there is more to this absence than convenience and the protection of privacy. Thatcher and Reagan give the impression that once the Leader was 'grown up', family was irrelevant; and family life, with their own children, appears as a distraction, a way the ambitious might lose torque. In Fraser's case, he frequently makes much of owing the success of their family life, the growth of their children, to Mrs Fraser. He is also reported to have kept in continual, close contact with his mother. However, all in all, our Strong Leaders invite scepticism about the nurturing benefits of family life: they are exemplars, in fact, of those whose ambitions have allowed little room for the intermixing of selves in families, as they are inept in equal, direct relations anywhere else.

Such contradictions are of the essence of Strong Leadership, whose programme of enterprise and order rests on unacknowledged ambivalence. Moreover, the doctrine of inequality can be wheeled in when the contradiction becomes too obvious. Reagan's administration may turn out to have been one of the most unsavoury this century, but always there is the excuse that heroes, leaders, the 'strong', have licence while the rest keep good order. Mrs Thatcher's Cecil Parkinson, entrepreneur extraordinaire and flagrant in his abuse of the family ethic, had to be stood down for a time as an example to the troops, but it was not long before he was back in a senior Cabinet post. Morality in Strong Leadership is 'realistic' in the sense that it is always political even internally or psychologically: the individual accepts the dividedness, speak with the voice of 'ought' and 'should' but then gets away with what he or she can, suffers remorse when necessary and cultivates a sharp tongue and a swift boot for those who, trying to integrate their warring selves and to understand their ambivalence, are neither so high-minded nor so expedient as the 'strong'.

For me, these are the unacceptable aspects of Strong Leadership. It is a politics of moralizing and expediency in a push/pull alternation that must eventually lead to cynicism. It entails turning our backs on the arduous task of knowing ourselves and other people, calling on us to 'externalize' or 'project'. It entails a divided existence where each initiative must be matched by heightened guilt; it entails a 'political' view of other people — they are competitors or rivals, superiors or inferiors, never just friends and companions. It entails a kind of piety towards convention, a lim itation on thought and hope, and an attitude that locates meaning and purpose outside and above the human community itself. This last encourages us to imagine ourselves only as deserving or not, never fortunate, or a product, in part, of other people's concern and interest. It breeds the ultimate hubris of Strong Leadership's form of individualism: the belief that, like God, we have a separate platform from which to judge our fellows.

One cannot write a book of this kind without feeling the pressure of the questions: have they succeeded, were they right, is Strong Leadership working? However, I cannot answer directly. Leadership is embedded in politics (this is as true of Group Leadership and Inspiring Leadership) which makes independent assessment in the McKinsey management style, impossible.

There are empirical difficulties too. To take Thatcherism as an example: almost a decade has passed and there have been many strong statements about its results, but commentators who try to do a broad summing up find the task beyond them. In fact, though they begin in a brisk, cost-benefit manner, they are soon speaking of something far less precise, a 'new mood', a 'change of attitude' in Britain, and they turn to analyzing Thatcherism as a philosophy and a way of life. There are figures, of course, on the rising pound, rising self-employment and home ownership, and these can be interpreted as milestones on the road to Strong Leadership's desired society. Yet how are they to be weighed against the pull of contrary forces (politics is surely more like a tug of war than a journey)? There are complaints that Thatcherism's pursuit of productivity has divided and atomized British society; Mrs Thatcher may be right that class barriers are down, but a once tolerant and seemly Britain may now be uncomfortably shrewd and go-getting. There are complaints that talent and initiative in the arts, the crafts, in teaching and social work, have been discouraged, that the only risk-taking wanted is the business kind. There have even been highly-placed reactions to Thatcherism's use of the courts in the cause of official secrecy that suggest a loss of freedom.

All these are the sort of judgements of Strong Leadership that will be made whether there is sufficient evidence or not. Group Leadership favours welfare and sees Mrs Thatcher's reforms to the National Health Service as the usual Strong Leader's attack. Inspiring Leadership, favouring social diversity and ideas, will predictably complain of conventionalism and resent the favour shown entrepreneurs. (David Hockney's letter from Los Angeles accusing Thatcherism of making a dull Britain and being a threat to tolerance of homosexuals is a little weakened by his admission that governments previous to hers were as bad.) The problem is how to measure the important things and how to compare and balance them. What value is there in Britain's regained self-esteem? Is it widespread? Is self-esteem the old patriotism or something more? Are the universities more alive now than before the Thatcher 'assault'? In some intellectual fields or in all? The union movement, modernizing fast, could be said to have been woken from a long and costly doze. Is there more freedom in Britain, or less, or a redistribution? Has there been a fall in compassion, or is Strong Leadership right to suspect the Nanny state of mostly attitudinizing?

I incline to the view that, just as Strong Leaders are only able to be what they are, only able to operate within the limits set by their upbringing and personality, so there are political moods or 'climates' within which some things are easier to do because the wind, as it were, is favourable, while other things are harder. I am definitely not suggesting Strong Leaders, or any other type of leader, should be given their head, that opposition should cease. Nor that there is an automatic, 'lazy susan' mechanism that brings round without effort a periodic difference in political emphasis. On the contrary, just because one emphasis is dominant, its opponents should work harder to limit its excesses and prepare the ground for their own return to influence.

The job of political criticism — necessarily a bit out of date and more abstract than the work of politicians themselves and the media's political commentators — starts with reinterpreting the best-foot-forward themes of those who are setting the mood. It locates the 'sub-text', the entailments as I have called them, in the political script. It must then propose how the effects are to be judged and, keeping to its brief to be *critical*, how the wishes and ideas that are politically out of court can be kept alive and kept influential though repressed. In other words, political criticism helps to see that the dominant mood, for example, for Strong Leadership, does not scoop the pool.

This attitude is based on the work of a psychoanalytic theorist of small groups, and on early attempts to extend his ideas and observations to aggregate social and political life. In Wilfred Bion's theories, Group Leadership has its day, as does Inspiring Leadership and Strong Leadership — and the climate each reflects and propagates is different, becomes persuasive, and tends to suppress the others. In one climate welfare efforts have a prevailing wind, while creativity and entrepreneurialism are left to wallow. In another, quick, comprehensive reform, based on an innovative (and sometimes Utopian) set of ideas, holds sway. In the third climate, that of Strong Leadership, an 'enterprise culture', hostility to unconventional ideas and a suspicion of welfarism and other collective efforts dominate the field.

The question of whether it has worked must therefore be answered differently. In the first place, there is the question of how effective Strong Leadership is in realizing its own best ideas — resolute, getting things done, tending the economic 'basics', establishing a mood of vigorous self-reliance and courage in the face of competitors and enemies, etc. It is quite possible for Strong Leadership (or any of the others) to be judged a failure in its own terms. Effort may be being wasted in putting down its political rivals or it may be limited to rhetoric, or bogged down in over-fussy attention to detail or in constructing symbolic shells, so that little is achieved even by its own standards.

The second question is the fate of those things Strong Leadership's rivals, Group Leadership and Inspiring Leadership, stand for. Strong Leadership can be criticized, in other words, not because it has failed to live up to its own programme but, on the contrary, because it is successful in that but at too heavy a cost, its rivals too completely vanquished. (Mrs Thatcher speaks of ending the influence of socialism 'for ever and ever'.) Compassion is not just reorganized but made an embarrassment, communal bonds are neglected till they shrivel up and die. Imagination and tolerance of diversity are turned into 'irresponsibility' and even subversion. Needless to say, if this happens, some of the fault may lie with those institutions — welfare organizations, churches, the relevant political party; intellectuals, the press, schools and universities, and again the relevant political party — whose nerve failed them so that they fell in with the dominant Strong Leadership mood or retreated from the scene, losing, in either case, close contact with their own emotional and intellectual constituency.

Individually, the admission of ambivalence is the acceptance of internal conflict and contradiction. This leads to some modification of the desire to be morally and psychologically 'monolithic', always above reproach and critical of others for not falling into line, and without a weak spot others would take advantage of. Admitting mixed motives and contradictory desires leads away from hypocrisy and towards understanding and live-and-let-live. Allowing that there is some good in one's rivals reduces the sharpness of both contest and control. Politically, there is danger in the myth of *un*-ambivalence in that the Strong Leader, realistic up to a point about power and its uses, finds no reason to stop amassing power. Number 1, he or she can be a yet bigger number 1. The drive to centralize power in oneself contradicts the view that good politics requires continuing, strong opposition and, while too much conflict can tear the body politic apart, too little — the Strong Leader in charge of everything and the mood of Strong Leadership wholly dominant — kills it just as effectively. It is perhaps the ultimate irony in Strong Leadership that they, the most combative of leaders, ride a psychological and ideological escalator to the deadly harmony of complete control. One does not know which to resist the harder: Strong Leadership's hard-edged competitiveness and belligerence, or its insistence on our 'all working together' with an extravagant display of patriotic piety — the looming leader or the tyranny of the team.

Sources

I believe that this short account of my sources will better meet the different demands of a general readership and an academic and professional one than the conventional footnotes plus bibliography. The items are arranged so that they follow the sequence of topics in the text, though major sources for each leader (often with helpful bibliographies) are listed first.

INTRODUCTION

Gary Wills, *The Kennedy Imprisonment* (Little Brown, Boston, 1982), is the major revisionist work on Kennedy (and the Kennedys), showing how charismatic (what I call Inspiring) Leaders are intrinsically, if not by definition, anti-institutional: their free-wheeling style overrides organized checks and balances and dissipates settled loyalties. This is the sour side of 'charisma' and 'inspiration'. There is another side, of course, the 'winds of change' that must blow if overgrown conventions are not to stifle human energies and hopes. Cory Aquino, in the Philippines, created and exploited such a force, even if events have shown that she has to use something like the tools of Strong Leadership to consolidate her position. The Kennedy-like Harold Wilson is remembered, with a Schlesinger-like phrase, in Anthony Shrimsley, *The First Hundred Days of Harold Wilson* (Wiedenfeld & Nicolson, London, 1964). In his introduction to *Harold's Years 1964–1976*, 'Impressions' from the *New Statesman* and the *Spectator* (Quartet Books, London, 1977, Kingsley Amis documents his hopes and disillusionment with 'the new man' and the sense of 'unreality' surrounding 'Harold's Years'. This sense of having encountered something unreal is a frequent aftermath of the excitement Inspiring Leaders create. Also, Amis's chosen way of passing the pre-Thatcher period (he pairs Heath with Wilson), which is to gather contemporary 'impressions' of the storm just over, is testimony to the evanescence that marks outbreaks of charisma: to do justice to it, you must get the *feeling*, especially if you have since plumped for a politics of 'hard results'. The same thought occurs when I compare two accounts of Trudeau and 'Trudeaumania'. Richard Gwyn, *The Northern Magus. Pierre Trudeau and Canadians*, McLelland & Stewart, Toronto, 1980) complete with a cool, Trudeau-like portrait of the author, is about the feeling, while George Radwanski, *Trudeau* (Signet, Agincourt, Ontario, 1979 (1978)), though earlier, concentrates on the facts. Both are necessary, overlapping and persuasive.

The only lengthy treatment of David Lange, still early and superficial, is *David Lange, Prime Minister, A Profile* by Vernon Wright (Unwin Paperbacks with Port Nicholson Press, Wellington, 1984). Lange's partnership with his finance chief, Roger Douglas, is curiously paralleled in Australia by Hawke's with his Treasurer, Paul Keating — 'charisma' and Strong Leadership in tandem being perhaps an unavoidable concession to the economic times. Robert Harris, *The Making of Neil Kinnock* (Faber & Faber, London, 1984), suggests parallels between Kinnock and Lange (as Muldoon, whom Lange replaced, was an antipodean Thatcher though effective only at Fraser's level). They have in common, as did Whitlam and Trudeau, a tremendous personal and professional investment in talk, government by wit and words. James Walter, *The Leader, A Political Biography of Gough Whitlam* (University of Queensland Press, St Lucia, 1980), tackles, with a range of psychoanalytic tools, the glamour of the man, a glamour evoked vividly in Graham Freudenberg, *A Certain Grandeur, Gough Whitlam in Politics* (Sun Books, Melbourne, 1978; Macmillan, 1977). See also my own comparisons between Trudeau and Whitlam, 'Whitlam, Whitlamism and The Whitlam years', in B. Grant (ed.), *The Whitlam Phenomenon* (Fabian Papers) (McPhee Gribble/Penguin Books, Ringwood, 1986).

For the Group Leader, there is no better text than Jimmy Carter, *Keeping Faith, Memoirs of a President* (Collins, London, 1982); its title is a *sine qua non* of Group Leadership. Similar themes, and the same tone, are in Michael Foot, *Another Heart and Other Pulses, The Alternative to the Thatcher Society* (Collins, London, 1984). Roy Hattersley, *A Yorkshire Boyhood* (Chatto & Windus, London, 1983), recounts the making of a Group Leader: he is cheerfully proud of his early parochialism and delicacy, his failures at school and in sport, his being 'usually on the losing side' — all told with self-deprecating humour. The Group Leader fears unprotected separateness where the Strong Leader fears to be socially swamped, and Hattersley's testimony to this is exquisite (the 'Miss Roberts' is not, I believe, the young Mrs Thatcher!):

> We would be detained at Miss Roberts's pleasure . . . without the comforting presence of Miss Roberts herself. Perhaps more composed children welcomed the absence of their tormentor. But to me the sight of her sitting, erect and disapproving behind her desk, would have been immensely reassuring . . . as long as Miss Roberts was there, looking at her errant pupils, I was confident that we had not been forgotten. Without her, I grew increasingly certain that she would never return to release us, and that our lifeless bodies would be discovered by a search-party of parents long after the weekend was over.

A. F. Davies, 'The Demand for Political Psychology' in his posthumous *The Human Element, Three Essays In Political Psychology* (McPhee Gribble/Penguin, Melbourne, 1988), is sharply unimpressed by 'The Great Dictators', Hitler, Stalin and Mao. He shows the same disdain for the politically ambitious of a more ordinary kind, using biography as a weapon against their fundamental claim that they should be treated 'differently'. In the media, 'charisma' is a debased word, but Robert Tucker, in particular, sees it clear-headedly and long ago persuaded me that, refurbished by psychological insights known only peripherally to Max Weber, it is an essential concept for understanding political and other leadership: see Robert C. Tucker, 'The Theory of Charismatic Leadership', *Daedalus*, Summer, 1968, pp. 731–56.

There are remarks on 'narcissism' and charisma in my own book *Political Ensembles* (Oxford University Press, Melbourne, 1985) especially pp. 133–7. This book sets out types of leaders — Strong, Group, Inspiring — and shows how a style of leading creates, and is created by, a distinctive following, linking leader and follower through a shared sense of self and social relations. It also places the types of leading and following in different political traditions which, in turn, link to different experiences and beliefs about personal and social matters usually thought far removed from politics, including family life, gender relations, childhood. I also try to show how thinking itself is shaped to the same patterns, and how modes of thought underpin different leader-follower and political 'ensembles'. In addition, these are linked to competing traditions of thought in sociology and political theory, and in psychoanalysis. These are called 'promptuaries', there and in this chapter. Finally, there is a short essay on political 'climates' or moods — what they are, how they arise, how they change. These remarks lead to the suggestion in Chapter 1 in this book, 'The Rage for Strong Leadership', that politics and leadership change together, though what the pattern of the change is (circle? spiral? ladder-like?) is unclear.

The psychoanalytical literature relevant to the three promptuaries is cited in *Political Ensembles*, where there is also a fuller exposition of them. The third promptuary, 'selfhood and meaning', involves the study of narcissism, identity and similar ideas, and rests on an epistemology — a theory of the bases of our thinking and experiencing — which rejects the division between subjective and objective, self and other in favour of 'potential space' (Winnicott), 'transformational objects', etc. (Bollas) and other ideas that express interaction, synchronicity or somesuch. British psychoanalysis has a whole school of this persuasion: Gregorio Kohon (ed.), *The British School of Psychoanalysis: The Independent Tradition* (Free Association Books, London, 1986). This opens with an influential article by Christopher Bollas, 'The Transformational

Object'. Leadership studies have not yet been much influenced by these ideas which, of course, have exceptional promise for understanding leader-follower linkages. In fact, where the political science 'message' is that we need 'transforming' leadership, the promptuary is Abraham Maslow's and other 'humanist' and 'third-way' psychologies. James McG. Burns, *Leadership* (Harper & Row, New York, 1978) — a prize-winning and influential book — makes 'transforming' leaders the goal, relegating others less noble and less inspiring to the inferior role of mere bargainers, or excluding them altogether. The tendency to reserve the term leadership for the *type* of leadership preferred is seen even in the more interesting (and much shorter) book by Robert C. Tucker, *Politics as Leadership* (University of Missouri Press, Columbia, 1981). It appears characteristic of American writing on leadership to equate it with value and virtue, to judge it before observing it, and even to mix it up with popularity and sheer 'personality'.

More serious is another version of the third promptuary, a sophisticated extension of Maslow, which fixes types of leadership to stages of psychological 'development'. This reduces political psychology to rating political leaders on the adequacy of their personality development. Robert Kegan and Lisa Laskow, 'Adult Leadership and Adult Development: A Constructionist View' in Barbara Kellerman (ed.), *Leadership: Multidisciplinary Perspectives* (Prentice Hall, Englewood Cliffs, 1984), is an excellent illustration of this approach. (Interestingly, their three *stages* closely resemble my three *types*.) The Kleinian-influenced management writer, Alistair Mant, escapes this facile developmentalism but, in a generally lively and thoughtful book, he goes rather too close to another error: making the third option — in psychology or in politics and leadership — the best one. Mant, *Leaders We Deserve* (Martin Robertson, London, 1983), has two real leadership types and a third, ideal one; or he has two types — the paranoid, zero-sum leader (cf. the Strong Leader) and the secure, imaginative and more 'feminine' leader — one of which appears in the worst light, the other in the best. Leaders may be inspiring, charismatic and visionary, 'third-way' ideals, but this is at some cost to their rootedness in real social relations and willingness to do the hard work, i.e. with the creative leader comes 'narcissism'. *Political Ensembles* has an extensive discussion of the psychological 'downside' of the 'brightest and the best' type of leadership.

THATCHER

Hugo Young & Anne Sloman (eds), *The Thatcher Phenomenon* (BBC Books, London, 1986), originally broadcast in the early summer of 1985, is an invaluable guide to the range of opinion about Mrs Thatcher among those who have worked close to her. John Cole, *The Thatcher Years, A Decade of Revolution in British Politics* (BBC Books, London, 1987), brings us almost up to date, as does a more specialized but less critical and profound book, Rodney Tyler's *Campaign!*, *The Selling of the Prime Minister* (Grafton Books, London, 1987). Bruce Arnold, *Margaret Thatcher, A Study in Power* (Hamish Hamilton, London, 1984), has a polemical interest, a small 'l' liberal's complaint about a leader who enjoys power.

There are several more or less biographical studies: Russell Lewis, *Margaret Thatcher, A Personal and Political Biography* (Routledge & Kegan Paul, London, 1975 and 1983); Nicholas Wapshott and George Brock, *Thatcher* (MacDonald and Co. (Future Paperback) 1983); Patricia Murray, *Margaret Thatcher, A Profile* (W. H. Allen, London, 1980) (a 'new and revised' edition of her 1978 book) — from which the Anna story comes; Patrick Cosgrove, *Margaret Thatcher Prime Minister* (Arrow Books, London, 1979) (a revision of his early *A Tory and Her Party*, Hutchinson, London, 1978); A. J. Mayer, *Madam PM and Her Rise to Power* (Newsweek Books, New York, 1979) — an American version; Hugh Stephenson, *Mrs Thatcher's First Year* (Jill Norman Ltd, London, 1980); Margaret Jones, *Thatcher's Kingdom* (Collins, London, 1984) — an Australian correspondent's view; and others.

For Anna the best source is Anna Harriette Leonowens, *The English Governess at the Siamese Court, Recollections of six years in the royal palace at Bangkok*, introduction by Robin Duke (The Folio Society, London, 1980). Duke's introduction surveys the facts on the author's life and contains the quotations from Margaret Landon as well as presenting the broadly sceptical view of Leonowens's historicity my remarks imply. ply. He quotes the 'present king of Siam' as saying Hollywood's *The King and I* is 'closer to the real thing' in its portrayal of King Mongkut 'than he appears in the original book'.

Other sources I have used on Mrs Thatcher are headed by her 'selected speeches 1975–1977', *Let Our Children Grow Tall* (Centre for Policy Studies, Conservative and Unionist Party, London, 1977) and the Verbatim Service of the London Press Service, which gives transcripts of occasional speeches, interviews, etc. Various publications of the British Information Service have been useful too. In 1981, the Tory research library kindly allowed me to read the annual reports of the Conservative and Unionist Party, 1965–77. These gave me confidence in my belief that Mrs Thatcher is the core of Thatcherism. In 1965 (p. 88) her scorn is already of vintage quality: the local councillors' job, if the Central Government carried the burden of collecting rates, 'would be absolutely marvellous. He could demand everything, the sky would be the limit, and he could blame the Government always if he did not get it . . . In these circumstances, I should very much like to be a local councillor. One would get the best of both worlds'.

For the most part, though, I have had to rely — as any citizen must — on the newspapers and weeklies: *The Listener, The Guardian Weekly*, occasionally the English papers but mostly the news services' and correspondents' reports in Australian papers, *The Age* (Melbourne), *The Sydney Morning Herald, The Australian, The Times on Sunday*, etc. A recent review of Thatcherism in *Contemporary Record*, vol. 1, no. 3, Autumn 1987, The Journal of the Institute of British Contemporary History, has a particular good section on Mrs Thatcher's Cabinet style which might be put alongside the picture I have composed. The best account of her, as a person and in politics, in any journal I have seen is the *New Yorker* profile (from which I have quoted), John Newhouse, 'The Gamefish', February, 1986. *Foreign Affairs* (USA), Summer 1986, carries a comparatively up-to-date account of Thatcherism's foreign policy (pp. 932–8).

Other books consulted were: Peter Calvert, *The Falklands Crisis: The rights and the wrongs* (Francis Pitner, London, 1982); Max Hastings and S. Jenkins, *The Battle For The Falklands* (Michael Joseph, London, 1983); Peter Eddy, Magnus Linklater, with Peter Guillman, *The Falklands War* (Andre Deutsch, London, 1982); Francis Pym, *The Politics of Consent* (Hamish Hamilton, London, 1984); R. Behrens, *The Conservative Party from Heath to Thatcher* (Saxon House, London, 1980); Zig Layton-Henry, *Conservative Party Politics* (Macmillan, London, 1980); T. F. Lindsay and M. Harrington, *The Conservative Party 1918–79* (Macmillan, 1979, 2nd edn); Robert Blake, *The Conservative Party from Peel to Thatcher* (Fontana, London, 1985); Anthony Sampson, *Macmillan: A Study in Ambiguity* (Penguin, Harmondsworth, 1967). I have drawn on two of my own, earlier articles on Thatcher: 'Ambivalence, Dilemma, and Paradox: The Nature and Significance of Leader-Follower Ties, with Comments on the Leadership of Margaret Thatcher', *Political Psychology*, vol. 5, no. 4, 1984 and 'Why Thatcher has no feel for the Commonwealth', *The Age* (Melbourne), 22 August 1986.

Finally, on Mrs Thatcher's training in public rhetoric, see Max Atkinson, *Our Masters' Voices, The Language and Body Language of Politics* (Methuen, London, 1984). This is a useful work for studying any political leader as he or she speaks, appears on television, etc. A Dartmouth college research team has been studying facial expressions in nightly news clips, for example in the Carter–Reagan debate of 1980. Oliver Sacks reports that his brain-damaged patients showed a special ability to 'read' their President without being taken in by the contrived semblance of coherence and rationality the rest of us are vulnerable to. *The Man Who Mistook His Wife For A Hat* (George Duckworth, London, 1985).

REAGAN

The outstanding work is Gary Wills, *Reagan's America: Innocents at Home* (Doubleday, Garden City, 1987), and the indispensable book for its facts on Reagan's background and childhood is Anne Edwards, *Early Reagan* (Williams

Morrow, New York, 1987). Alan Brinkley, 'Invitation to a sinless world', *Times Literary Supplement*, 22 May 1987, a review of Wills's work, raises interesting questions about the place of image and myth in American society, wondering if Wills is not as implicated in them as Reagan is. Michael Rogin's *Ronald Reagan: The Movie* (University of California Press, Berkeley, 1987), is the source for the Edgar Alan Poe story. These works arrived late in my analysis of Reagan (though our accounts check out rather well) and I worked mainly from journalists' books: Lou Cannon, *Reagan* (G. P. Putnams and Sons, New York, 1982); Laurence l. Barrett, *Gambling with History* (Doubleday, New York, 1983); Lee Edwards, *Ronald Reagan, A Political Biography* (Nordland, Houston, 1981); Hedrick Smith (ed.), *Reagan: The Man, The President* (Pergamon, Oxford, 1981); Doug McLelland, *Hollywood on Reagan* (Winchester, 1983). More analytic and/or academic sources are: Paul D. Erickson, *Reagan Speaks, The Making of an American Myth* (New York University Press, New York, 1985); Jeanne J. Kirkpatrick, *The Reagan Phenomenon, and other foreign policy speeches* (American Enterprise Institute for Public Policy Research, Washington, 1983); Fred. I. Greenstein (ed.), *The Reagan Presidency, An Early Assessment* (Johns Hopkins University Press, Baltimore, 1983); Betty Glad, 'Black-and-White Thinking: Ronald Reagan's Approach to Foreign Policy', *Political Psychology*, vol. 4, 1983 (pp. 33–76) and her 'Ronald Reagan's Mid-Life Crisis and Turn to the Right' (unpublished manuscript); Norman Holland, 'Ronald Reagan's L-Shaped Mind' in A. P. McIntyre, *Aging and Political Leadership* (Oxford University Press/State University New York Press, Melbourne/Albany, 1988); R. K. Riemens, S. Hellweg, P. Kipper, S. L. Phillips, 'An Integrative Verbal and Visual Analysis of the Carter–Reagan Debate', *Communication Quarterly*, vol. 33, 1985 (pp. 34–42); Gary G. Hamilton and Nicole Woolsey Biggart, *Governor Reagan, Governor Brown, A Sociology of Executive Power* (Columbia University Press, New York, 1984).

Newspapers and weeklies were the other main source for interviews, speeches, news conferences and reports. Regular official publications, including *The Congressional Record* and the *Weekly Compilation of Presidential Documents* were also useful. Occasional pieces of comment were influential, for example, Professor Stanley Hoffman's pieces on Reagan's foreign policy in *The New York Review of Books* (see 'The New Orthodoxy'), 16 April 1981 and 'Reagan Abroad', 4 February 1982) and Alex Brummer's 'Reagan Goes Mourning Again' in *The Guardian Weekly*, 31 May 1987. Leslie H. Gelb, 'The Mind of the President' was published in *The New York Times Magazine*, 6 October 1985.

Two confessional books deserve listing together: the President's own (with Richard G. Hubler) *Where's The Rest Of Me?* (Karta Publishers, New York, 1981) (originally published in 1965) and David A. Stockman, *The Triumph of Politics, The Crisis in American Politics and How It Affects the World* (Bodley Head, London, 1986). For the Dorian Gray idea, see Oscar Wilde, *The Picture of Dorian Gray* (Penguin, Harmondsworth, 1985). In A. P. McIntyre, *Aging and Political Leadership* (details above) I have a chapter called 'Ronald Reagan's Dorian Gray Complex'. This lists in note 1 some psychoanalytic works on Wilde's novel. Wilfred Bion's theory of thinking appears in his *Elements of Psychoanalysis* (Hogarth, London, 1968), and in *Second Thoughts, Selected Papers on Psychoanalysis* (Karnac Books, London, 1974) (originally published in 1967). Donald Meltzer's *Sexual States of Mind* (Clunie Press, Perthshire, 1973), contains the remarks relevant to latency and Reagan on pp. 162–3.

FRASER

The best sources are John Edwards (with drawings by Patrick Cook), *Life Wasn't Meant To Be Easy, A political profile of Malcolm Fraser* (Mayhem, Sydney, 1977); Philip Ayres, *Malcolm Fraser, A Biography* (Heinemann, Melbourne, 1977); D. M. White and D. A. Kemp, *Malcolm Fraser On Australia* (Hill of Content, Melbourne, 1986) (extracts from Fraser's speeches and addresses). Useful adjuncts are: P. G. Tiver, *The Liberal Party: Principles and Performance* (Jacaranda Press, Milton, Queensland, 1978); Graeme Starr, *The Liberal Party of Australia, A Documentary History* (Drummond/Heinemann, Melbourne, 1980); and Patrick O'Brien, *The Liberals: Factions, Feuds and Fantasies* (Viking and Penguin Australia, Ringwood, 1985). The last contains both criticism and support, especially in Chapter 2, 'Fraser and Fraserism: Myths and Realities', and refers widely to the relevant literature.

There is very little academic work to draw on. A. Patience and B. Head (eds), *From Whitlam to Fraser* (Oxford University Press, Melbourne, 1987), and their follow-up, *From Fraser to Hawke* (Longman Cheshire, forthcoming 1988), are useful as guides to arriving and then departing Fraserism. Several good journalistic accounts of Fraser's coming to power, including the constitutional crisis that preceded it, are available, for the most part built around the 1975 election. Most have chapters on Fraser the man: C. J. Lloyd and A. Clark, *Kerr's King Hit* (Cassell, Melbourne, 1976); Paul Kelly, *The Unmaking of Gough* (Angus & Robertson, Sydney, 1976). Paul Kelly's *The Hawke Ascendency* (Angus & Robertson, Sydney, 1984), leads the field on Fraser's defeat in 1983, but see also Robert Haupt with Michelle Grattan, *31 Days to Power: Hawke's Victory* (Allen & Unwin, Sydney, 1983); and Anne Summers, *Gamble for Power: How Bob. Hawke Beat Malcolm Fraser* (Nelson, Melbourne, 1983). A former Fraser Minister, Sir James Killen, made observations on Fraser which I've quoted in the text: *From Killen: Inside Australian Politics* (Methuen Haynes, Melbourne, 1985). Don Chipp, another Fraser Minister for a short time before he founded the Australian Democrats, gives his observations on Fraser in Don Chipp and John Larkin, *Don Chipp: The Third Man* (Rigby, Melbourne, 1978). As I was preparing this manuscript there appeared the memoirs of a senior public servant, J. W. C. Cumes, *A Bunch of Amateurs* (Macmillan, Melbourne, 1988), which confirms the image of Fraser as very aggressive in his dealings abroad. (The book also contains an excellent profile of Hayden as, in my terms, a Group Leader.) The single most important academic study of Fraser is a short one. I have quoted it extensively in the text: D. Brereton and J. A. Walter, 'Question Time Performance and Leadership Style: A Study of Whitlam and Fraser', *Australian Journal of Politics and History*, vol. 24, 1978 (pp. 301–16). D. A. Kemp, 'A Leader and a Philosophy', is reprinted in Henry Mayer (ed.), *Labor to Power* (Angus & Robertson, Sydney, 1973).

Resident in Australia, naturally I was closer to Fraserism than to its British and American counterparts. I was, above all, a participant-observer in Fraser's four elections. The profile of Fraser is influenced by my observations of him on television and radio, by my bulging files of newspaper clippings: reportage, 'profiles', interviews and transcripts. There seems no point in citing all of these, but they represent a wide sampling of the Australian media, for example, *The Bulletin, The Age* (Melbourne), *The Australian Women's Weekly, The Herald* (Melbourne), *Quadrant, The Catholic Weekly, The National Times, Sydney Morning Herald, Checkpoint* (The Liberal Party's in-house journal), *Ad Hoc* (a student-Liberal publication), a newsletter for old-age pensioners, etc.

Other references in the text are to Plato, *The Republic*, translation H. D. P. Lee (Penguin, Harmondsworth, 1955); R. L. Stevenson, 'The Strange Case of Dr Jekyll and Mr Hyde' (Heinemann, London, 1924 (1886)); and Bruno Bettelheim, *The Uses of Enchantment, The Meaning and Importance of Fairy Tales* (Alfred Knopf, New York, 1976).

CONCLUSION

Some years ago, A. F. Davies published a short note 'Political and Literary Criticism — Some Resemblances' in the first *Melbourne Journal of Politics*. This became 'Literary and Political Criticism' in his *Essays in Political Sociology* (Cheshire, Melbourne, 1972). A splendid essay 'The Demand for Political Psychology' opens Davies's *The Human Element* (cited above). Following this essay on the uses of political psychology, Davies writes of 'Guilt in Politics', and in 'The Politics of Being Central' he reflects on the dangers of politics for the full, examined life. John Carroll, *Guilt, The Grey Eminence Behind Character, History and Culture* (Routledge & Kegan Paul, London, 1985), puts the 'conservative' case for guilt. (Davies critically reviews this work.) I wrote about friendship in *Political Ensembles* (cited earlier) and again, under the title 'Freud, Friendship and Politics', in Roy Porter and Sylvana Tomaselli (eds), *The Dialectics of Friendship* (Tavistock, London, 1988). Both contain bibliographies. I began to write about 'political climates' in the last chapter of *Political Ensembles*. Arthur M. Schlesinger Jr., *The Cycles of American History* (Houghton Mifflin, Boston, 1983), is one of those writers who are reviving the idea of moods in politics and history.

Wilfred Bion, *Experiences in Groups* (Tavistock, London, 1961), has been widely influential beyond Britain, in North and South America and in Australia and New Zealand. The extension of Bion's small-group observations and concepts to political climates (and cycles) is work hardly begun. An interesting example comes from Britain where a team of group analysts and others set up a project to monitor the effects of Thatcherism on the society as a whole. In the extracts below (summaries of summaries) Thatcherism appears as a 'Fight–Flight' mood — Bion's term, which I have rephrased as 'structure' and Strong Leadership — and it is seen to submerge the opposite values, of community and even ideas, which are embodied in the other group positions, Dependency (Group Leadership) and Pairing (Inspiring Leadership). The attempt to take broad emotional soundings in any particular political era is exciting. It calls, however, on skills not usually available to political commentators and political scientists, and it requires that those who have them (group analysts and the like) change their focus of interest, develop new concepts and modify their techniques. The observations refer to the early months of Mrs Thatcher's first government:

> Greater inequalities . . . increase the anxieties of the winners and survivors about protecting their gains against the attacks of those impoverished by the process . . . the demand for law and order is intensified (Summer 1980). Withdrawal . . . retreat . . . flight for survival . . . Holidays were a return to sanity; returning to normal life is a return to madness . . . There is a demand for teaching . . . as opposed to thinking for oneself . . . a wish to go back to old knowledge . . . The redundant . . . are seen as an embarrassment, a source of contamination (Autumn 1980). Individuals feel increasingly let down by the institutions to which they look to meet their needs. Institutions seem to be engaged in a search for a 'clean' model of the world . . . they are constructs of power, antagonistic to humans, concerned with cleaning things out . . . People are no longer sure what is the optimum number of people to join forces with . . . To survive, I'm forced back on myself and my family [but] to achieve I have to be connected into society . . . The government is increasingly perceived as being highly insensitive, uninterested in the people it purports to represent and pursuing an obsessional preoccupation of its own . . . where can we put our trust? (Early 1981). Rules are increasingly being invoked in organisations. Role and status differentiations are also expressed more

sharply . . . 'Splitting' comes from a sense of being beleaguered. Amidst turbulence, rules give certainty and professional role boundaries are defended to confer a sense of identity; but it means that people are much less able to act with personal authority. They huddle in smaller and smaller groups, with mounting anxiety about what is going on outside . . . Once you're out of a job . . . you've got to hold inside envy and jealousy of colleagues who are doing the work you'd like to do . . . Holding these feelings inside yourself corrodes you . . . (Spring 1981). Fear of violence . . . provided the dominant theme . . . Anti-Thatcher feelings . . . People have to look elsewhere for humanity, for ideas about the future. Anger and rebelliousness are becoming much more overt . . . Into this climate came the Royal wedding, offering hope, renewal, involvement — at least for the day. For most it was a unifying experience: one felt greater belonging to a family and country [though] re-evocation of hierarchies of church and state also brought out the negative . . . Rituals have been destroyed in our society (whatever happened to harvest festival? . . .) . . . One encouraging snippet: during a recent power-cut which shut off the traffic lights in Winchester the traffic moved more freely . . . (Summer 1981)

The source for these extracts is O. Khaleelee and E. Miller, 'Beyond the small group: society as an intelligible field of study', in Malcolm Pines (ed.), *Bion and Group Psychotherapy* (Routledge & Kegan Paul, London, 1985).

Index